Legitimacy in Global Governance

Legitimacy in Global Governance

Sources, Processes, and Consequences

Edited by
Jonas Tallberg, Karin Bäckstrand,
and Jan Aart Scholte

OXFORD
UNIVERSITY PRESS

OXFORD
UNIVERSITY PRESS

Great Clarendon Street, Oxford, OX2 6DP,
United Kingdom

Oxford University Press is a department of the University of Oxford.
It furthers the University's objective of excellence in research, scholarship,
and education by publishing worldwide. Oxford is a registered trade mark of
Oxford University Press in the UK and in certain other countries

© Oxford University Press 2018

The moral rights of the authors have been asserted

First Edition published in 2018

Published in the United States of America by Oxford University Press
198 Madison Avenue, New York, NY 10016, United States of America

British Library Cataloguing in Publication Data
Data available

Library of Congress Control Number: 2018937427

ISBN 978–0–19–882687–3

Preface

Legitimacy is crucial if global governance is to deliver on the many challenges confronting contemporary states and societies, from climate change to trade protectionism and human rights abuses. Yet as this book goes to press the legitimacy of global governance appears to be increasingly contested. Britain's vote to leave the European Union, the election of Donald Trump as US president, and the general rise of anti-globalist populism all suggest growing popular discontent with global governance institutions (GGIs). These developments point to a range of important questions that scholarship has yet to address in a systematic fashion: To what extent are GGIs perceived as legitimate by various audiences? What are the sources of that legitimacy (or its absence)? By what processes are GGIs legitimated and delegitimated? What are the consequences of legitimacy (or its lack) for the functioning and problem-solving effectiveness of GGIs?

The purpose of this volume is to advance an agenda for systematic and comparative research on the dynamics of legitimacy in global governance. The volume makes four contributions by: (1) developing and refining a sociological approach to legitimacy; (2) considering a full spectrum of actors, both state and societal, as audiences of legitimacy claims; (3) advocating a comparative approach to the study of legitimacy in global governance, across institutions, issue areas, countries, societal groups, and time; and (4) offering the most comprehensive treatment so far of the legitimacy of GGIs, spanning three analytical themes, namely, of sources of legitimacy, processes of legitimation and delegitimation, and consequences of legitimacy.

This book results from the first two years of a six-year research program on *Legitimacy in Global Governance* (LegGov), carried out by researchers from the Departments of Political Science at Lund and Stockholm Universities, as well as the School of Global Studies at the University of Gothenburg. The program is funded by Riksbankens Jubileumsfond and coordinated by Jonas Tallberg at Stockholm University.

The idea to produce a joint edited volume first arose in April 2016 at a LegGov project meeting. Successive drafts of the chapters were subsequently presented at several LegGov workshops. The process of writing this book has been as important as its final outcome, by pushing our research group to confront thorny conceptual, theoretical, and methodological issues associated with our research agenda. It has been a stimulating intellectual journey, involving conversations among researchers with cross-cutting expertise in areas such as global governance, comparative regionalism, political theory, development studies, and environmental politics. We thank all contributors for their collegial spirit, critical input, and tremendous patience. For indispensable, dedicated, and meticulous editorial assistance we are greatly indebted to Karin Sundström, PhD candidate at Stockholm University.

We have also benefited from excellent external input. In June 2017, members of LegGov's International Scientific Advisory Board offered very constructive comments on the book manuscript. We would like to express our particular gratitude to Steven Bernstein, Heba Raouf Ezzat, Adebayo Olukoshi, Diana Tussie, Yu Keping, and Michael Zürn for their sharp and helpful engagement. Further special thanks go to Steven Bernstein and Diana Tussie for their excellent concluding commentaries in the volume. LegGov's three postdocs—Bart Bes, Nora Stappert, and Soetkin Verhaegen— also provided very helpful comments on the manuscript.

We are also most grateful to senior editor Dominic Byatt and the publishing team at Oxford University Press for their continuous support and professional handling of the book. Two anonymous reviewers for Oxford University Press challenged us to further clarify the book's contribution and theoretical position in relation to debates on legitimacy in global governance.

Finally, our gratitude extends to Riksbankens Jubileumsfond, whose generous funding of the LegGov program has made the book possible.

As editors we of course take full responsibility for any remaining errors and omissions.

Contents

Contents

List of Figures

List of Tables

List of Abbreviations

ADB	Asian Development Bank
AIIB	Asian Infrastructure Investment Bank
APEC	Asia-Pacific Economic Cooperation
APF	Anti-Privatization Forum
APP	Asia-Pacific Partnership on Clean Development and Climate
ASEAN	Association of South East Asian Nations
AU	African Union
BCBS	Basel Committee on Banking Supervision
BRIC	Brazil, Russia, India, and China
CBD	Convention on Biological Diversity
CETA	Comprehensive Economic and Trade Agreement
CJN!	Climate Justice Now!
COP	Conference of the Parties
CP	comparative politics
CSO	civil society organization
CSR	corporate social responsibility
EC	European Community
ECJ	European Court of Justice
EITI	Extractive Industries Transparency Initiative
ESS	European Social Survey
EU	European Union
FSC	Forest Stewardship Council
G7	Group of Seven
G8	Group of Eight
G20	Group of Twenty
GAC	Government Advisory Committee
GATT	General Agreement on Tariffs and Trade
GFATM	Global Fund to Fight AIDS, Tuberculosis and Malaria

GGI	global governance institution
GRI	Global Reporting Initiative
HDI	Human Development Index
IAEA	International Atomic Energy Agency
IASB	International Accounting Standards Board
ICANN	Internet Corporation for Assigned Names and Numbers
ICC	International Criminal Court
IEA	International Energy Agency
IGO	intergovernmental organization
IMF	International Monetary Fund
IO	international organization
IR	international relations
IRENA	International Renewable Energy Agency
ISO	International Organization for Standardization
KP	Kimberley Process
MAI	Multilateral Agreement on Investment
MERCOSUR	Southern Common Market
MSC	Marine Stewardship Council
NAFTA	North American Free Trade Agreement
NATO	North Atlantic Treaty Organization
NAZCA	Non-State Actor Zone for Climate Action
NGO	non-governmental organization
NSG	Nuclear Suppliers Group
OECD	Organisation for Economic Co-operation and Development
OIC	Organization of Islamic Cooperation
OSCE	Organization for Security and Co-operation in Europe
SADC	Southern African Development Community
SAPSN	Southern African People's Solidarity Network
SDGs	Sustainable Development Goals
TGN	transgovernmental network
TPA	transnational private arrangements
TPP	Trans-Pacific Partnership
TRIPS	Trade-Related Aspects of Intellectual Property Rights
TTIP	Transatlantic Trade and Investment Partnership
UN	United Nations
UNASUR	Union of South American Nations

UNDP	United Nations Development Programme
UNEP	United Nations Environment Programme
UNESCO	United Nations Educational, Scientific, and Cultural Organization
UNFCCC	United Nations Framework Convention on Climate Change
V-Dem	Varieties of Democracy
WCD	World Commission on Dams
WFTO	World Fair Trade Organization
WHO	World Health Organization
WTO	World Trade Organization
WVS	World Values Survey

List of Contributors

Hans Agné is Associate Professor of Political Science at Stockholm University, Sweden.

Karin Bäckstrand is Professor of Environmental Social Science at Stockholm University, Sweden.

Steven Bernstein is Professor of Political Science at University of Toronto, Canada.

Magdalena Bexell is Associate Professor of Political Science at Lund University, Sweden.

Lisa M. Dellmuth is Associate Professor of International Relations at Stockholm University, Sweden.

Catia Gregoratti is Lecturer in Politics and Development at Lund University, Sweden.

Kristina Jönsson is Associate Professor of Political Science at Lund University, Sweden.

Jan Aart Scholte is Professor of Peace and Development in the School of Global Studies at the University of Gothenburg, Sweden.

Fredrik Söderbaum is Professor of Peace and Development Research in the School of Global Studies at the University of Gothenburg, Sweden.

Thomas Sommerer is Associate Professor of Political Science at Stockholm University, Sweden.

Jonas Tallberg is Professor of Political Science at Stockholm University, Sweden.

Diana Tussie is Director of the Department of International Relations at the Latin American School of Sciences, FLACSO, Argentina.

Anders Uhlin is Professor of Political Science at Lund University, Sweden.

Fariborz Zelli is Associate Professor of Political Science at Lund University, Sweden.

Part I
Introduction

1

Introduction

Legitimacy in Global Governance

Jonas Tallberg, Karin Bäckstrand, and Jan Aart Scholte

Today's more global world requires substantial global governance. Consider climate change, Internet communications, disease epidemics, financial markets, cultural heritage, military security, trade flows, and human rights. All manifest the significant global challenges that mark contemporary society. Meeting global challenges and providing global public goods with national and local government alone is at best suboptimal and at worst detrimental. Shortfalls of global governance invite uncoordinated climate policies, a fragmented Internet, perennial financial crises, transcultural misunderstanding, arms proliferation, trade protectionism, and human rights abuses behind a screen of state sovereignty. Global governance institutions (GGIs)—such as the United Nations (UN), the World Health Organization (WHO), the Group of Twenty (G20), and the Forest Stewardship Council (FSC)—are therefore essential for realizing and preserving collective welfare in the twenty-first century.

Like all types of governance arrangements, GGIs are more likely to operate smoothly if they enjoy legitimacy. Under conditions of legitimacy, people who are subject to and affected by a governing framework perceive its exercise of authority to be appropriate (Weber 1922/1978; Suchman 1995). When audiences view a governance arrangement as legitimate, they have confidence in its rule and are more likely to endorse and comply with its policies (Parsons 1960; Meyer and Rowan 1977; Dahl and Lindblom 1992). Without legitimacy, authority is likely undermined or must depend on coercion, secrecy, and trickery to obtain sway—and governance is often less effective as a result.

Experience shows various situations where the presence of legitimacy has significantly bolstered GGIs. For instance, societal beliefs across the world in the rightful authority of the UN have arguably helped this organization to construct a wide-ranging human rights regime since the 1940s. Likewise, legitimacy perceptions from member governments vis-à-vis the Organisation for Economic Co-operation and Development (OECD) have allowed this institution to make influential recommendations across a large swathe of policy domains. Meanwhile legitimacy in the form of consumer confidence has figured strongly in the success of certain non-state GGIs such as the World Fair Trade Organization (WFTO).

However, in many other cases shortfalls of legitimacy have severely weakened GGIs. For instance, resistance in key countries blocked plans for an International Trade Organization in the 1940s, a European Defence Community in the 1950s, a New World Communication and Information Order in the 1980s, and a Multilateral Agreement on Investment in the 1990s. Electorates in Denmark, France, Ireland, and the Netherlands have rejected successive European Union (EU) treaties, resulting in scaled-back ambitions, while United Kingdom voters decided in 2016 to leave the EU altogether. Weak legitimacy of the International Monetary Fund (IMF) has often hampered implementation of its macroeconomic prescriptions across all world regions. Certain governments' anticipation of domestic reluctance to carry the costs of climate mitigation weakened the Kyoto Protocol of 1997 and may well compromise the successor Paris Agreement of 2015. Thus, legitimacy deficits carry the risk of insufficient and ineffective global governance for today's global challenges.

If legitimacy has this central importance for global governance, then it is vital to understand how these beliefs in appropriate authority operate. That is the core concern of this volume: to develop an agenda for systematic and comparative research on legitimacy in global governance. In complementary fashion, the chapters address different aspects of the overarching question: *to what degree, why, how, and with what consequences GGIs gain, sustain and lose legitimacy*. This involves studying not only legitimacy as an attribute that GGIs may possess to varying degrees, but also legitimation and delegitimation as processes of justification and contestation intended to shape legitimacy beliefs. How far do various audiences regard GGIs to be legitimate? What are the sources of that legitimacy (or its absence)? By what processes are GGIs legitimated and delegitimated? What are the consequences of legitimacy (or its lack) for the functioning of GGIs? How are these legitimacy dynamics in global governance similar to or different from the workings of legitimacy in the nation-state and other forms of governance? In the broadest sense, the volume considers what systematic attention to legitimacy can tell us about world politics, and what experiences from world politics suggest for understanding legitimacy in contemporary politics generally.

To this end, the volume promises four contributions for advancing the research frontier on legitimacy in global governance. First, it further develops a *sociological approach* to GGI legitimacy. Existing research has been primarily normative, examining how far GGIs conform to philosophical standards such as justice and democracy (Buchanan and Keohane 2006; Christiano 2010). In contrast, this volume joins recent efforts to theorize and investigate beliefs among state and societal actors regarding the legitimate authority of GGIs (see, e.g. Hurd 1999; Bernauer and Gampfer 2013; Zaum 2013a; Tallberg and Zürn 2017). The focus is not on whether, in normative terms, GGIs ought to be considered legitimate *in principle*, but whether, why, how, and with what consequence they enjoy legitimacy *in practice*. A sociological approach to legitimacy can reveal the processes through which those who are subject to rules grant or withhold legitimacy vis-à-vis global governance institutions.

Second, the volume moves beyond the traditional focus on states as the principal audience for GGI legitimacy (cf. Franck 1990; Hurd 2007) and considers a *full spectrum of actors* from states to social movements. In today's more globalized world politics, legitimacy for GGIs comes not only from governments, but also from civil society organizations, business associations, political parties, media channels, and ordinary citizens. This volume therefore conceptualizes the audiences of GGIs to encompass both state and wider societal actors.

Third, this volume advocates a *comparative approach* to the study of legitimacy in global governance. Existing empirical research on legitimacy in global governance has relied heavily on single-case studies (cf. Hurd 2007; Binder and Heupel 2015; Dellmuth and Tallberg 2015). In contrast, comparative analysis can help both to highlight the specificities of individual cases and to identify general features that are common across multiple cases. Several chapters in this volume spell out theoretical frameworks and empirical designs for comparative examination of GGIs: across different issue areas, different policy functions, different institutional designs, and different memberships. Moreover, the volume suggests how comparative analysis may fruitfully combine quantitative and qualitative methods in an integrated and complementary fashion.

Fourth, this volume offers the most *comprehensive treatment* so far of the sociological legitimacy of global governance. Existing work in this area has tended to focus on specific aspects of legitimacy in global governance: i.e. how one or the other particular factor has shaped the politics of GGI legitimacy (cf. Johnson 2011; Ecker-Ehrhardt 2012; Bernauer and Gampfer 2013; Zaum 2013a). In contrast, this volume addresses all three broad analytical themes in research on legitimacy in one coherent endeavor: the sources of legitimacy for GGIs; the practices of legitimation and delegitimation in relation to GGIs; and the consequences of legitimacy for the problem-solving effectiveness of GGIs, as well as competition between them.

In making these contributions, the volume adopts an empirical approach to the study of legitimacy. The conceptual distinctions, the theoretical conjectures, and the methodological strategies laid out in this book ultimately serve the goal of gaining knowledge about legitimacy in global governance through empirical assessment. This empirical approach to legitimacy is open to a variety of theoretical perspectives. The chapters in the volume correspondingly explore a multitude of theories in International Relations (IR) and political science.

This empirical approach to legitimacy is problem-driven, rather than dictated by a particular theoretical agenda or methodological preference. Indeed, multiple logics are probably at play at the same time around GGI legitimacy. For instance, factors influencing citizens' legitimacy beliefs may be located at several levels: i.e. with the predispositions of individuals; with the qualities of GGIs; and with the broader social structures in which both citizens and institutions are embedded. Similarly, processes of legitimation and delegitimation likely involve deliberate strategies as well as non-deliberate practices, just as GGI legitimacy may have consequences for problem solving through mechanisms that involve instrumental calculation and norm conformance.

The rest of this introductory chapter sets the scene for these contributions in subsequent chapters. The next section below provides working definitions of key concepts—global governance and legitimacy—as these notions are understood in this volume. A third section situates this volume within existing literature on legitimacy in global governance. The remainder of the chapter then introduces the themes of the volume—the sources, the practices, and the consequences of legitimacy—and positions the contributions of the chapters in relation to these themes.

Core Concepts: Global Governance and Legitimacy

Given that both "global governance" and "legitimacy" can be understood in multiple ways, with considerably different implications, it is vital at the outset to clarify the conceptualizations that guide this volume. Thus "global governance" is understood here neither as merely "international organizations" nor as "world government," but as the full range of institutional regulatory arrangements that operate beyond the territorial confines of the nation-state. Meanwhile, "legitimacy" is approached in this volume in a sociological rather than a normative sense.

Global Governance

As understood in this volume, "governance" is a generic term that encompasses the various processes of regulating society. Governance occurs through the formulation and administration of rules and regulatory institutions in the collective life of a given population. "Rules" include general principles as well as specific measures; they cover formal laws and standards as well as informal norms. "Regulatory institutions" are understood here as the established organizations (tribal councils, corporate boards of directors, domestic governments, etc.) that perform governance functions. Taken in sum, governance aims at bringing order, predictability, and directed change to a society (Kooiman 2003; Hermet et al. 2005; Bevir 2013).

Importantly, governance involves more than government (Rosenau and Czempiel 1992). Indeed, the concept of governance has gained greater currency since the 1980s out of growing recognition that regulatory processes in contemporary society are not limited to the nation-state. Today, societal rules are also generated on other scales besides the national (e.g. governance through global, regional, and local institutions) and in other sectors besides public governance (e.g. regulation through market and civil society actors). As a result, the question of legitimacy is no longer, as in classical political theory, an issue concerning the nation-state alone.

Among the various additional fields of societal regulation, "global governance" as understood here refers to regulatory processes beyond the nation-state, whether on a regional or planetary scale (Rosenau 1999; Barnett and Finnemore 2004; Weiss and Wilkinson 2014). Global rules encompass both voluntary measures and legally binding regulations, ranging across principles such as human rights, laws such as EU directives, standards such as Internet protocol addresses, and codes of conduct such as corporate social responsibility (CSR) schemes. While states are often party to the formulation and administration of global rules, global governance also involves various types of non-state actors. In sum, global governance can be conceived as structures and processes of coordination among governments, intergovernmental organizations, and non-state actors across the private-public divide with a collective purpose to make and implement global rules and norms for managing transnational problems (Hempel 1996).

As organizations with rule-making power beyond the state, GGIs come in various formats. Some are IGOs, formally created and operated bodies with multiple state members and a permanent secretariat (Karns et al. 2015; Cogan et al. 2016). Well-known IGOs include the UN, the EU, the North Atlantic Treaty Organization (NATO), and the World Trade Organization (WTO). Other GGIs take form as transgovernmental networks (TGNs), informal collaborations among national ministries that make rules outside of traditional international law and work without a distinct permanent supporting office (Slaughter 2004; Djelic and Sahlin-Andersson 2006; Hale and Held 2011: part I). Prominent TGNs include the G20, the Basel Committee on Banking Supervision (BCBS), and the Nuclear Suppliers Group (NSG). A third category of GGIs are transnational hybrid institutions (THIs), which make global rules through a mix of governmental and non-governmental actors (Hale and Held 2011: part I; Raymond and DeNardis 2015). Examples of THIs include the Global Fund to Fight AIDS, Tuberculosis and Malaria (GFATM) and the Kimberley Process (KP) to halt trade in conflict diamonds. Still other GGIs are transnational private arrangements (TPAs) of market and/or civil society actors with little if any direct state participation (Hall and Biersteker 2004; Graz and Nölke 2008; Büthe and Mattli 2011). Cases of TPAs include the Global Reporting Initiative (GRI) and the Marine Stewardship Council (MSC).

GGIs also vary in other ways besides their organizational form. As already noted, GGIs may be global or regional in their geographical coverage. They may be general purpose or task-specific in their issue scope (Lenz et al. 2015). GGIs also vary in their level of authority (advisory, binding) and their type of governance functions (executive, legislative, judicial). As explored further in Chapter 4, such variations may have implications for the nature and extent of legitimacy that the GGI obtains.

Legitimacy

As noted above, legitimacy has two main alternative conceptual meanings: normative and sociological. Normative legitimacy refers to an authority's right to rule based on its conformity to certain philosophically formulated values and principles, such as democracy, justice, and fairness. This is the notion of legitimacy that is studied in normative political theory (e.g. Buchanan and Keohane 2006; Christiano 2010). In contrast, sociological legitimacy refers to the beliefs or perceptions within a given audience that an exercise of authority is appropriate (e.g. Weber 1922/1978; Tallberg and Zürn 2017). Normative and sociological inquiries of legitimacy are thus guided by different questions. Normative studies typically ask: "By what ethical standards should we evaluate an authority's right to rule, and how do particular governance arrangements measure up against these standards?" Meanwhile, sociological inquiries ask: "To what extent, on what grounds, through what processes, and with what consequences is a governing authority perceived to be legitimate by a given audience?"

Most research to date on legitimacy in global governance has been normative. One strand of research has explored normative values associated with the input side of global governance, such as participation, transparency, and accountability (e.g. Christiano 2010; Held 1995; Dahl 1999; Scholte 2011a; Archibugi et al. 2012). Another strand of scholars has emphasized values associated with the output side of global governance, assessing the extent to which GGIs produce outcomes that contribute to efficiency, justice, and fairness (e.g. Pogge 2002; Buchanan and Keohane 2006; Scholte et al. 2016; Westergren 2016).

In contrast to the predominant normative approach to legitimacy in global governance, this volume pursues a sociological track. It examines how multiple audiences (elites as well as citizens at large, state and non-state actors alike) perceive a GGI's exercise of authority as appropriate and rightful. With a sociological conceptualization of legitimacy, the volume builds on several other recent contributions (Hurd 2007; Reus-Smit 2007; Tallberg and Zürn 2017). Central to the sociological approach is a focus on legitimacy (as an attribute of an institution, based on audience beliefs) and (de)legitimation (as a process of justification and contestation of an institution's exercise of authority, with the aim of affecting audiences' legitimacy beliefs).

Whereas legitimacy in a normative sense may be fixed in a particular abstract philosophical argument, legitimacy in a sociological sense may vary over time, across audiences, between institutions, and so on. Nor is the sociological legitimacy of a GGI necessarily based on a single logic, but may be shaped by multiple sources. Legitimacy beliefs are often operationalized as an individual's statements of confidence or trust in a political institution (e.g. Caldeira and Gibson 1995; Norris 2009), but the conceptualization of legitimacy adopted here is open to alternative measurements as well, such as observed behaviors of endorsement or resistance.

That said, legitimacy goes beyond mere support for a governance arrangement. Whereas approval of a GGI could be driven by instrumental cost-benefit calculation, legitimacy involves a reservoir of confidence that is not dependent on short-term satisfaction with the distributional outcomes of a given regime (Easton 1975). Legitimacy presumes that audiences would regard an institution's exercise of authority as appropriate even if the organization were to take a decision that goes against their narrow self-interest. This is how the legitimacy of national legislatures, executives, and courts is commonly conceptualized, and the notion applies also to the legitimacy of GGIs. So, for instance, the legitimacy of the European Court of Justice (ECJ) must rest on an appreciation of how it performs its function for the common good, and not merely on narrow satisfaction with particular judgments (Caldeira and Gibson 1995).

Also key in this volume's conceptualization of legitimacy is the notion of "audience": namely, the circle(s) of actors who hold or withhold beliefs of appropriate authority vis-à-vis a governance arrangement. Audiences of GGIs include both state and societal actors, ranging from government elites to civil society organizations, business actors, and ordinary citizens. In addition, audiences comprise both "constituencies" (i.e. groups which are bound by the authority of a governance institution) and "observers" (i.e. circles which fall outside the jurisdiction of an institution but may still hold views about the appropriateness of its exercise of authority) (Tallberg and Zürn 2017). These concepts and distinctions are explored in more detail later (Bexell and Jönsson, this volume).

Legitimacy beliefs often vary across and within audiences. Determining the legitimacy of a GGI is therefore not a binary call of high or low, given that legitimacy perceptions tend to spread across a continuum, as well as to fluctuate across countries, societal groups, and other audiences. Hence, rather than drawing a blanket conclusion that a particular GGI does or does not enjoy legitimacy, it is better to identify differing types and degrees of legitimacy beliefs across the institution's various audiences.

It is also vital to consider that the legitimacy beliefs of audiences are socially embedded. These perceptions are not generated in a vacuum, but emerge from a context of societal norms about the appropriate exercise of authority. In this vein Mark Suchman understands legitimacy as "a generalized perception or assumption that the actions of an entity are desirable, proper, or appropriate *within some socially constructed system of norms, values, beliefs, and definitions*" (1995: 574, emphasis added). These social constructions vary across time and space, such that, for example, a norm of absolute monarchy once underpinned prevailing beliefs in legitimate government, but the idea has few followers today.

The social embeddedness of legitimacy beliefs suggests that sociological and normative conceptions of legitimacy may be empirically related while still being analytically distinct (Keohane 2006; Bernstein 2011; Beetham 2013). Thus the normative may shape the sociological inasmuch as audiences when making their judgments about appropriate authority may be influenced by the academic-philosophical thinking which circulates in their particular historical context. Conversely, the sociological may shape the normative inasmuch as political theory tends to reflect the time and place of its formulation. Showing such an interplay, both today's normative theory and today's prevailing societal perceptions emphasize criteria such as democracy and justice as grounds for legitimacy.

However, fulfillment of normatively justified standards is no prerequisite for sociological legitimacy. It may even be that legitimacy perceptions go against certain normatively justified legitimacy standards. For example, the UN Security Council might fare poorly when evaluated against a central normative standard like democracy; yet many audiences could still regard the institution as legitimate for other reasons (e.g. effective peacekeeping). Conversely, a GGI such as the International Criminal Court (ICC) may conform well to a relevant normative standard, such as the rule of law, but some audiences could still perceive the institution as illegitimate (e.g. for slow responses to violations).

An important implication of the social embeddedness of legitimacy is the possibility for actors to affect legitimacy beliefs through practices of legitimation and delegitimation. Social construction does not preclude agency, but opens up spaces for actors to draw on prevailing norms to shape legitimacy perceptions (Suchman 1995; Finnemore and Sikkink 1998). Legitimation and delegitimation are processes of justification and contestation, whereby supporters and opponents of GGIs seek to influence audience perceptions of the legitimacy of these institutions (Tallberg and Zürn 2017). With these practices approval is deliberately expressed or withdrawn (Barker 2007; Hurrelmann et al. 2007).

Thus, proponents of GGIs may engage in legitimation practices that seek to cultivate confidence among state and societal actors in these institutions' right to rule (Symons 2011; Zaum 2013a; Gronau and Schmidtke 2016). Conversely, opponents of GGIs may engage in delegitimation practices that aim to undermine beliefs in these institutions' rightful authority (O'Brien et al. 2000; Gregoratti and Uhlin, this volume). Such legitimation and delegitimation practices may be discursive, institutional, or behavioral (Bäckstrand and Söderbaum, this volume). What practices are used, by whom, directed at what audience, and with what success or failure are intriguing questions for the sociological study of legitimacy.

State of the Art

Legitimacy is a topic with an enduring but until now mostly marginal place in the study of world affairs (Clark 2005: 2; Hurd 2007: 11). As detailed in this section, some large-scale theorizing in IR has assessed the role of legitimacy in relation to different conceptions of world order. In addition, some recent middle-range theorizing has examined more closely, and more sociologically, the dynamics of legitimacy beliefs towards GGIs. Yet there have been few attempts, as pursued in this volume (a) systematically and comparatively to investigate the sources, practices, and consequences of legitimacy in global governance; and (b) to explore legitimacy and legitimation in relation to a broader range of GGIs (covering TGNs, THIs and TPAs as well as IGOs) as along with a more comprehensive set of audiences (including general publics as well as elites).

In one stream of IR theory, realist scholarship has usually seen legitimacy as a tool of power that states exploit to advance their interests, but that does not constrain their actions (e.g. Morgenthau 1948; Krasner 1999). In this vein, E. H. Carr (1946) emphasizes how strong states can further their interests externally by cloaking them in internationally acceptable principles. Also from a realist perspective, Jack Goldsmith and Eric Posner (2005) challenge the idea that international law possesses some inherent legitimacy that can and should restrict the actions of (powerful) states.

In contrast, liberal institutionalist accounts of world politics have viewed legitimacy more positively, highlighting its functional usefulness to the collective of states (e.g. Buchanan and Keohane 2006; Alter 2008). For instance, Inis Claude

(1966) suggests that IGOs fulfill an important political function of collective legitimization (see also Slater 1969). For John Ikenberry (2001), the establishment of legitimate world orders after wars helps to reduce costs of enforcing the peace.

In a third vein of IR theory, certain constructivist scholars have devoted considerable attention to exploring how legitimacy is intersubjectively established, shaped, and challenged in relations among states (e.g. Clark 2005; Clark and Reus-Smit 2007a). For example, Ian Hurd (2007) demonstrates how states have created, used, and contested legitimacy in the UN Security Council. Also on constructivist lines, international law scholars Jutta Brunnée and Stephen Toope (2010) focus on the role of "shared understandings" in creating legal obligations. Other constructivists examine how the legitimacy of international law affects state behavior by creating a "compliance pull" (Franck 1990; Checkel 2001).

Meanwhile, a range of critical theories has examined how the generation of legitimacy can uphold (and the contestation of legitimacy can undermine) hegemonic global regimes. For example, neo-Gramscian research considers how ideology (as "false consciousness") produces legitimacy beliefs vis-à-vis governance by global capitalism and its ruling class (Cox 1987; Gill 2008). Poststructuralists examine how dominant discourses produce legitimacy perceptions in the disciplining "global governmentality" of neoliberalism (Larner and Walters 2004; Hansson et al. 2015). Postcolonial theory explores how prevailing knowledge structures create legitimacy perceptions (among elite as well as subaltern circles) vis-à-vis Western imperialism (Said 1978; Krishna 2009; Seth 2013).

Alongside this world-order theorizing, legitimacy and legitimation in global governance has also recently emerged as a topic in three strands of middle-range theorizing. First, students of public opinion have examined citizen support for GGIs as an indicator of their legitimacy, and explored what factors lead publics to ascribe appropriate authority to GGIs (e.g. Caldeira and Gibson 1995; Norris 2000; Hooghe and Marks 2005; Johnson 2011; Ecker-Ehrhardt 2012; Voeten 2013; Dellmuth and Tallberg 2015; Schlipphak 2015). Second, research on (de)legitimation processes has assessed practices that aim at boosting or undermining the perceived legitimacy of GGIs (e.g. Steffek 2003; Bernstein 2011; Quack 2010; Brassett and Tsingou 2011; Symons 2011; Zaum 2013a; Binder and Heupel 2015; Gronau and Schmidtke 2016). Third, some work has specifically examined legitimacy dynamics around private global governance (Bernstein and Cashore 2007; Dingwerth 2007, 2017; Black 2008; Pauwelyn et al. 2014). These three strands of middle-range theorizing usually focus on the legitimacy of GGIs in relation to a broader set of actors—both state and non-state. While this research offers promising input to the present volume, much of it has focused on specific GGIs and misses larger systematic and comparative analysis.

This brief review of existing research on legitimacy in global governance suggests that sociological aspects have so far not attracted full deserved attention. Most classical theory of world politics has only touched upon legitimacy, and then usually only in relation to interstate politics. Meanwhile, as indicated earlier, most contemporary scholarship on legitimacy in global politics has explored normative standards rather than actor perceptions. Certain recent public-opinion and legitimation-process research has opened important new ground, but it is for the present book to build knowledge towards a more comprehensive and comparative perspective on sociological legitimacy in global governance.

Themes and Contributions of the Volume

This volume moves beyond the state of the art by applying sociological analysis of GGI legitimacy to a broad spectrum of institutions and audiences, developing a comparative approach, and combining questions concerning sources, practices, and consequences of legitimacy in global governance. The remainder of this opening chapter lays out the contents and contributions of the volume in relation to these three central themes in turn. The discussion of each theme first examines the main lines of debate around the issue and then introduces the relevant chapters, highlighting their central arguments and contributions. Taken together, the chapters significantly expand the research agenda on global governance.

As a prelude to the three more specific themes, Hans Agné in Chapter 2 explores more generally the turn toward legitimacy in global governance research. Agné suggests that this turn is partly explained by shortcomings in normative research on global justice and democracy, and the potential of a sociological study of legitimacy to overcome those problems. The chapter discusses the merits and demerits of alternative conceptualizations of legitimacy in serving these purposes. Agné concludes in favor of a sociological understanding that is sensitive to normative philosophical underpinnings, thereby inviting further debate over the most productive conceptualizations of legitimacy for empirical global governance research.

Sources of Legitimacy

What makes actors accept or contest the authority of GGIs? Exploring the bases of legitimacy perceptions is imperative in order to understand when and why GGIs gain, sustain, and lose the confidence and trust of their audiences. The sources of legitimacy have long preoccupied political and sociological theory in relation to the nation-state (Weber 1922/1978; Arendt 1956;

Lipset 1960; Easton 1975; Habermas 1973/1976; Beetham 2013). Today, with the growth of governance beyond the state, this issue becomes pressing with regard to regional and global institutions as well.

Existing research on the grounds of legitimacy of GGIs generally highlights two main sources (Bodansky 1999; Scharpf 1999; Hurd 2007; Ecker-Ehrhardt and Wessels 2013; Dellmuth and Tallberg 2015). Studies that emphasize *input-oriented* sources of legitimacy posit that GGIs gain acceptance as a result of providing access, participation, and representation in their decision making. In contrast, research that privileges *output-oriented* sources of legitimacy argues that GGIs gain acceptance by generating benefits for state and societal actors.

This book moves beyond earlier research on sources of legitimacy in several important respects. To begin with, it proposes a more nuanced and comprehensive typology of institutional sources of legitimacy than the common distinction between input and output (Chapter 4). In addition, it theorizes a broader range of sources than earlier studies, complementing a conventional focus on institutional features with an examination of how individual predispositions (Chapter 3) and social structures (Chapter 5) shape beliefs in the legitimacy of GGIs.

Lisa Dellmuth in Chapter 3 examines factors in individual cognition and psychology that may influence legitimacy perceptions. Dellmuth surveys the full breadth of relevant political science research in order to advance an agenda for empirical studies of individual-level factors that shape citizens' legitimacy beliefs in global governance. The chapter focuses on five types of such explanations: namely, related to political knowledge, utilitarian calculations, social identity, values, and susceptibility to political communication. The chapter's threefold core argument maintains, first, that global governance scholarship needs to consider individual sources of legitimacy, and in this respect should build on previous insights from comparative politics and social psychology. Second, research on beliefs in GGI legitimacy needs to look comparatively across institutions, countries, and time. Third, future research on sources of GGI legitimacy can acquire better measures of legitimacy through the use of large-scale public opinion surveys and survey experiments.

In Chapter 4, Jan Aart Scholte and Jonas Tallberg query the widely prevalent input-output distinction of institutional sources of GGI legitimacy and suggest instead a typology which builds on a related but analytically sharper distinction of procedure and performance. Moreover, Scholte and Tallberg emphasize that legitimacy perceptions derive not so much from procedure/input or performance/output per se, but from certain *qualities* of those phases of a policy cycle. Among such features, the chapter suggests that three—democratic, technocratic, and fairness qualities—figure most prominently in generating audience beliefs in GGI legitimacy. Thus Scholte and Tallberg arrive at a novel 2×3 typology whereby the institutional sources of GGI legitimacy can be classified as democratic, technocratic, and fair procedure and performance. The chapter further illustrates a range of indicators for these institutional qualities and considers how these sources of legitimacy may vary across types of GGIs, countries, societal groups, and time. The result is a wider, tighter, and more systematic understanding of the institutional grounds for GGI legitimacy.

In Chapter 5, Scholte addresses the possible role of social structure in shaping legitimacy beliefs towards global governance. Social-structural sources relate to the ways that people live together in society: for example, as regards culture, ecology, economy, geography, history, and political regime. Such sources are structural in the sense of emanating from the ordering patterns of social life. After addressing relevant ontological and epistemological issues of structural analysis, the chapter considers various social structural forces that could shape legitimacy beliefs in global governance, including norms, hegemonic states, capitalism, discourses, modernity, and social stratifications. Throughout, the chapter reflects on methodological possibilities and challenges of incorporating structural sources into empirical research on legitimacy in global governance.

Practices of Legitimation and Delegitimation

Following the chapters on sources of legitimacy, a second theme of the volume concerns practices of legitimation and delegitimation. Here the book moves from studying legitimacy as an attribute of an institution—i.e. whether and why a GGI is viewed as exercising authority appropriately—to exploring processes of justification and contestation which seek to shape audiences' perceptions of GGI legitimacy (Hurrelmann et al. 2007; Bernstein 2011; Brassett and Tsingou 2011; Tallberg and Zürn 2017). What practices are available to GGIs and their supporters in the promotion of legitimacy, as well as to those who contest GGI claims to authority? Who are the audiences at which legitimation and delegitimation attempts are directed? Are legitimation and delegitimation practices effective in shaping legitimacy beliefs and, if so, under what conditions?

Existing literature on this topic is dominated by studies of top-down legitimation efforts: that is, the practices used by GGIs in attempts to legitimize their authority (e.g. Gronau and Schmidtke 2016; Zaum 2013a). Some earlier research has focused on discursive or rhetorical practices, as revealed through official texts or speech acts, whereby GGIs legitimize themselves with verbal justifications of their policies and activities (Halliday et al. 2010; Reyes 2011; Steffek 2003). Other work has attended to institutional legitimation practices, as exhibited through organizational structures and procedures of GGIs. For example, a GGI might through initiatives on transparency and consultation open up to a broader range of audiences (Grigorescu 2007; Scholte 2011a;

Tallberg et al. 2013). Legitimacy crises for GGIs frequently trigger legitimation practices to regain the confidence of audiences (Reus-Smit 2007; Eckersley 2007). Finally, research on delegitimation of GGIs through contestation practices is still nascent. Despite evidence that non-governmental organizations (NGOs) and social movements challenge the authority of GGIs (e.g. O'Brien et al. 2000; Bandy and Smith 2005; Della Porta and Tarrow 2005), few studies have explored variation in the format, use, targets, and impacts of delegitimation practices.

Moreover, as explored in Chapter 8 of this volume, strategies to (de)legitimize GGIs do not always have their intended impact and indeed can sometimes have opposite effects. For example, actions aimed at delegitimizing a GGI may backfire and actually increase overall legitimacy perceptions of the institution. Conversely, a GGI's legitimation efforts may have unintended consequences of deepening opposition to the institution.

To take this research forward, Karin Bäckstrand and Fredrik Söderbaum in Chapter 6 develop a framework for categorizing legitimation and delegitimation practices, while Magdalena Bexell and Kristina Jönsson in Chapter 7 explore the conceptualization of GGI audiences, and Catia Gregoratti and Anders Uhlin in Chapter 8 suggest how civil society protest may be studied as attempts at delegitimation. A common theme across the three chapters is the "legitimacy nexus" between GGIs and their audiences (Symons 2011: 2258).

Bäckstrand and Söderbaum build on earlier research to develop a wide-ranging typology for empirical analysis of legitimation and delegitimation practices. The framework is novel in three respects. First, while earlier literature has primarily studied legitimation, this classification encompasses both legitimation and delegitimation practices. Second, while most previous research has examined top-down legitimation practices by GGIs and their member states, this typology includes also bottom-up legitimation and delegitimation practices from various societal audiences. Third, the framework captures a full variety of legitimation and delegitimation practices, classified in the chapter as being discursive, institutional, and behavioral in character.

Whereas Bäckstrand and Söderbaum categorize legitimation and delegitimation practices, Bexell and Jönsson identify types of audiences at which these practices are directed. The concept of "audience" focuses attention to interactions between those who seek to shape legitimacy perceptions and those whose perceptions would be shaped. Different communicative practices may have different implications for different audiences. The chapter develops a theatre metaphor to suggest that audiences play an active part in the performance of GGI (de)legitimation. To adapt the concept of audiences for empirical analysis, Bexell and Jönsson introduce further categories for classifying the relationships between GGIs and the multitude of actors that may hold legitimacy beliefs about them.

In Chapter 8, Gregoratti and Uhlin turn attention to civil society protest as a specific delegitimation practice vis-à-vis GGIs. The authors argue that, while existing research has commonly portrayed protest as a challenge to the legitimacy of GGIs, when and how this delegitimation happens is not well theorized. To advance such understanding, the chapter proposes a distinction between protest which targets a GGI as a whole (diffuse protest) and protest which targets particular processes and policies of the GGI (specific protest). The chapter also distinguishes between protest by actors which the GGI recognizes to be a significant audience and protests by actors which lack this status.

Consequences of Legitimacy

What are the consequences of GGIs gaining, maintaining, or losing legitimacy? It is a long-established wisdom in domestic politics that legitimacy makes national political institutions more effective (e.g. Weber 1922/1978; Dahl and Lindblom 1992). Legitimate institutions make actors more willing to engage in political discussions, to pool resources, and to implement collective decisions. In contrast, political institutions whose legitimacy is weak must rely on coercion, compensation, and manipulation, which typically undermine their long-term effectiveness.

Previous research features two main positions on the effects of legitimacy in global governance. One side of the argument maintains that the legitimacy of GGIs does not affect the behavior of states and societal actors. Realists traditionally assume that states act on the basis of self-interest and relative power rather than on legitimacy (Waltz 1979; Mearsheimer 1994/1995). This skeptical position is shared by the so-called enforcement school, which dismisses legitimacy as a source of compliance with international rules (Downs et al. 1996). In contrast, a second position maintains that the legitimacy of GGIs matters for actor behavior, for instance, by exercising a "compliance pull" (Franck 1990). It is also commonly suggested that legitimacy is particularly central to GGIs, since they, unlike domestic political institutions, have few alternative means to secure compliance (Hurd 1999).

The volume's contributions on this third theme build on the argument that legitimacy does matter for GGIs' effects on world politics. Along these lines, Thomas Sommerer and Hans Agné in Chapter 9 propose a framework for analyzing when and how the legitimacy of GGIs affects problem-solving effectiveness. Then, Fariborz Zelli in Chapter 10 explores how legitimacy can be an asset for GGIs in a landscape of increasing institutional complexity.

Sommerer and Agné outline a new research agenda on the consequences of legitimacy for the problem-solving effectiveness of GGIs. Growing attention to sources of legitimacy and processes of legitimation in global governance has so far not been matched by systematic research on its consequences. This chapter sets the stage for such progress by disaggregating consequences into empirically meaningful components, and outlining a research strategy to study these different impacts. Specifically, Sommerer and Agné highlight four sequential types of consequences, relating to: (a) the resources committed to a GGI; (b) the scale of policy output produced by a GGI; (c) actor compliance with GGI policies; and (d) problem-solving effectiveness of the GGI.

Zelli explores the consequences of legitimacy in view of the growing institutional complexity of global governance. GGIs do not operate as autonomous entities, but are entwined in dense patchworks of institutions with partly overlapping and competing mandates. Zelli suggests potential causal consequences of the legitimacy of a GGI for the institutional complexity of its issue field. Specifically, the analytical framework set out in the chapter theorizes the consequences of legitimacy crises for three dimensions of institutional complexity: the degree of complexity of the institutional architecture; the effectiveness of the GGI within this architecture; and the modes of governance used by the GGI to navigate this architecture. The chapter illustrates the potential of this framework with examples relating to climate change, energy, and trade governance.

Commentaries

In lieu of a self-evaluating conclusion, the volume winds up with two outside perspectives on its contributions. In the first commentary, Steven Bernstein finds that the volume's sociological and comparative approach marks a major step forward in the empirical study of legitimacy in global governance. Previous diagnoses of legitimacy problems of GGIs have not been matched by empirical analyses of why, how, and with what consequences these institutions gain or lose legitimacy in the first place. At the same time, Bernstein highlights three significant challenges for the ambitious research program developed in the volume. First, a focus on actor beliefs and strategies may come at the expense of attention to evolving norms and cultural factors that may underpin actors' notions of what legitimacy requires. Second, it is important to differentiate political communities of legitimation, which may vary widely in composition, power, and relevance across institutions and geographies, with significant implications not only for who matters, but also for what gets legitimated, and with what consequences. Third, theory needs to link sources, strategies, and consequences of legitimacy across different types of GGIs.

In the second commentary, Diana Tussie argues for greater attention to issues of power and markets in future research on global governance legitimacy. Tussie highlights the need to examine the effects of geopolitical change on legitimacy in global governance. In times of transition, the sources of legitimacy are themselves points of contestation. Global power transitions—together with voter contestation of GGIs—expose the limits of the liberal order and intimate a return of contending conceptions of world order. Tussie further argues that markets need to be brought back into the picture. Given the fragile legitimacy of GGIs, domestic governance must not be undermined by international markets. States must have scope to achieve a social bargain in which their citizens are protected and markets are restrained, such that international corporate actors do not gain extraordinarily at the expense of the general public. Hence the concluding reflective commentaries underscore the truism that no volume can ever have the final word on its subject. Nevertheless, with its systematic and comprehensive attention to sources, processes, and consequences, this book charts a new agenda of research on legitimacy and (de)legitimation in global governance. Central to this ambition is innovation in the conceptualization and theorization of legitimacy and legitimation in global governance, as well as the identification of viable strategies for wide-ranging and comparative empirical research.

2

Legitimacy in Global Governance Research

How Normative or Sociological Should It Be?

Hans Agné

Chapter 1 painted a broad picture of what legitimacy means and does in a complex international system of global and regional governance. To sharpen and deepen that picture, this chapter asks why legitimacy currently attracts increased attention in research on global governance (as inter alia represented by this volume), and how legitimacy should be defined for that research agenda. With particular attention to recent developments in international political theory as well as empirical research concerned with normative problems, it interrogates the concept of sociological legitimacy that lies at the heart of this volume, clarifying its meanings, possibilities, and limitations. It thereby offers a theoretical basis for conceptual decisions that shape the following chapters on the sources, processes, and consequences of legitimacy.

The chapter makes a stand-alone argument in three steps with regard to the legitimacy scholarship. First, it highlights an increasing interest in legitimacy among scholars who have previously been concerned with democracy in global politics. Legitimacy has in recent years often supplemented, and sometimes replaced, the concept of democracy in accounts of transnational and global politics. Second, the chapter develops a functionalist explanation of this turn to legitimacy in research on global governance. An important reason for the shift is that attention to legitimacy helps scholars to address problems that arise when theorizing global democracy. Third, and more extensively, it argues that the conception of legitimacy which most helps to overcome problems in global democracy research has a normative sociological character. A normative sociological conception relates legitimacy to beliefs held by those who are subject to and/or participate in a given political institution (e.g. Weber 1922/1978; Hurd 2007; Tallberg et al., this volume), rather than to beliefs held by political theorists as they seek to provide rational answers to normative questions (cf. more purely normative conceptions of legitimacy, e.g. Simmons 1999; Buchanan 2002; Westergren 2016). Still, legitimacy should not be treated as involving any and all political beliefs of subjects, and in particular should exclude beliefs that are motivated by individual self-interest alone (contra, e.g., Dellmuth and Tallberg 2015; Jerdén 2016; Macdonald 2015; but similar to Hurd 2007). The latter qualifications distinguish the *normative* sociological (as against a purely sociological) conception of legitimacy that is expounded below.

Thus the purpose of the chapter is to develop and defend interpretations of legitimacy that address, more successfully than in the past, specific problems in earlier research on democracy in global governance. How relevant can a conception of legitimacy constructed for this quite specific purpose be for other aims of research on global governance?

The desire to overcome certain problems in democratic theory is clearly but one reason among several to research legitimacy in global politics at this point in time, as other chapters in this book make clear. Still, there are reasons to think that its implications for the concept of legitimacy are broadly relevant. Democracy has a special relationship with sociological as well as normative sociological legitimacy which it does not share with purely normative legitimacy. They are driven by the same conviction: that politics is qualitatively different when pursued in accordance with values shared by the subjects of that politics. What counts is not whether subjects are right in their political views. Of prime importance is whether some part (e.g. a majority or an elite) of a particular audience (e.g. a nation or the whole of humanity) perceives that politics is right. The concluding section in the chapter returns to this point and argues that the wider relevance of the normative sociological conception of legitimacy is demonstrated by other contributions to this volume.

The rest of this chapter has one shorter and one longer part. The first and shorter part introduces debates on global democracy, observes how some scholars of that subject have recently paid increasing attention to legitimacy, and explains why that conceptual shift can help to address certain problems in global democracy research. The second and longer part of the chapter discusses how legitimacy should be defined in light of the explanation elaborated in the first part, while covering three questions: namely, whether legitimacy should be defined as a normative or a sociological concept; whether legitimacy research should base itself on the theoretical assumptions held by researchers or those held by research subjects; and whether or not legitimacy should be defined in opposition to self-interested beliefs.

From Global Democracy to Global Legitimacy

The idea of global democracy gained heightened political and intellectual importance in the 1990s. The end of the Cold War created room for more cooperative practices among the major states and the world as a whole. Academics responded by debating "models" of democracy to facilitate thinking about how the global world could be made more democratic. The models included the cosmopolitan idea to create a planetary parliament (Held 1995), the radical vision of a constituent power exercised by a multitude animated by political love (Hardt and Negri 2001), and pragmatic approaches to promote democratic values in existing international practices: e.g. authentic deliberation (Kuyper 2016), stakeholder accountability (Scholte 2004a; Macdonald 2008), and political equality (Näsström 2015).

These debates on global democracy have in recent years given more attention to legitimacy. Indeed, several of these scholars now prefer the concept of legitimacy to democracy and/or justice (e.g. Erman 2016; Macdonald 2015). Several of them have merged notions of democracy and legitimacy into a concept of democratic legitimacy (e.g. Macdonald 2012; Agné et al. 2015). Others have added legitimacy to their earlier concerns with global democracy (e.g. Bexell 2014; Dellmuth and Tallberg 2015; Held and McNally 2014).

To give a few specific examples, Saward has gone from defining global democracy in normative and institutional terms (2000) to defending a general theory according to which "provisionally acceptable claims to democratic legitimacy ... are those for which there is evidence of sufficient acceptance ... by appropriate constituencies" (2010: 146). Macdonald has gone from arguing that global democratization can and should proceed by making international agents directly accountable to stakeholders (Macdonald 2008) to arguing that the appropriate viewpoints from which to judge migration and international borders is neither democracy nor justice, but political legitimacy (Macdonald 2015). Erman (2016) argues that legitimacy is a more appropriate concept than democracy or justice for analyzing the normative standing of global governance institutions (GGIs).

So why are these scholars turning, or increasing their attention, to legitimacy in global and international politics at this moment in time? There are of course many possible reasons: new sources of data on global attitudes, such as online surveys and digital media; perceived changes in the legitimacy, power, and need for GGIs at this moment in time; and possible career benefits from relabeling study objects.

In order to address the question of how legitimacy should be defined, however, this chapter adopts a functionalist explanation of the conceptual shift from democracy to legitimacy in global governance research (or of the increasing attention to legitimacy in this context). From this perspective, conceptual changes are rational adaptations by scholars to perceived problems in research. Thus concepts which are seen to generate unresolvable problems decrease in prevalence and will be replaced by others. In contrast to the alternative explanations mentioned above, a functionalist perspective does not start from a set definition of legitimacy, but invites examination of alternative conceptions in light of the problem at hand. It leads to a fruitful question, therefore, namely whether increased attention to legitimacy in global governance research is a sound scholarly reaction to intractable difficulties around the concept of global democracy and—if so—what specific meanings of legitimacy are entailed by that problem.

Certainly past research on global democracy has had its successes, at least as measured by conventional quantitative indicators. For example, Google Scholar currently reports 4072 citations for the signpost contribution in the field, David Held's *Democracy and the Global Order* (1995). The same database reports that John Dryzek's *Deliberative Global Politics* (2006) has attracted 549 references. Works by Archibugi, Gould, Patomäki, Smith, and others have between them accumulated large numbers of citations.

Still, skepticism remains about the need and usefulness of the global democracy concept. Sometimes the critique is explicit (e.g. Dahl 1999; Miller 2010), but more commonly it is manifested in the indifference of the broader political studies community. For example, almost all existing empirical indices of democracy in political science take the territorial state as their unit of analysis. This is the case, e.g., for the Polity, Vanhannen, Freedom House, and, most recently, Varieties of Democracy (V-Dem) indices of democracy. These research instruments are thus broadly insensitive to qualities and difficulties of democracy among and beyond states. Meanwhile, empirical research on global democracy remains limited, and so far its assessments of democratic values in global practice are tentative (Scholte 2011a; Dingwerth 2014; Stevenson 2016; Kuyper 2016; Sénit et al. 2016). On the few occasions when empirical studies have addressed causal issues, the analyses have faced issues of extrapolation (Koenig-Archibugi 2011), aggregation of national data (Koenig-Archibugi 2015), or scope limitations (Agné 2016). Unhappier still for scholars who are interested in global democracy for normative reasons, their work appears so far to have had only the most marginal influence on real politics (Archibugi 2008).

Why, then, does research on global democracy find itself in a situation of relatively little intellectual and practical impact? One reason relates to inherent problems of the concept. In this regard critics have argued that global democracy is inaccessibly utopian (Dahl 1999), normatively and conceptually ill-conceived (Miller 2010), or even incoherent, insofar as global or international politics lack the necessary premises for democratic politics (Erman and Näsström 2013). As such, the global democracy concept does not offer a suitable basis either for normative thinking or for empirical studies. In this case, global democracy research also cannot develop a theory that is useful for change makers who want to improve the world. The turn from democracy to legitimacy in global governance research can then either remove an inapplicable concept or—even if the argument of inapplicability is rejected—temper expectations about what needs to be changed in global politics (cf. Erman 2016).

A second reason for the limited influence of global democracy research concerns the common reliance on a theoretical frame in which democracy is possible only in the presence of a demos or several demoi (Grimm 1995; Dahl 1999; Bohman 2007; Miller 2010; for a review, see Valentini 2014). The argument and the problem is that democracy presupposes a demos while no global demos is in place. From this perspective global democracy may be seen as possible only in a distant future when a global demos has in some mysterious way materialized. For the many political scientists who think that a demos of *some* kind is a necessary precondition—be it a governance structure that allows everyone affected by a decision to be included in making it (e.g. Valentini 2014), or a group with collective identity and internal solidarity (e.g. Miller 2010)—the turn to legitimacy in global governance research offers a preferable approach to studying when, how, and with what effects democracy, or good governance in general, operates at the global level. Instead of theorizing global political dynamics by presupposing a monolithic demos (or several demoi) that are either present or absent, the concept of legitimacy invites researchers to think about a condition for democracy—legitimacy—that varies across institutions, between policy issues, among audiences, and over time. To analyze the possibilities and effects of democracy (or some other form of good governance) under varying conditions of legitimacy provides richer ground for thinking about when democracy works than thinking about democracy under a single condition of there being a demos in place or not. Moreover, unlike the demos, legitimacy is not something that must for logical reasons exist before democratic procedures are inaugurated. Instead, legitimacy may emerge after or in tandem with democratic practices. Thus, it makes good sense for research to give increasing attention to legitimacy, and less attention to the demos or several demoi, as a precondition for democracy in global governance.

Having established a rationale for legitimacy as an alternative or supplement to democracy and/or the demos in global governance research, careful reflection is required on the precise conceptualization of the emergent concern.

Is Legitimacy a Normative or a Sociological Concept?

A standard distinction in research on legitimacy in international politics is between sociological/empirical and normative/moral interpretations of the term (Clark 2003). Alternative formulations of the same distinction include those of legitimacy and perceived legitimacy (Buchanan and Keohane 2006), philosophical and social-scientific legitimacy (Beetham 2013), and objective and attitudinal legitimacy (Taylor 1985). The widespread use of this binary makes it a good starting point for this part of the chapter. Should such interest in legitimacy as proceeds from a desire to overcome difficulties in earlier research on global democracy be based on a normative or a sociological interpretation?

Posing the question in this way presupposes that normative and socio-logical legitimacy can be suitably distinguished in the first place. This is a controversial assumption (Habermas 1996; Beetham 2013; Macdonald 2015; Miller 2010), and at some points below the discussion will relax the separation in order to consider the best ways forward for research. For the moment, however, the distinction between normative and sociological legitimacy is retained as much as possible in order to facilitate communication with the many global governance scholars (including the contributors to this volume) who regularly invoke the distinction.

Distinguishing Normative and Sociological Legitimacy

Normative legitimacy is commonly defined as the normative (moral or legal) right of a political institution to rule over its subjects (Beetham 2012; Buchanan 2002). On some conceptions normative legitimacy also entails an obligation of subjects to comply with the institution (Simmons 1999). Research on norma-tive legitimacy typically specifies and debates the necessary and sufficient conditions for institutions to have that right. Commonly discussed sources of normative legitimacy include democratic procedures, improvements to gen-eral welfare, and contributions to a just distribution of economic resources (Westergren 2016: ch. 6).

Normative approaches therefore adopt a philosophical-reflective method-ology. Such research clarifies and evaluates the moral standing of governing institutions in light of their conformity to specified moral principles. In normative thinking, therefore, legitimacy derives from a theorist's rational argumentation about philosophical issues, not from the opinions that some group of citizens happen to share or reject. Theorists may argue that norma-tively sound standpoints should to some extent reflect—and indeed inform and influence—the views held by real people (Sleat 2014). However, norma-tive legitimacy is not inherently fact-sensitive, and the grounds for legitimacy developed by a moral philosopher may have little correspondence to the actual views held by the subjects of a given regime (Cohen 2008).

In contrast, sociological legitimacy refers by definition to a *belief* among the subjects of a governing institution that it is legitimate (Weber 1922/1978). The exact features that subjects require from an institution for it to be sociologically legitimate are much debated. Different approaches highlight, for example: (a) protection of values defined in normative theory (Buchanan 2002; Buchanan and Keohane 2006); (b) protection of moral convictions and/or self-interests of subjects (e.g. Dellmuth and Tallberg 2015; Macdonald 2015); or (c) protection of moral convictions of subjects, excluding their self-interests (Hurd 2007; Reus-Smit 2007; Scholte and Tallberg, this volume). Importantly, however, these different second-order conceptions of sociological legitimacy do not undermine the first-order distinction between sociological legitimacy and normative legitimacy. After all, the beliefs of political subjects (sociological legitimacy) do not overlap perfectly with the beliefs held by professional theorists and philosophers (normative legitimacy).

Decoupling Purposes and Conceptions of Research

It is sometimes assumed that empirical research, which aims to develop and test causal explanations, cannot use normative conceptions of legitimacy and should instead go with some version of sociological legitimacy. In this vein Hurd argues that "the concept of legitimacy loses its explanatory purchase if it is equated to the concept of justness" (2007: 32; see also Tallberg et al., this volume). However, this position may generate misconceived disagreements on whether legitimacy should be interpreted either in normative or in socio- logical ways. Indeed, normative conceptions of legitimacy can be used for empirical or purely sociological research, and vice versa.

Normative conceptions enter empirical or positive research when a scholar investigates whether a particular governance institution (say, the Swedish government or the European Commission) empirically fulfills the researcher's own normatively motivated criterion. For example, the researcher could claim normatively that legitimacy rests on democracy and then explore the conse- quences of the presence or absence of democracy for other matters such as economic growth or international peace. Such research applies criteria result- ing from normative-theoretical reflection in empirical research to describe institutions as legitimate or not and then tests the effects of having or lacking those characteristics. Hence, there is no logical tension, let alone contradic- tion, between adopting a conception of legitimacy for normative reasons and using the same conception to conduct empirical and positive research (e.g. Agné 2016).

Conversely, research on sociological legitimacy can potentially serve nor- mative purposes: that is, helping to develop rational arguments for an insti- tution's moral right to govern. The rationally motivated right of an institution to rule is not constituted exclusively by its approximation to the normative ideals favored by political theorists, but also on its approximation to the normative ideals held by its subjects. For instance, if there is reasonable disagreement on what justice demands (e.g. between a nationalist social democrat and a cosmopolitan neoliberal), it can make sense for both parties—in case two institutions make conflicting claims to authority—to comply with the institution that is more legitimate from a sociological perspective. As an underlying principle, too, respecting the values of equality and democracy implies that governors should never ignore what the subjects of their rule believe is right, even if they as rulers think that people hold mistaken views (Westergren 2016: 16, 30–8). The normative relevance of sociological legitimacy is also assumed more broadly in particular branches of political theory (Habermas 1996; Saward 2010; Macdonald 2015; Miller 1999; Sleat 2014).

Admitting on these grounds that normative conceptions of legitimacy are relevant for empirical and sociological research, and vice versa, does not blur the difference between facts and values. Explanatory and normative theorizing remain different exercises. As Beetham underlines, "explaining what is differs from exploring the ground for what ought to be." The "fact-value distinction" is necessary for social scientists not to "intrude their own values into the situation under investigation" (Beetham 2013: 243). Yet upholding the fact-value distinction carries no implication that social scientists should disregard normative premises when they construct and test causal explanations. On the contrary, attention to normative legitimacy is necessary for "any understanding of the logic of reasons at work when people follow rules, keep obligations or seek to realize their ideals... Such 'logic' can only be grasped by an internal analysis of ideas and arguments, of the kind that is central to the practice of normative philosophy" (Beetham 2013: 243–4; see also Miller 1999: 43, 60).

Towards a Sociological Conception

In light of the above, both normative and sociological conceptions of legitimacy (as well as notions that integrate the two aspects) can be useful for conducting the empirically grounded research on GGIs, which remains a weak spot in global democracy research. But should research on legitimacy be led by sociological or normative conceptions? On the whole it would appear more productive to adopt a sociological approach or, to be more specific, a conception that refers to some sociological matters, e.g. the beliefs held by a particular group of people, as specified in normative theory. Two main reasons motivate this choice.

First, sociological legitimacy can explain elements and consequences of democracy in global governance in ways that normative legitimacy cannot. To recall, one of the difficulties with most existing research on democracy beyond the state is the reliance on the idea of a demos (or several demoi).

While problematic, the idea of a demos is not without purpose, however. To know when it is worthwhile to attempt to create democratic global institutions, we must first be able to explain when and how they are possible, function, and contribute to a common good or a fair distribution of goods among communities with different values. It is for the purpose of explaining such matters that a sociological conception of legitimacy is preferable both to the idea of a demos *and to that of normative legitimacy*. Theories about the effects of sociological legitimacy as well as those stipulating or implying that democracy requires a pre-existing demos attempt to explain compliance of people with political decisions by referring to non-institutional qualities of the people themselves (e.g. Weber 1922/1978; Miller 2010). However, rather than the premise of a singular unified demos, sociological legitimacy comes with the expectation of variation between audiences, institutions, and policy issues (as demonstrated in other chapters across this volume). Again in contrast to the idea of the demos, sociological legitimacy does not necessarily exist prior to democracy, and can possibly be conceived of also as a consequence of democracy. These explanations would be less effective—and some indeed would be tautological—if they rested on a normative rather than a sociological conception of legitimacy. This is because normative conceptions of legitimacy will themselves typically refer to the institutions or practices that potentially manifest democracy. Research on legitimacy in global governance should therefore steer towards sociological interpretations: this conceptual choice allows to generate and test new, context-sensitive, and non-tautological explanations of how democracy (or other notions of good governance) function in a global context.

A second reason for favoring a sociological conception is that it is productive for normative research agendas, namely to identify conditions for GGIs to obtain the right to rule. Global governance contexts generally involve greater value pluralism and organizational heterogeneity than domestic governance. In their search for unifying principles, normative theorists may neglect the diversity of moral intuitions that often characterize global contexts. Because the capacity for moral reflection is limited among all persons—including philosophers—there is a relatively greater risk for mistakes in normative reasoning when the task of moral reflection is to clarify the relatively more complex and diverse normative structures often found in global governance. To limit these risks it is important to reveal (as sociological research does) the reasons why, and extent to which, real people do or do not accept GGIs. Hence, turning to a sociological conception of legitimacy also holds some promise to overcome difficulties of logical applicability and excessively high normative standards that challenged earlier research on global democracy.

For sociological legitimacy to be relevant in respect of normative issues, the researcher must in some way delimit *a priori* the reasons for which an audience might perceive an institution to be legitimate. If no such limitations are made, "sociological legitimacy" may refer to, for example, beliefs that an institution exploits subordinated people in an effective way. Such beliefs would not carry much normative relevance, let alone be comparable for normative purposes to beliefs that the same institution distributes resources justly or makes decisions democratically. But can researchers delimit these normative reasons a priori and still pursue positive research, e.g. to test the effects of sociological legitimacy on the functioning of democracy or problem-solving capacity? As elaborated in the next section, exploring the normative relevance of sociological legitimacy is not only coherent with, but also beneficial for, pursuing positive research aims. Hence the empirically most useful conception of legitimacy is not purely sociological, but normative sociological.

Who Should Decide What Constitutes Sociological Legitimacy?

To recall, a second-order definition of sociological legitimacy identifies the qualities that subjects must perceive in a governing institution for them to consider it legitimate. To protect the integrity and distinctiveness of their respective fields, normative and empirical researchers tend to take contrasting positions on whether the nature of these qualities should be decided by the researchers or by the research subjects. So far, however, the literature has not carefully and explicitly debated this issue.

A first position is that the institutional features which are relevant for legitimacy should be decided by the researcher, using procedures of rational argumentation in normative theory. Normative theorists tend to favor this standpoint, since it allows them to recognize the reality of sociological legitimacy without needing to qualify the validity of their philosophical arguments by observations of sociological legitimacy. Legitimacy is then defined as a fundamentally normative concept, which is empirically realized through the institutional conditions which meet the theorist's criteria. The implication for empirical research is that the meaning of legitimacy depends on choices made in normative theory about which empirical qualities are necessary and sufficient for an institution to have a moral right to rule (e.g. Buchanan 2002; Erman 2016; Westergren 2016; Simmons 1999). In this approach, only perceptions by subjects that relate to the standards identified by normative theorists count as sociological legitimacy. Thus legitimacy in this case would not include perceptions of any conditions that subjects themselves decide to associate with the term legitimacy. Buchanan (2002: 689) illustrates this position in saying that:

Sometimes it is unclear whether "legitimacy" is being used in a descriptive or a normative sense . . . I am concerned exclusively with legitimacy in the normative sense, not with the conditions under which an entity is believed to be legitimate. However, a normative account of legitimacy is essential for a descriptive account. Unless one distinguishes carefully between political legitimacy, political authority, and authoritativeness, *one will not be clear about what beliefs in legitimacy are beliefs about.* (emphasis added)

The second position—i.e. that political subjects themselves should decide the institutional features which are relevant for legitimacy—can be favored by empirical and positive researchers as a way to protect their results from philosophical objections. The typical way of proceeding then is to define sociological legitimacy operationally in terms that allow subjects with different normative convictions to reveal their beliefs in legitimacy through one and the same empirical measurement. Survey questions that ask respondents about their confidence in, or support for, particular institutions are examples of such operationalizations, which seek to capture belief in legitimacy independently of the researcher's normative convictions. In this vein, Dellmuth and Tallberg measure sociological legitimacy with respect to the United Nations (UN) by reporting respondent views on "confidence in the UN," which in their interpretation may include perceptions motivated by "instrumental concerns," "private interests," and the "individual welfare" of the respondents (2015: 455).

Notice that even broad categories such as "confidence" and "support" do not give equal room for all normative viewpoints on legitimacy. On the one hand, to identify legitimacy with confidence presumes (controversially in normative theory) a concept of representative rather than direct democracy, in which subjects trust other agents rather than themselves to make decisions (e.g. Pitkin 1967 versus Barber 1984). On the other hand, to identify legitimacy with support for policies is to subscribe (again controversially in normative theory) to a consensus rather than an agonistic or conflictual conception of legitimacy (e.g. Habermas 1996 versus Mouffe 1999) in the context of democratic politics. However, the impossibility to get completely rid of normative assumptions in the definition and operationalization of sociological legitimacy does not imply that all sociological conceptions are equally premised on substantive assumptions about what is right. The critical question remains, therefore: Should the scholar or the subjects of research decide the second-order definition of sociological legitimacy? As argued below, problems in past work on global democracy suggest that these decisions should be made by the researchers rather than the researched.

As indicated earlier, researching legitimacy in global governance may help to alleviate the relatively underdeveloped state of empirical research to test preconditions for democratic or other normatively interesting global decision practices. However, if such research does not define concepts carefully before using them to gather data, the studies will obviously have an insufficient idea of what data have been collected. For this reason, the researcher, not the research subjects, should decide second-order definitions of sociological legitimacy.

To elaborate this point, subjects may support or have confidence in governance institutions for a wide range of reasons, including some that can seem morally dubious. For instance, subjects may believe that the authority promotes distributive justice, but they might also believe that it effectively dominates people of a particular race, class, or sex. Drawing such different predispositions for action, support, or confidence into one conception does not provide for a sufficiently precise formulation to guide empirical investigations into the causal mechanisms through which sociological legitimacy produces effects. Care for quality in empirical research and positive theory therefore requires that the researcher, not the research subject, defines the institutional or other features whose perceptions count as sociological legitimacy.

Uncompromising positivists, who renounce normative theory as ideology, may reject such a normative sociological conception of legitimacy by arguing that, if empirical research provides no reason to prefer one second-order definition of legitimacy to another, it would be less arbitrary and more scientific to let research subjects decide second-order definitions of legitimacy. On this view, it is unproblematic and even useful to describe, for instance, Nazi Germany as to some extent sociologically legitimate. While it might be objected that science extends beyond positive theory and empirical research, the ultra-positivist position is still worth considering. The next section does so by examining a commonly suggested restriction to the scope of second-order definitions of legitimacy: namely, that the beliefs inherent in legitimacy cannot be motivated by self-interest alone.

Does Self-Interest Contradict Sociological Legitimacy?

We saw in an earlier section that some scholars of global governance define legitimacy as acceptance of an institution based on "instrumental concerns," "private interests," "individual welfare," together with normative values (Dellmuth and Tallberg 2015: 455). Others suggest that beliefs motivated by individual self-interests have nothing to do with legitimacy:

> [L]egitimacy is an endorsement of the state by citizens at a moral or normative level. It is normative by conceptual definition. It is analytically distinct from that form of political support derived from personal views of goodness. What is sometimes called "performance legitimacy" is plausible only in terms of how citizens evaluate state performance from a public perspective. A citizen who supports the regime "because it is doing well in creating jobs" is expressing views of legitimacy. A citizen who supports the regime "because I have a job" is not. (Gilley 2006: 502)

The question then is whether legitimacy should be defined in contrast to, or in ways compatible with, the notion of acceptance based on self-interest.

One argument for excluding self-interest from legitimacy is that it may help to explain stability in political institutions. A social order is more stable when support for governance institutions rests on legitimacy rather than self-interest alone (e.g. Weber 1922/1978; Hurd 2007). Yet is this sufficient reason to remove self-interest from the concept of sociological legitimacy? After all, self-interests need not be less stable than moral convictions. Observing for example an academic seminar in political theory for some time, it is clear that participants may change normative convictions more often than self-interests, such as requesting a salary for the time they spend together. Hence, if the adequacy of a definition of sociological legitimacy depends on its ability to explain stability in political institutions, then it is not sustainable to invoke a presumed difference in stability between self-interests and normative convictions.

A second and somewhat more promising argument for the standard distinction between self-interest and sociological legitimacy is that actions driven by self-interest have a less stable dynamic than actions driven by legitimacy beliefs. In situations driven by self-interest:

> any loyalty by actors toward the system or its rules is contingent upon the system providing a positive stream of benefits. Actors are constantly recalculating the expected payoff to remaining in the system and stand ready to abandon it immediately should some alternative promise greater utility. Such a system can be stable while the payoff structure is in equilibrium, but the actors are constantly assessing the costs and benefits of revisionism. In this way, self-interested actors are onto-logically inclined to revisionism rather than to the status quo.   (Hurd 2007: 39)

This inclination toward revisionism among self-interested actors, however, must be compared to the social instability which is generated by shifts in normative beliefs or changing opportunities to approximate them in practice. Just as actors driven by self-interest monitor expected payoffs, actors driven by norms monitor that the political machinery conforms to their normative expectations. When a governance institution fails to meet this moral stand-ard, then revisionism will be as likely among normatively committed actors as it is among self-interested actors. Subjects who are willing to sacrifice their self-interest to establish a higher good no longer delivered by their common institution, or who experience a new situation in which their original con-ception of the good can be realized more completely than the present insti-tutional structure does, will have as strong reasons for changing or breaking the political institution as self-interested actors losing gains will have. Hence this second possible reason for excluding beliefs motivated by self-interest from sociological legitimacy also does not hold.

A third reason for excluding self-interest from the sources of sociological legitimacy is that such a conception provides for a richer political and social theory. To include self-interest is to invite rational-choice theory to the core of social legitimacy. To be sure, sociological legitimacy can in principle be combined with rational-choice explanations. However, collapsing the distinction between the two kinds of theory reduces opportunities to think differently and to debate multiple explanations (and their possible combinations) in political and social theory at large. Such an outcome should deeply trouble any social scientist, including advocates of the ultra-positivist position noted in the foregoing section. The burden of proof should therefore be shifted to scholars who allow beliefs based on self-interest to be constitutive of legitimacy (e.g. Macdonald 2015; Dellmuth and Tallberg 2015; Jerdén 2016).

Proponents of the latter position could argue that the pursuit of self-interest is generally normatively defensible, and therefore we should make room for self-interested beliefs in the concept of legitimacy. This assertion may seem too blunt, but it gains plausibility if we imagine a political context where subjects are regulated by institutions which are constructed to serve a normative aim, such as the protection of basic individual rights (Macdonald 2015). In this situation, subjects who comply with those institutions may in their individual decision making be relieved of the moral burden to prioritize normative aims. As long as the institutions protect moral aims, subjects may act morally *and* self-interestedly at the same time (cf. Hurd 2007).

Under such conditions, beliefs motivated by self-interest are not so easily rejected as irrelevant for normative sociological legitimacy, since in these situations self-interested behavior serves the common good. Yet the argument appears insufficient to motivate a definition of sociological legitimacy that includes beliefs based on self-interest alone. In particular, the argument does not hold in respect of global governance. Political institutions at the global level are weak and rarely able to steer the actions of self-interested individuals to achieve a common global good. Only when strong institutions are in place to protect a common good can individual self-interest coexist with public virtues. When—as in global governance—political institutions are weak and fragmented, political subjects themselves have to protect the normative convictions needed for effective political institutions, often by creating new institutions. Hence, there are sound reasons to exclude by definition beliefs motivated by self-interest alone from concepts of sociological legitimacy in respect of global governance. This conclusion also reinforces the earlier point that researchers, not research subjects, should hold the ultimate responsibility to define what legitimacy means.

Conclusion

In light of the forgoing discussion, legitimacy prevails when the subjects of an institution believe or perceive that it has qualities which—for reasons ultimately decided by the analyst—are sufficient for those subjects to think that they should accept the institution. Depending on the institution in question, acceptance may include compliance with its decisions, voluntary provision of resources to the institution, or abstention from obstructive behavior vis-à-vis the institution. While there may be many reasons why subjects think that they should accept an institution, all are not sufficient for the institution to be legitimate. Beliefs about an institution based on self-interest should not be seen as constitutive of legitimacy in global governance.

This argument was primarily motivated by a wish to overcome limitations in earlier research on global democracy. But is it also more broadly useful? A brief exploration of the wider research agenda represented by this volume suggests a positive answer. First, all chapters in this volume have a sociological, or a normative sociological, conception of legitimacy. If the functional explanation of the turn to legitimacy suggested in the first part of this chapter is correct, this is the conceptual choice one should expect scholars to make, although not all contributors to this volume were previously engaged in research on global democracy. Second, most or all contributions to this volume rely on normative theories or judgments when defining sociological, or normative sociological, legitimacy. Acceptance of institutions grounded in self-interest alone does not qualify as sociological legitimacy. Again, if the functional explanation suggested in this chapter is correct, and the implied argument for excluding self-interested motivations from the concept of legitimacy applies, one should expect scholars to make exactly this choice.

Even as legitimacy may have overtaken democracy in thinking about global governance we should not lose sight of the latter. As argued, concerns with democracy inform conceptual decisions about legitimacy. Moreover, the conceptual problems in global democracy research that have contributed to the turn to legitimacy could also provoke an improved understanding of democracy. Global democracy can therefore be retained as an important normative ideal as well as an unexploited resource to explain political outcomes (Agné 2018). Finally, normative understandings of democracy in global politics are likely to shape perceptions constitutive of legitimate global governance (Scholte and Tallberg, this volume). Renewed efforts to clarify the meanings and functions of democracy are therefore intrinsically related to the study and practice of legitimacy in global governance.

Part II
Sources of Legitimacy

3

Individual Sources of Legitimacy Beliefs

Theory and Data

Lisa M. Dellmuth

As previous chapters have established, legitimacy beliefs among citizens are central to the functioning of global governance institutions (GGIs). It matters significantly for the viability and effectiveness of a political body that citizens believe that its authority is appropriately exercised (Weber 1922/1978; Suchman 1995). Contemporary history shows that this general point for governance arrangements is applicable also to GGIs (cf. Steffek 2004; Tallberg and Zürn 2017).

Now that Part I has set the broad scene of this book—addressing overall themes and the overarching concept of legitimacy itself—Part II turns more specifically to sources of legitimacy beliefs. A key aspect of understanding the legitimacy of GGIs is to identify the sources of these beliefs: that is, the circumstances in which citizens regard a GGI's authority to be appropriate and desirable. The present chapter focuses on sources of legitimacy that lie with the individual citizens who make the legitimacy judgments and constitute GGIs' audiences, i.e. individual sources. What individual features make citizens more or less likely to consider GGIs legitimate? The following two chapters then consider grounds of legitimacy that arise from GGIs themselves (institutional features) and the societies in which citizens and institutions are embedded (social structural sources).

To this end, the chapter develops an agenda for exploring the predispositions of individuals that favor or inhibit the development of legitimacy beliefs vis-à-vis GGIs. The chapter reviews relevant existing literature in social psychology, comparative politics, and international relations (IR). While not all of these works refer explicitly to "legitimacy beliefs," they often invoke closely related relevant concepts such as "diffuse support" or "confidence."

This chapter is divided into three sections. The first section prepares the ground for the subsequent discussion on individual sources of legitimacy beliefs by reviewing how such legitimacy beliefs are commonly conceptualized and measured in existing literature. What challenges confront the measurement of legitimacy beliefs? The section concludes that evidence from existing cross-national data sets is severely limited. Such data sets tend to provide only single-item measures concerning the European Union (EU) and the United Nations (UN). Little comparable data is available on legitimacy beliefs across different types of GGIs, across issue areas, across world regions, across countries, across social groups (i.e. that would allow to compare the beliefs held by citizens and specific elite groups), and over time. The section concludes with a discussion of how such shortcomings in data can be addressed.

The second section engages with the core purpose of the chapter: exploring individual-level explanations for variation in citizens' legitimacy beliefs. The section focuses on five types of such explanations found in the existing literature: namely, political knowledge, utilitarian appraisals, social identity, values, and susceptibility to political communication. This survey shows how existing theories draw on, and sometimes combine, insights from social psychology, comparative politics, and IR. The section identifies several promising individual-level explanations, but also concludes that the scope of most arguments remains unclear, as few studies engage in comparative inquiries of the individual drivers of legitimacy beliefs across GGIs, issue areas, world regions, countries, social groups, and time.

Finally, the conclusion summarizes the chapter's message in three key points. First, future research on the legitimacy of GGIs could usefully draw on the rich literature in social psychology and comparative politics regarding public opinion towards domestic political institutions (cf. Caldeira and Gibson 1992; Tyler 2006). Second, as also argued in Chapter 2, more systematic inquiries are needed to explain variation in legitimacy beliefs across GGIs, issue areas, world regions, countries, social groups, and time. Third, explanations of legitimacy beliefs can be advanced by (a) including a broader range of questions that tap legitimacy beliefs in existing large-scale cross-national surveys, and (b) using survey experiments.

Conceptualization and Measurement of Legitimacy Beliefs

As a first step in developing an agenda for exploring individual-level explanations of legitimacy beliefs, this section discusses challenges and possibilities in conceptualizing and measuring citizens' legitimacy beliefs as such. This question has been contentious since the first research on legitimacy perceptions vis-à-vis the EU (e.g. Merritt and Puchala 1968; Dalton and Duval 1986). The establishment of a liberal trade program for Europe in the Single European Act in 1986 and the Maastricht Treaty in 1992 further spurred interest in public perceptions of the EU's legitimacy. Increased data collection on the EU through the Eurobarometer surveys (Loveless and Rohrschneider 2011: 8) and on other GGIs through the World Values Survey (WVS) enabled the first survey data analyses on legitimacy beliefs vis-à-vis the EU and other GGIs (e.g. Eichenberg and Dalton 1993; Norris 2000).

This early survey work generated some interesting findings. For example, Lindberg and Scheingold (1970) had previously diagnosed a state of "permissive consensus" among European citizens that enabled elites to promote European integration largely unconstrained by public pressure. In contrast, Eichenberg and Dalton twenty years later drew on Eurobarometer data to argue that the "conventional wisdom...that European citizens merely provided a 'permissive consensus'" no longer applies, as "public opinion is exercising a growing influence on national policymakers and on the institutions of the EC [European Community] itself" (1993: 507–8). More recently, survey data have led scholars to conclude that the EU faces a "constraining dissensus" (Hooghe and Marks 2009), whereby national identities and ideologies may limit EU policymakers' room for maneuver.

Conceptualization

Public opinion research on legitimacy beliefs draws upon, and bridges, social psychology and political systems theory. Most of the literature on the EU's legitimacy has focused on "public support" for European integration, building on early contributions in systems theory about "diffuse support" and "specific support" as well as studies of political institutions in the United States (Easton 1965, 1975; Tanenhaus and Murphy 1981; Caldeira and Gibson 1992).

Eichenberg and Dalton (1993) define public support as a political "attitude," thereby linking the study of public support to probably the most distinctive and indispensable concept in social psychology, where "attitude" is commonly defined as an evaluative judgment about a stimulus object (cf. Eagly and Shelly 1993: 1). More recent studies have explored public support for GGIs other than the EU, such as the UN (Ecker-Ehrhardt 2016), international economic institutions (Edwards 2009), and international courts (Voeten 2013; Ecker-Ehrhardt 2016).

Other proxies for legitimacy are "trust" (e.g. Torgler 2008; Zmerli 2010) and "confidence" (e.g. Norris 2000; Dellmuth and Tallberg 2015). These two terms have been developed in a large literature on political trust in the domestic context (e.g. Uslaner 2002; Bühlmann and Kunz 2011) and are well anchored in system theory (e.g. Easton 1975). For Easton, trust or confidence (which he uses as synonyms) arise when people expect that "the political system (or some part of it) will produce preferred outcomes even if . . . the authorities were exposed to little supervision or scrutiny" (Easton 1975: 447). Here "outcomes" may refer to the procedures, the polity, and the performance of a political system, while preferences may relate to an individual's self-interests as well as altruistic interests. This understanding of trust or confidence has informed much research on the sociological legitimacy of GGIs (Johnson 2011; Voeten 2013; Dellmuth and Tallberg 2015, 2016a, 2016b; Tallberg et al., this volume). However, others advocate to exclude narrow self-interest as a component of confidence in sociological legitimacy (Agné, this volume).

To study legitimacy beliefs empirically, scholars typically use different measures of support as indicators for legitimacy (e.g. Caldeira and Gibson 1995; Dellmuth and Chalmers 2017; Mau 2005; Rohrschneider 2002; for an overview, see Westle 2007; but see Karp et al. 2003: 276, who view support as a precondition for European institutions to build legitimacy). Others use trust (Harteveld et al. 2013: 543) or confidence (Dellmuth and Tallberg 2015: 461) as empirical measures for legitimacy as a theoretical concept. In sum, the existing public opinion literature typically studies legitimacy through indicators of confidence, trust, and support. The next section examines the concrete survey data that is available to measure these indicators.

Measurement

Several cross-national survey data sets include measures of legitimacy beliefs vis-à-vis GGIs. However, these data sets are scattered across institutions and geographical areas and also have significant gaps in the operationalization of central concepts.

To begin with, the WVS has in recent waves asked questions about people's confidence in GGIs. Table 3.1 lists all GGIs included in different data-collection waves of the WVS. The overview distinguishes between GGIs active in four broad issue areas: economic affairs, security, regional integration, and multi-issue global cooperation.

While the WVS enables comparative research across institutions, there are important limitations. Table 3.1 illustrates that the included GGIs are almost exclusively regional organizations, which means that questions about confidence in a GGI are asked in disparate and non-comparable country samples. The WVS covers only a few GGIs with a global membership, in the sense of including member states from more than one world region: namely, the International Monetary Fund (IMF), the North Atlantic Treaty Organization (NATO), and the UN.

In terms of the number of countries in which questions about these GGIs were asked, more encompassing public opinion data are available on the UN

Table 3.1. Question about confidence in GGIs in the WVS, 1990–2014

Issue area	Wave 2 (1990–4)[a]	Wave 3 (1995–8)	Wave 4 (1999–2004)	Wave 5 (2005–9)	Wave 6 (2010–14)
Economic affairs		TLC	TLC	CER, IMF	TLC, CER
Security	NATO		NATO	NATO	
Regional integration	EU	EU, ASEAN, AU/OAU, NAFTA, Andean Pact, Mercosur, SAARC, APEC, OAS/OEA	EU, ASEAN, Arab League, AU/OAU, NAFTA, Andean Pact, Mercosur, SAARC, ECO, APEC, OAS/OEA, SADC/SADEC, EAC	EU, Arab League, AU/ OAU, NAFTA, Mercosur, APEC, OAS/ OEA, CARICOM, CIS	EU, ASEAN, Arab League, AU/ OAU, NAFTA, Mercosur, SAARC, APEC, CARICOM, CIS, UNASUR, AMU, GCC
Multi-issue		UN	UN	UN	UN, Organization of the Islamic World

Notes: see http://www.worldvaluessurvey.org. African Union (AU), Arab Maghreb Union (AMU), Asia-Pacific Economic Cooperation Conference (APEC), Association of Southeast Asian Nations (ASEAN), Caribbean Community and Common Market (CARICOM), Commonwealth of Independent States (CIS), Cooperation Council for the Arab States of Gulf (GCC), Closer Economic Relations (CER), East African Community (EAC), Economic Cooperation Organization (ECO), Free Commerce Treaty (*Tratado de Libre Comercio*, TLC), International Monetary Fund (IMF), North American Free Trade Agreement (NAFTA), North Atlantic Treaty Organization (NATO), Organization of African Unity (OAU), Organization of American States (OAS) or Organización de Estados Americanos (OEA), South Asian Association Regional Cooperation (SAARC), Southern African Development Community (SADC/SADEC), Union of South American Nations (UNASUR). Question wording: I am going to name a number of organizations. For each one, could you tell me how much confidence you have in them: is it a great deal of confidence, quite a lot of confidence, not very much confidence, or none at all?

[a] The confidence question was not included in the first wave from 1981 to 1984.

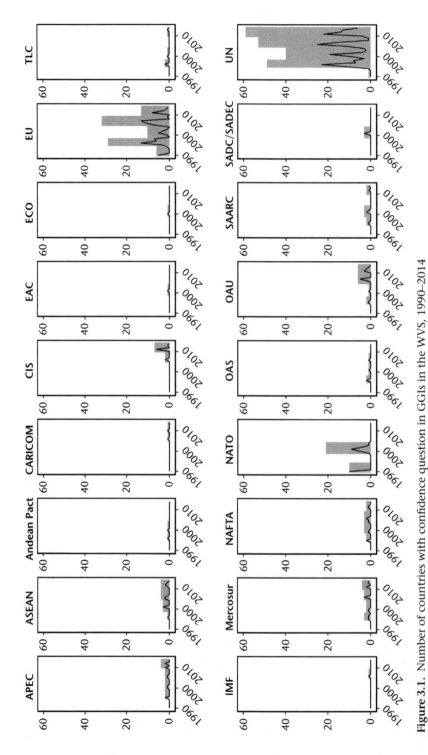

Figure 3.1. Number of countries with confidence question in GGIs in the WVS, 1990–2014

Note: author's own presentation, based on WVS data, waves 2–6. The solid lines depict the number of countries for each year, whereas the grey shades show the number of countries for each wave.

than on any other global institution and on the EU more than on any other regional institution (see Figure 3.1). The black lines in Figure 3.1 depict the yearly variation in included countries, whereas the grey spikes show the total number of countries included in the four-year waves.

Next to the WVS, a number of other cross-national surveys provide opportunities for comparative analysis of legitimacy beliefs. Table 3.2 shows years when regional survey series (such as the Asian Barometer, Afrobarometer, and Eurobarometer, as well as the global Gallup Voice of the People series) have included measures of legitimacy beliefs. (Table 3.2 does not include the many questions that have been used to measure public support for the EU, since these questions do not include items on other GGIs.) However, questions measuring legitimacy beliefs are typically not asked in all member states of a GGI, and the data are fragmented across disparate regional samples. In particular, questions about regional governance organizations are usually only asked in the member states of these institutions. Exceptions are questions about the EU in the Afrobarometer and Gallup surveys. Additional problems for comparability arise when the wordings of questions and the categories of answers change within and across survey series.

Another issue pertains to the specific measures used to tap legitimacy. As Table 3.2 shows, most questions refer to "trust" or "confidence" in GGIs, which as indicated earlier are conventional indicators of legitimacy beliefs. However, it becomes more problematic when the Eurobarometer asks whether people think that their country's membership of the EU is "a good thing, neither good nor bad, or a bad thing." Although this question may capture legitimacy beliefs to some extent, it may also lead people to think about the benefits of membership, which relates to specific rather than diffuse support (see also Agné, this volume). Similar problems arise with questions in the Afrobarometer about a country's say in, and benefits from, GGIs. Meanwhile, Gallup includes questions about whether people have "a positive, negative, or neutral opinion" of GGIs, which is problematic since, like the Eurobarometer formulation, it may push people to indicate specific rather than diffuse support. Respondents may think that they need to relate their answers to an opinion about specific aspects of GGIs, such as policy, procedure, or issue area.

Existing data sets are also of limited value in studying the temporal evolution of legitimacy beliefs, an issue which merits more attention (Niedermeyer and Sinnott 1995: 5). A rare exception is the biennial European Social Survey (ESS), which has since 2002 included questions about trust in the European Parliament and the UN. To date, almost no studies have examined how far transformations in legitimacy beliefs in GGIs may be explained by factors such as policy change, changes in elite discourse, or triggering events such as global crises or natural disasters. Moreover, the few available analyses of this kind relate only to the EU, looking at the effects on legitimacy of policy

Table 3.2. Questions on legitimacy beliefs in regional survey series and global surveys other than the WVS, 1990–2014

GGI[a]	Asia Europe Survey[b]	Asian Barometer Surveys[c]	Afrobarometer[d]	Eurobarometer and Candidate Countries Eurobarometer[e]	European Social Survey[f]	Gallup Voice of the People[g]	Latinobarometer[h]
AU/OAU			2002, 2003, 2005, 2008, 2009			2005	
Andean Pact							2001–3, 2009–10
ASEAN	2000						2001, 2010, 2011
Inter-American Development Bank							
COE				1999, 2000, 2001, 2002, 2003			
EAC			2002, 2003, 2005, 2008, 2009				
ECHR				1999, 2001, 2002, 2003			
ECOWAS			2002, 2003, 2005, 2008, 2009				
EU	2000	Wave 2 (2005–8)	2002, 2003, 2005	1990–2014	2002, 2004, 2006, 2008, 2010, 2012, 2014[i]	2004, 2005, 2012	2002, 2003
FAO						2011, 2012	
IMF		Wave 2 (2005–8)	2002, 2003, 2005			2004, 2005	2001–3, 2009–11
ICC							
ICJ				1999, 2000, 2001, 2002, 2003		2005	
ISO						2011, 2012	
Mercosur							2001–3, 2009–11
NAFTA	2000						
NATO				2001, 2002, 2003, 2004, 2009		2004	
OAS/OEA						2004	
OECD							
OSCE				1999, 2000, 2001, 2002, 2003			2001, 2009–11

SADC/SADEC		2002, 2003, 2005, 2008, 2009				
SICA	2000					
UN	2000	Wave 2 (2005–8)	1997, 1999–2014	2002, 2004, 2006, 2008, 2010, 2012, 2014	2004, 2005, 2005, 2011, 2012, 2013	2011 2001–3 2009–11
UNASUR						
UNESCO			1999, 2000			2009, 2010
UNHCR					2011	
UNICEF					2011, 2012	
WHO					2011, 2012 2005, 2012, 2013	
World Bank	2000	Wave 2 (2005–8)	1995, 2001, 2004, 2010	2002, 2003, 2005	2004, 2005	2001, 2002, 2009–11
WTO	2000		2001, 2004	2002, 2003, 2005	2004, 2012	2002

Notes: [a] Council of Europe (COE), Economic Community of West African States (ECOWAS), European Court of Human Rights (ECHR), Food and Agriculture Organization (FAO), International Criminal Court (ICC), International Court of Justice (ICJ), International Organization for Standardization (ISO), Organisation for Economic Co-operation and Development (OECD), Organisation for Security and Cooperation in Europe (OSCE), Central American Integration System (SICA), United Nations Educational, Scientific and Cultural Organization (UNESCO), United Nations High Commissioner for Refugees (UNHCR), United Nations Children's Fund (UNICEF), World Health Organization (WHO).

[b] The Asian Barometer Surveys (see http://www.asianbarometer.org) should not be confused with the Asiabarometer. For each that you are aware of, please let us know your impression of the following organizations. Here is a scale: 1 means very bad and 10 means very good. (Skip items that the respondent have not heard of.)

[c] Please indicate to what extent you trust the following institutions to operate in the best interests of society. If you don't know what to reply or have no particular opinion, please say so. (Trust a lot; Trust to a degree; Don't really trust; Don't trust at all; Don't know.) Some items refer to specific bodies such as the European Parliament.

[d] See http://www.afrobarometer.org. In your opinion, how much does the [GGI] do to help your country, or haven't you heard enough to say? (Do nothing no help; Help a little bit; Help somewhat; Help a lot; Don't know.) Giving marks out of ten, where 0 is very badly and 10 is very well, how well do you think the following institutions do their jobs? Or haven't you heard enough about the institution to have an opinion? (0 very badly—10 very well; Don't know.)

[e] Candidate Countries Eurobarometer. Different question wordings over time. I would like to ask you a question about how much trust you have in certain institutions. For each of the following institutions, if you have heard of them, please tell me if you tend to trust it or tend not to trust it. (Tend to trust; Tend not to trust; Don't know.) Generally speaking, do you think that (our country's) membership of the European Union (of the European Community common market) is: a good thing, neither good nor bad, or a good thing? (A good thing; Neither good nor bad; A bad thing; Don't know; Not applicable.)

[f] See http://www.europeansocialsurvey.org. Using this card, please tell me on a score of 0–10, how much you personally trust each of the institutions I read out. 0 means you do not trust an institution at all, and 10 means you have complete trust. (1 No trust at all—10 Complete trust; Don't know.)

[g] See https://www.icpsr.umich.edu/icpsrweb/ICPSR/series/223. And is your overall opinion of the [organization] positive, neutral, or negative? (Positive; Neutral; Negative; Don't know; Not applicable.) Do you have a positive (Good), or neutral (Neither good nor bad) opinion of the following international organizations or have you never heard of them?

[h] See http://www.latinobarometro.org/. The answer categories of this question vary slightly over time: From the list of institutions in the card, please mention all that you know and give it a grade from 1 to 10, being 1 Very bad and 10 Very good. (10 Very good—1 Very bad; Don't know.)

[i] This question item deals with the European Parliament.

change (Dellmuth and Chalmers 2017), elite communication (Gabel and Scheve 2007a), and economic crises (Braun and Tausendpfund 2014).

The limited data on GGIs other than the EU means that longitudinal analyses of developments in legitimacy beliefs for a worldwide sample of countries are difficult to realize. In the WVS, data across four or five waves are only available for four GGIs (see Figure 3.2): the EU, the North American Free Trade Agreement (NAFTA), the Southern Common Market (Mercosur), and the UN. The lack of over-time studies of legitimacy beliefs is a clear gap in the existing literature, as only longitudinal analyses can tell if legitimacy beliefs have changed over time and if existing explanations for legitimacy hold across time periods.

Given these limitations of existing survey data, how should researchers wishing to study legitimacy beliefs move forward? First, it would benefit cumulative research to have more systematic inclusion of legitimacy measures across existing large-scale surveys and a more systematic coverage of countries in these surveys. Such a move toward systematization would greatly facilitate comparability of data across and within surveys. To the extent that surveys would also include several measures of legitimacy beliefs, this would make it

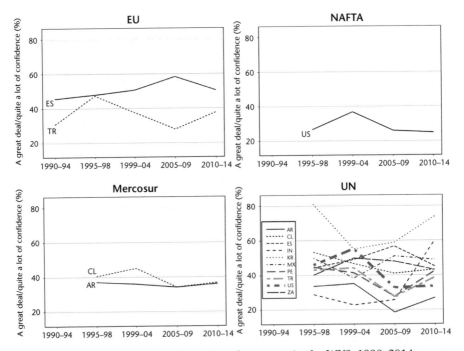

Figure 3.2. Countries with data for at least four waves in the WVS, 1990–2014

Note: author's own presentation, based on WVS data, waves 2–6. The country abbreviations refer to Argentina (AR), Chile (CL), India (IN), Mexico (MX), Peru (PE), South Africa (ZA), South Korea (KR), Spain (ES), Turkey (TR), and the United States (US).

possible to explore how different legitimacy measures relate to each other (Caldeira and Gibson 1992), and whether existing findings might be driven by the choice of survey measures and their placement in questionnaires.

Second, researchers could study legitimacy beliefs through survey experiments, building on methodological advances in social psychology and comparative politics. Survey experiments have clear advantages in avoiding methodological problems that arise from poor data availability and difficulties in identifying causal effects (Bernauer and Gampfer 2013; Chong and Druckman 2007; Maier et al. 2012; Mutz 2011; Schuck and de Vreese 2006). Like opinion surveys, survey experiments are administered to randomly selected representative samples of the target population of interest, implying that the results of these studies can be generalized to the overall target population. However, unlike the merely observational data from opinion surveys, survey experiments allow the establishment of causal inferences by subjecting sub-samples to different treatments. Such an approach avoids the problems that plague efforts to establish causal inferences from observational data alone (e.g. reverse causality, spurious correlations, selection bias, and multicollinearity). The random assignment of respondents to treatment groups and a control group ensures that the observed treatment effects do not systematically derive from uncontrolled influences.

Survey experiments enable researchers to test theories about the sources of legitimacy beliefs for which there are no data available in existing large-scale opinion surveys. By administering experiments on representative samples of one or several populations, researchers can engage in cross-national comparisons of legitimacy beliefs without relying on cross-national survey data. This method has been used to study effects on legitimacy beliefs of citizens' susceptibility to elite communication (Dellmuth and Tallberg 2016b) as well as citizens' evaluation of GGIs' institutional qualities (Dellmuth et al. 2017).

In sum, research on legitimacy beliefs vis-à-vis GGIs confronts challenges in terms of the conceptualization and measurement of such beliefs. While existing studies certainly make choices about definitions, indicators, and the like, these methodological decisions are seldom explicitly discussed. Moroever, existing data sets face clear limitations in terms of coverage and comparability. Greater attention to these issues in future research could advance the systematic study of the sources of beliefs in GGI legitimacy.

Individual-Level Explanations of Legitimacy Beliefs

Having set out key framing challenges about conceptualization and measurement, the chapter can turn to its more specific concern with individual-level factors that might help to explain variation in legitimacy beliefs towards GGIs.

Over the past two decades, a growing number of scholars have begun to explore individual-level explanations of legitimacy beliefs. These contributions often draw on rich intellectual traditions in political psychology (Tyler 2006), sociology (e.g. Weber 1922/1978), and comparative politics (Easton 1975). Yet, so far, most of these studies have focused on public opinion towards the EU, with only limited attention to other GGIs. This following discussion reviews existing research on five main types of individual-level explanation: i.e. pertaining to political knowledge, utilitarian appraisals, social identity, values, and susceptibility to political communication. By addressing circumstances of the individual who holds the legitimacy beliefs, these explanations are distinct from the institutional and structural sources of legitimacy beliefs that are discussed in the next two chapters.

Political Knowledge

One potential key cognitive factor shaping legitimacy beliefs is political knowledge held by individuals. When correct political information becomes extensive and organized in people's minds, it amounts to what is variously referred to as "sophistication" (Luskin 1990), "awareness" (Zaller 1992), "knowledge" (Delli Carpini and Keeter 1996), and "cognitive mobilization" (Inglehart 1970). These substantially overlapping concepts all refer to organized cognition (Luskin 1990). Knowledgeable individuals are more likely to be exposed to, and able to process, new political information (Zaller 1992; Delli Carpini and Keeter 1996: 192–3).

Political knowledge theories have predicted that knowledgeable citizens tend to be more supportive of GGIs. Based on Inglehart's (1970) argument that high levels of cognitive mobilization enable citizens to identify with the European political community, scholars have argued that these circles may find GGIs more familiar and less threatening (cf. Janssen 1991). In addition, more knowledgeable citizens are usually integrated into transnational networks of communication where people tend to be supportive of multilateral organizations and global governance (cf. Norris and Inglehart 2009: ch. 6), leading to higher levels of support for the EU (Inglehart et al. 1991; Caldeira and Gibson 1995). Evidence also suggests a positive association between political knowledge and support for a number of GGIs: the European Court of Justice (ECJ) (Caldeira and Gibson 1995), the EU (Anderson 1998), as well as the UN, NAFTA, the World Trade Organization (WTO), and the IMF (Dellmuth and Tallberg 2016b). Similarly, Ecker-Ehrhardt (2012) shows that awareness affects beliefs in the problem-solving capacity of the EU, the UN, the WTO, the IMF, and the Group of Eight (G8).

However, the direct causal link from political knowledge to legitimacy beliefs is far from settled. Indeed, it remains unclear why all types of information—e.g. about the failings as well as the benefits of GGIs—should generate greater support (cf. Karp et al. 2003: 275–6). No systematic research exists either about the types of knowledge about GGIs that shape transnational resistance networks, where the focus is on delegitimating global governance (e.g. Tarrow 2005; Della Porta 2016).

Also in the vein of political knowledge theories is the argument that people's level of political awareness influences the extent to which they make use of heuristics when forming legitimacy beliefs (Karp et al. 2003; Harteveld et al. 2013). This proposition suggests that people with less political knowledge about GGIs are more prone to construct evaluative judgments about GGIs based on the information that they hold about the political institutions they know best (typically domestic bodies). Indeed, convincing evidence indicates that people with more confidence in their domestic government also have more confidence in the EU (e.g. Anderson 1998; Muñoz et al. 2011; Sattler and Urpelainen 2012; Armingeon and Ceka 2014; Muñoz 2017), the African Union (AU), the Union of South American Nations (UNASUR) (Schlipphak 2015), the UN (Dellmuth and Tallberg 2015, 2016b), the World Bank, and the IMF (Johnson 2011).

A recent comparative analysis of the EU, UN, IMF, WTO, and NAFTA confirms the positive association between confidence in domestic and global institutions, and suggests that this relationship is driven both by people's use of heuristics and by an antecedent factor of social trust (Dellmuth and Tallberg 2016b). In contrast, evidence is not convincing for a "support transfer," where individuals who do not support domestic political institutions tend to support the EU. The evidence for this latter claim comes only from 1994 and 1995, and the measures for the dependent variables in these analyses tap specific rather than diffuse support (Sánchez-Cuenca 2000; Kritzinger 2003).

We need more studies testing comparatively the linkages between political knowledge and legitimacy beliefs, using survey instruments that draw on the methodological advances in the political knowledge literature (cf. Delli Carpini and Keeter 1996; Mondak 1999; Dolan 2011). Existing studies rely on self-reported knowledge indicators, where people are typically asked whether they have heard of a particular global institution, which is not a very reliable measure of knowledge. We need more and better data on factual knowledge about a large number of GGIs (Dellmuth 2016).

Ultimately, political knowledge matters because it can enhance a GGI's "epistemic virtues." This quality refers to a GGI's ability to interact with its audiences in ways that facilitate critical assessment of the GGI's activities. Buchanan and Keohane (2006) argue that such epistemic virtue is a precondition for a GGI's moral right to rule. Clearly a GGI cannot have a probing critical conversation with its audiences if they are not knowledgeable.

Utilitarian Appraisals

Utilitarian appraisals refer to citizens' judgments about the costs and benefits of GGIs for them personally. In this vein economic theories relate legitimacy beliefs to how GGIs impact on an individual's pocketbook, either in terms of personal wellbeing ("ego-tropic considerations") or the relative economic performance of their sub-national region or country ("sociotropic considerations"). The explanatory power of economic considerations has been theorized and convincingly demonstrated in the context of the EU (e.g. Eichenberg and Dalton 1993; Gabel 1998a, 1998b; Christin 2005). Economic theories assume that people are affected differentially by globalization, for example, in terms of income levels, vulnerability due to low education and occupational skills, economic performance of home country, or geographical proximity to borders.

In terms of ego-tropic considerations, there is evidence that wealthy EU citizens are more likely to benefit from capital liberalization, since they can exploit the greater investment opportunities provided by more open financial markets, which leads them to think more favorably of the EU (e.g. Gabel and Palmer 1995; Gabel 1998c; Hooghe and Marks 2005). Rohrschneider and Loveless (2010) have refined existing theories about ego-tropic considerations by examining how national contexts influence the linkages between self-interested economic considerations and EU legitimacy. Specifically, they show that citizens in less affluent countries are more inclined to evaluate the EU on the basis their own personal economic prospects. In contrast, evidence suggests that individuals in richer countries evaluate the EU chiefly on political criteria such as democracy. Ego-tropic considerations have also been shown to be relevant in the context of legitimacy beliefs towards the IMF, the World Bank, and the WTO. Dissatisfaction with one's household income appears to trigger negative attitudes towards these international economic institutions (Edwards 2009).

In terms of sociotropic considerations, survey evidence suggests that people from wealthier countries that are net contributors to the UN budget are less supportive of the UN (Dellmuth and Tallberg 2015). In the context of the EU, research suggests that the net contributors to the EU budget are less supportive of the regional institution than the net beneficiaries (e.g. Anderson and Reichert 1995; Gabel and Palmer 1995; Hooghe and Marks 2005; Karp et al. 2003; Harteveld et al. 2013). However, not all studies find evidence of such a link (Rohrschneider and Loveless 2010). Moreover, research that demonstrates an effect of net benefits from the EU's budget on public support for the EU usually does not theorize this link. That is, this work fails to demonstrate how the specific types of funding that constitute these net transfers are relevant to individual citizens. Indeed, recent research shows that European spending only increases support for the EU in the case of redistributive spending that creates clear winners and losers, which makes EU spending visible even among the less politically knowledgeable. Such supranational spending generates more supportive attitudes among those who perceive themselves as "winners" of needs-based spending (Dellmuth and Chalmers 2017). There is also evidence that the effect of EU spending on support for the EU is stronger among the politically aware and those who have a European identity (Chalmers and Dellmuth 2015). In the context of the IMF, the World Bank, and the WTO, Edwards (2009: 194) has examined both ego-tropic and sociotropic considerations. He shows that, while a "bad (and deteriorating) situation, both for the nation as well as individuals, implies a greater sensitivity to the distributional effects of the [international economic institutions]," pocketbook explanations have more explanatory power than sociotropic considerations.

Social Identity

A third strand of research on individual-level sources of legitimacy highlights the effects of social identity on support for and confidence in GGIs. These theories conceive of identities as relatively stable predispositions formed early in life through socialization and interactions with family, friends, neighbors, and teachers (Norris and Inglehart 2009: ch. 6). Identity theories of legitimacy have especially addressed the multilevel polity of the EU, where evidence suggests that people have overlapping identities (Risse 2002; Hooghe and Marks 2005).

From this perspective, a person's local, regional, national, and European identities shape how they view the EU. Individuals with more broadly inclusive European identities tend to feel less threatened by regional integration processes and are hence more supportive of the EU than individuals with entrenched national or other exclusive identities (e.g. Carey 2002; McLaren 2002, 2004; Hooghe and Marks 2005; de Vreese and Boomgaarden 2005; Chalmers and Dellmuth 2015). For example, Harteveld et al. (2013: 548) show how identity can "function as a buffer against more short-term notions, such as (perceived) costs and benefits" related to the economic impact of EU integration. Indeed, indicators of European identity typically have more explanatory power than indicators of material self-interest or sociotropic considerations when explaining support for the EU (e.g. Hooghe and Marks 2005; Chalmers and Dellmuth 2015). There is also evidence for such a link in the context of the UN, where people who identify with a world community are more positively predisposed towards the UN (Furia 2005; Norris 2000; Torgler 2008; Dellmuth and Tallberg 2015).

Values

Values theories focus on how a person's norms and moral beliefs shape their attitudes towards political institutions. The boundaries of the concepts "attitude" and "values" in this literature often blur. Values are commonly defined as standards or criteria for guiding action, for developing and maintaining attitudes towards relevant objects (Rokeach 1968: 160).

In the case of global governance, literature concerning values has usually focused more specifically on cosmopolitanism as a worldview. Broadly speaking, cosmopolitans associate their identity with humanity as a whole, adhere to universal ethics, and hold open attitudes towards people from other places and cultures. Such values of globalism, universalism, and humanism may, in turn, shape attitudes towards GGIs (cf. Inglehart and Rabier 1978; Ecker-Ehrhardt 2012), and are prevalent across social groups and countries regardless of their affluence (Furia 2005). The existing public opinion literature emphasizes two main causal mechanisms linking cosmopolitan values and legitimacy beliefs in GGIs. First, citizens identifying with a global community may be more likely to be exposed to information about GGIs and more positively predisposed toward that information (Dellmuth and Tallberg 2015; Dellmuth 2016). Second, as cosmopolitans treat humanity as a whole as a relevant identity group, they feel concrete moral and political obligations from this identification (Furia 2005). In addition, cosmopolitans may be more likely to appreciate GGIs as problem solvers for transboundary policy challenges affecting all humans (Ecker-Ehrhardt 2016).

Values theories have advanced our understanding of individual legitimacy beliefs by discussing causal linkages from values to legitimacy beliefs. Yet studies do not agree on the causal sequence: namely, whether cosmopolitan values precede beliefs in GGI legitimacy; or whether cosmopolitan values result from positive attitudes towards GGIs (Norris 2009: 20). Furthermore, the explanatory power of values other than cosmopolitanism remains unexplored. Moral beliefs and ideologies may shape individuals' attitudes toward global governance, but with the exception of one recent study (Ecker-Ehrhardt 2016) they have not been systematically linked to legitimacy beliefs.

Susceptibility to Political Communication

A final type of individual-level explanation of legitimacy beliefs focuses on citizens' susceptibility to political communication. This literature problematizes the assumption that people hold well-formed and enduring attitudes, which they can "look up" in memory to form their political judgments. Instead, this research suggests that individuals may have relatively loose opinions about political institutions, which make them susceptible to communication about these institutions, as put forward in the early study by Converse (1964). Whether citizens' legitimacy beliefs are more or less easily affected by political communication depends not only on properties of the process of political communication (such as the source, message, and object), but also on characteristics of the recipient of the communication (such as their prior experiences, opinions, and beliefs) (Tyler 2006).

Drawing on social psychology, elite communication theories suggest than legitimacy beliefs may be shaped through communication by political parties, civil society organizations, and governments (e.g. Chong and Druckman 2007). As elaborated in the next chapters of this volume, political and societal elites often compete in trying to influence citizens' perceptions of GGIs through legitimation and delegitimation practices. Typical means are press releases, social media, public speeches, and policy papers. This competition is consequential. There is robust evidence that mass publics express more favorable attitudes towards the EU when political elites send a consistent and positive message about European integration. Vice versa, more polarized elites reduce public support for the EU (Gabel and Scheve 2007a, 2007b).

Most of existing research on the effects of elite communication in global governance focuses on the EU, where the evidence is mixed (Loveless and Rohrschneider 2011). Some studies find support for an impact of elite communication on public support for the EU (de Vreese and Boomgaarden 2005). Others find that partisan ideology moderates the effect (Maier et al. 2012). Yet others find no effect at all (Chalmers and Dellmuth 2015).

Much less research addresses effects of elite communication beyond the EU. That said, one recent comparative study shows how elite communication shapes people's legitimacy beliefs vis-à-vis the UN, IMF, WTO, NAFTA, and EU (Dellmuth and Tallberg 2016a). This research demonstrates that elite communication has greater effects on citizens' legitimacy beliefs when the public perceives the communicating elites to be credible, when messages are negative in tone, and when the communication refers to GGIs with which citizens are more familiar.

The last finding ties in well with theorizing on individual-level predispositions that make citizens more or less susceptible to framing effects (Chong and Druckman 2007). Generally, the literature suggests that citizens are more impressionable when it comes to communication on issues that are less familiar to them, where they have not acquired an information and knowledge base for stable political attitudes. Conversely, framing effects diminish when individuals are more engaged and knowledgeable, making their opinions less open to capture. When citizens are already exposed to a broad array of arguments, they are less affected by biased representations of issues in elite communication (Chong and Druckman 2007; Nicholson 2011; Bechtel et al. 2015). This theoretical expectation has been verified empirically in studies which document the moderating impacts of knowledge and deliberation on the ways that political issues are framed (Druckman and Nelson 2003; Karp et al. 2003).

Taken together, the five types of individual-level studies discussed in this section have enhanced our understanding of the drivers of citizen beliefs in the legitimacy of GGIs. However, most existing work is limited to the EU and advancing this agenda requires wider testing and more comparative analysis.

Conclusion: an Agenda for GGI Legitimacy Scholars

This chapter has reviewed existing literature relevant to individual-level sources of legitimacy beliefs in GGIs. Following a discussion of the conceptualization and measurement of legitimacy beliefs per se, the chapter has assessed five types of individual-level explanations: in terms of political knowledge, utilitarian appraisals, social identity, values, and susceptibility to elite communication. This concluding section draws the overall argument together in three steps.

First, better understanding of legitimacy beliefs in global governance will require more engagement with insights from comparative politics and social psychology (cf. Kaltenthaler and Miller 2013). As the review of individual-level explanations has demonstrated, research in comparative politics has been at the forefront in integrating lessons from social psychology. With the exception of research on the EU, IR scholarship lags behind in theorizing the importance of individual-level attributes, such as political knowledge, cosmopolitan identity, and susceptibility to political communication, for the development of legitimacy beliefs.

Second, research on individual-level sources of GGI legitimacy needs more comparative work. Despite a burgeoning literature on individual-level factors that shape attitudes towards the EU, few studies examine other GGIs, and there are almost no comparative assessments of legitimacy beliefs across GGIs, issue areas, world regions, countries, social groups, and time. Exploring whether and how individual-level explanations of legitimacy beliefs work similarly or differently in varying GGI contexts is an important task for future research.

Third, insufficient data are currently available for comparative assessments of individual sources of legitimacy beliefs regarding GGIs. To redress this situation, researchers should refine and improve measures of legitimacy beliefs and their covariates in existing large-scale surveys. Work should also draw on the methodological insights from social psychology and comparative politics with respect to survey experiments (Chong and Druckman 2007). Most large-scale surveys currently face limitations in terms of measurement, coverage, and comparability, but such obstacles can be overcome through greater attention to the requirements of comparative legitimacy research. One example is the cooperation between the Legitimacy in Global Governance research program in Sweden and the WVS 7 on a new battery of questions on legitimacy in global governance. In addition, survey experiments constitute an attractive alternative to observational data. This method allows for resource-efficient collection of data that are comparable across GGIs and countries. In addition, survey experiments benefit from the advantages of generalizable population-based samples and the internal validity of experiments (cf. Mutz 2011; Maier et al. 2012; Dellmuth and Tallberg 2016a; Dellmuth et al. 2017).

All told, this discussion of existing evidence about the sources of citizens' legitimacy beliefs vis-à-vis GGIs shows that these perceptions depend on a range of individual predispositions. While the core of public opinion research on legitimacy beliefs focuses on individual sources, taking theory forward will also require consideration of how individual sources such as instrumental self-interest and social identity are shaped by contextual factors such as the institutional qualities of GGIs (see Scholte and Tallberg, this volume), the social structures in which citizens are embedded (see Scholte, this volume), and the social transmission of information about GGIs (see Bäckstrand and Söderbaum, this volume). Given the increasing importance of legitimacy beliefs for the viability of GGIs in a time of ever greater politicization of global institutions, the individual sources and circumstances explaining global governance legitimacy beliefs warrant further attention, examining legitimacy beliefs comparatively across GGIs, issue areas, world regions, countries, social groups, and time.

4

Theorizing the Institutional Sources of Global Governance Legitimacy

Jan Aart Scholte and Jonas Tallberg

Where do legitimacy beliefs come from in respect of global governance institutions (GGIs)? On what bases do people (elites as well as general publics) perceive that a GGI exercises authority in an appropriate way, thereby warranting their confidence and trust? The question of the grounds for legitimacy perceptions—i.e. the reasons why people endorse a given governing authority—has long occupied political and sociological theory in relation to the nation-state. Today, with the growth of governance beyond the state, this issue becomes pressing with regard to regional and global institutions as well.

While Chapter 3 examined sources of legitimacy associated with citizen predispositions (individual features), the present chapter considers grounds of legitimacy that arise from GGIs themselves (institutional or organizational features). Chapter 5 subsequently turns to the role of societal factors in promoting or undermining legitimacy in global governance (social structural features).

To identify and classify institutional sources of GGI legitimacy, this chapter in its first section examines existing literature concerning such bases on which subjects regard governing authorities to exercise rightful rule. This review shows that a century of theorizing has identified a diverse array of possible institutional touchstones for legitimacy beliefs. That said, this past work has not delivered a fully consolidated operational typology of the organizational sources of sociological legitimacy, particularly as they relate to political authority beyond the state. Better analytical tools are wanted for distinguishing and measuring those institutional features of a GGI that elicit perceptions of appropriate rule amongst its audiences.

With the aim of offering such an improved classificatory scheme, the second part of the chapter synthesizes and extends existing theory through a novel typology. This taxonomy is built around two axes. On the one hand, it distinguishes institutional procedure and institutional performance as central aspects of GGI policymaking. On the other hand, it identifies the democratic, the technocratic, and the fair as qualities of procedure and performance. Interweaving these two axes, the typology identifies six institutional features as possible sources of GGI legitimacy: democratic procedure, democratic performance, technocratic procedure, technocratic performance, fair procedure, and fair performance. Such a classification of the legitimacy-generating features of GGIs is both more encompassing and analytically sharper than earlier categorizations. The typology also offers promising prospects for empirical application in quantitative as well as qualitative research.

The third part of the chapter elaborates on these empirical possibilities with a discussion of why and how the relative salience of the different institutional sources of GGI legitimacy might vary across four dimensions. To begin with, the significance of these sources might fluctuate across GGIs (e.g. by institution type, issue coverage, or functional orientation). Second, the prominence of these sources might vary across countries (e.g. by regime type, level of economic development, or cultural values). A third plausible dimension of variation is across societal groups (e.g. by age, ethnicity, gender, or socioeconomic status). Finally, the relative importance of these institutional sources of legitimacy might vary across time (e.g. as new norms about appropriate global governance develop and take hold).

Institutional Sources of Legitimacy: an Array of Possibilities

This chapter is primarily concerned to develop a typology for classifying institutional sources of legitimacy perceptions in respect of GGIs, i.e. the reasons that audiences hold for regarding organizations such as the United Nations (UN) and the African Union (AU) to exercise authority appropriately. It should be specified again that the present analysis addresses *features of GGIs* that may generate legitimacy beliefs. This focus is different from that of Chapter 3, which considered individual sources of legitimacy, and Chapter 5, which explores social-structural sources of legitimacy. This chapter's focus on institutional sources of legitimacy is important not least because it identifies qualities of GGIs that members and staff can address with strategies to enhance the legitimacy of their organization in the eyes of its audiences. Equally, the conceptual framework can guide opponents of GGIs in their efforts to delegitimate these governance agencies.

To lay the ground for this chapter's proposition of a novel typology, the following paragraphs review a range of classifications from earlier general political thought on the institutional sources of legitimacy. This survey begins with Weber, then considers a range of other theories of legitimacy as related to the modern state, and finally examines recent work on the institutional sources of legitimacy in respect of GGIs.

Systematic theorization of the grounds for legitimacy perceptions began with Max Weber a century ago. Weber's classic *Economy and Society* initially roots legitimacy beliefs in affect ("emotional surrender"), value rationality ("belief in the absolute validity of the order"), religion ("belief that salvation depends on obedience to the order"), and/or "interest situations" (1922/1978: 33). Later in the text Weber distinguishes three core grounds of sociological legitimacy, namely, rationality (based on legality), tradition (the sanctity of immemorial conditions), and charisma (devotion to the exceptional character of an individual person) (1922/1978: 215). In Weber's schema democracy as a source of legitimacy evolves out of charismatic authority (1922/1978: 266–7). As indicated later in the present discussion, Weber's various propositions appear to have some—but also limited—relevance to contemporary GGIs. In any case his distinctions were offered as a heuristic device rather than as a taxonomy that would be operationalized in empirical research.

Subsequent social research has offered other conceptions of the institutional bases of sociological legitimacy. For example, Seymour Martin Lipset distinguished between legitimacy (as a matter of evaluative beliefs) and effectiveness (as a matter of instrumental calculation) (1960: 77–8). In contrast, Jürgen Habermas a decade later very much linked legitimacy to effectiveness, suggesting that the European state faced a "legitimation crisis" when it could not deliver on its welfare promises (1973/1976: Part III). Meanwhile, David Easton proposed that governments obtained consent of the governed on the grounds of ideology (moral convictions), structure (belief in institutions), or the personal qualities of rulers (1975: 452). A more recent schema developed by Robert D. Lamb has suggested that authority is accepted as legitimate to the extent that it is perceived to be predictable (non-arbitrary and transparent), justifiable (conforming to core values), equitable (with fair distribution), accessible (with assurance of voice), and respectful (of human dignity) (2014: 28–30).

Thus, even a brief survey reveals considerable variation in past conceptualizations of the institutional grounds of legitimacy. Existing social science does not provide a clear and consistent account of the features of governance organizations which elicit legitimacy perceptions among the governed. Indeed, other prominent contemporary theorists of legitimacy such as Rodney Barker and David Beetham have not offered classificatory schema of sources at all (Barker 1990; Beetham 2013). Nor are most of the distinctions suggested by Lipset, Habermas, Easton, and Lamb sufficiently precise to be readily translated into concrete indicators and measures for empirical research. Moreover, all of the classifications of institutional sources of legitimacy noted so far are directed at the modern state; it cannot be assumed that they apply equally to governance beyond the state.

The study of legitimacy perceptions with respect to suprastate authorities began in the 1970s, primarily in terms of public opinion research on European integration (Inglehart 1970; Dalton and Duval 1986; Hewstone 1986). This vein of work has continued to the present (Hooghe and Marks 2009; Koopmans and Statham 2010; de Wilde and Zürn 2012; Hobolt 2012). However, these studies have not systematically identified, in typological form, the institutional features that can shape various audiences' legitimacy beliefs. Nor has this research extended beyond European regionalism to wider global governance.

Research that specifically theorizes institutional sources of legitimacy vis-à-vis global governance first arose in the 1990s. This work arguably responded to more pronounced popular contestation during this decade of the Bretton Woods institutions, the European Union (EU), the Multilateral Agreement on Investment (MAI) initiative, and the World Trade Organization (WTO) (Beetham and Lord 1998; Hurd 1999; Gill 2000; O'Brien et al. 2000). These public protests often targeted alleged undemocratic procedures and unfair outcomes of GGIs. In addition, against a backdrop of accelerated globalization, other voices at this time were decrying shortfalls in effective problem solving from GGIs (Commission on Global Governance 1995). Correspondingly, the past two decades of efforts to theorize the institutional sources of GGI legitimacy have generally highlighted questions of democracy, technocratic effectiveness, and fairness, albeit not always very systematically.

The first important attempt at greater conceptual systematization developed around notions of "input" and "output" legitimacy of GGIs. In this vein, Fritz Scharpf distinguished between process (i.e. the ways that decisions are made) and substance (i.e. the results of decisions) as grounds for the endorsement of authority, in this case of the EU (Scharpf 1999). Later Vivien Schmidt urged additional separate consideration of "throughput" legitimacy in relation to the internal governance of EU institutions (Schmidt 2010). These distinctions helpfully note that audience perceptions of GGI legitimacy can be gained (or lost) at different stages of a policy cycle: namely, in respect of decision formulation, decision implementation, and decision outcome.

The premise of input/throughput (henceforth combined as "procedural") accounts is that process criteria are important for perceptions of legitimacy. In this vein, actors accept an institution's exercise of authority because of how the organization was set up and operates. Procedural accounts have an early antecedent in Weber's notion of legal-rational sources of legitimacy. On these lines, governance is regarded as appropriate because properly appointed authorities follow properly formulated decision-taking processes. So, for example, audiences might accord legitimacy to the Forest Stewardship Council (FSC) because its policymaking is perceived to involve a broad range of stakeholders. Alternatively, actors might deny the legitimacy of the Group of Twenty (G20) because it is seen to operate outside of formal public international law. For procedural approaches, legitimacy of a GGI derives from the way that the institution functions, irrespective of the consequences of its decisions and policies.

In contrast, other accounts of GGI legitimacy sources emphasize output (henceforth "performance"). On these lines, perceptions of legitimacy derive from audience evaluations of a governing institution's outcomes. With a focus on performance, GGIs might gain or lose legitimacy depending on whether audiences see them as enhancing or undermining desired conditions in society. For example, the United Nations Framework Convention on Climate Change (UNFCCC) might attract legitimacy if actors perceive it to enhance ecological sustainability. Meanwhile, the Kimberley Process (KP) might obtain legitimacy if audiences regard it to advance peace. Alternatively, the World Bank might struggle to hold legitimacy if subjects believe that this institution fails to reduce poverty. For performance approaches, legitimacy of a GGI derives from its impacts, irrespective of how the institution made the relevant policy.

In practice, procedural and performance sources of legitimacy may coexist in manifold combinations, as audiences assess a GGI's right to rule by invoking both aspects. Towards one end of the spectrum, legitimacy perceptions will be stronger where both procedure and performance criteria are seen to be met. Toward another end of the spectrum, legitimacy perceptions will be weaker where audiences evaluate both process and outcome negatively. In other cases, audiences' assessments of a GGI's procedure and performance may be mixed, both within and between the two aspects. For example, many might rate the North Atlantic Treaty Organization (NATO) poorly on transparent procedures, but highly on security outcomes.

Yet, as the preceding illustrations indicate, there is more to the sources of GGI legitimacy than procedure or performance per se. Slightly simplified, this distinction captures two *aspects* of policymaking, rooted in two different stages of the policy cycle, which may affect legitimacy beliefs. However, to get at more specific grounds for legitimacy beliefs one must also examine more precisely the *quality* of procedure and performance. Thus, the examples above referred to *transparent* procedures, *effective* performance, etc. Building on Scharpf's work, it might be tempting to equate procedure with democracy and performance with effectiveness. However, this conflation would exclude the possibility that democracy and effectiveness could be qualities of both procedure and performance. For example, democracy could be an outcome in cases where a GGI's activities generate more transparency and participation.

Likewise, effectiveness could be a quality of policy processes if a given institutional procedure produces more and faster decisions. In addition, it is plausible that other qualities of procedure and performance besides democracy and effectiveness could shape legitimacy perceptions. It is therefore important that a typology of sources of GGI legitimacy supplements the procedure/performance dichotomy with an appreciation of the multiple qualities of process and outcome that may matter.

Ian Hurd moves in this direction with his three-way distinction of "favourable outcomes," "fairness," and "correct procedure" as institutional grounds for the perceived legitimacy of intergovernmental organizations (IGOs) (2007: 67). The first category corresponds broadly to Scharpf's notion of effective outputs. Hurd then highlights fairness (of either procedure or outcome) as an additional important institutional source of GGI legitimacy. The third category of "correct procedure" suggests that respect of agreed decision-making rules is more important for perceptions of GGI legitimacy than democratic process. However, this conceptualization arguably reflects Hurd's interest in the legitimacy that *states* accord to *IGOs*, as distinct from the present volume's concern with the legitimacy that *people* accord to *GGIs* in the broader sense. Wider publics (i.e. beyond government officials) are arguably more concerned that GGIs heed democratic voice and control than that such bodies adhere to legal-bureaucratic routines. Moreover, like Scharpf's input-output approach, Hurd's schema omits the possibility that GGIs could obtain or lose legitimacy in terms of effective procedures or democratic performance.

Addressing some of these shortfalls, Jonas Tallberg and Michael Zürn (2017) develop a 2×2 matrix of sources of GGI legitimacy which overcomes equations of process with democracy and outcome with effectiveness. This typology distinguishes legitimacy derived from "procedure" and "performance" on the one hand and from "democracy" and "purposiveness" on the other. In this schema, democracy can be a quality of policymaking processes (with transparency, participation, and accountability) as well as a policy outcome (with protection of democratic rights and processes). Likewise, what this typology calls purposiveness can be a quality of procedure (with efficiency, expertise, and legality) as well as results (with problem solving and welfare gains).

While this 2×2 scheme is analytically tighter and more comprehensive than earlier conceptualizations of the sources of GGI legitimacy by Scharpf and Hurd, the typology includes some significant ambiguities. In particular, the designation "purposive" is rather sweeping, tending to encompass anything that is not covered by democracy. In addition, the schema proposed by Tallberg and Zürn rather downplays fairness as a source of legitimacy beliefs and does not recognize that fairness is a value that could relate to procedure as well as performance.

In sum, a century of theorizing has identified a range of possible institutional sources of legitimacy, for governance in general as well as GGIs in particular. Yet on the whole the resulting schemas are narrow, fuzzy, and/or difficult to operationalize. What is wanted is a typology that encompasses more possible sources, distinguishes them more clearly from each other, and allows for easier application in empirical research.

A Novel Typology

To advance along these lines, the following section develops a new typology of institutional sources for GGI legitimacy beliefs by means of a 2×3 matrix (Table 4.1). Like any analytical construct, this typology has limitations, which are acknowledged below. Nevertheless, the schema covers many key institutional features of GGIs that may lend or deny these institutions legitimacy—and does so more systematically and precisely than earlier efforts.

In this schema, the two rows make the distinction between procedure and performance that has evolved out of earlier thinking about input and output legitimacy. Hence the matrix distinguishes between sources of legitimacy that pertain, on the one hand, to the ways that GGIs are perceived to conduct themselves and, on the other hand, to the results that GGIs are perceived to produce.

Meanwhile, the columns in the matrix highlight a threefold distinction between democratic, technocratic, and fair as three generic qualities that may apply to both the procedure and the performance of GGIs. The category of democratic procedure and performance is taken forward from earlier schema, and is used to capture perceptions that affected publics have due voice in and control over governance arrangements. The category of technocratic procedure and performance is used to capture audiences' perceptions that a governing authority is effective in the light of best available knowledge and policy instruments. The term "technocracy" is not invoked here with any negative connotations and rather seeks to convey a sense of expertise-based problem solving (Fischer 1989). Finally, the category of fair procedure and performance captures perceptions that process and outcome are just, equitable, and impartial vis-à-vis

Table 4.1. Institutional sources of legitimacy

	Democratic	Technocratic	Fair
Procedure	Participation Accountability	Efficiency Expertise	Impartiality Proportionality
Performance	Democracy promotion in wider society	Problem solving Collective gains	Human dignity Distributive justice

implicated actors. Thus, in a further development of the Tallberg and Zürn matrix, which placed all non-democratic sources of legitimacy in the category of "purposive," this typology carefully distinguishes between technocratic and fair qualities of procedure and performance, and puts these qualities on a par with democratic qualities.

A next step is to identify specific institutional features, within each of the six combinations, that generate audience perceptions of legitimate global governance. Thus, what would qualify as "democratic procedure," "technocratic procedure," and "fair procedure"? Similarly, what would count as "democratic performance," "technocratic performance," and "fair performance"? Such more precise institutional features can in turn guide the selection of indicators for empirical research on sources of GGI legitimacy.

In terms of *democratic procedure*, one prominent legitimacy source could be participation, namely, that all affected parties have due involvement in and deliberation around a GGI's policymaking processes (Held 1995). Also significant in democratic procedure could be accountability, namely, that a GGI through transparency, consultation, review, and redress adequately answers to the publics that it affects (Scholte 2011a). Meanwhile, legitimacy through *democratic performance* could be achieved when a GGI's activities increase popular participation and public accountability in wider society (Pevehouse 2005; Keohane et al. 2009).

As for *technocratic procedure*, legitimacy could emanate from efficiency or expertise in institutional processes. Efficiency could lie in the number and speed of a GGI's policy decisions, while expertise could involve basing policy decisions on the best knowledge and skills (Majone 1998; Bernstein 2005). Meanwhile, *technocratic performance* could rest on problem solving (i.e. the fullest and fastest realization of results) and collective gains (i.e. the largest benefits for society) (Keohane 1984; Scharpf 1999). For example, some recent empirical research concludes that citizen perceptions of IGO problem solving constitute a strong base for legitimacy beliefs (Ecker-Ehrhardt 2012; Dellmuth and Tallberg 2015).

With respect to *fair procedure*, this quality could stem from institutional features such as impartiality (i.e. policymaking processes are followed consistently and without discrimination) and proportionality (i.e. members contribute to GGI resourcing in accordance with their relative means). Thus, for example, perceptions of double standards have undermined legitimacy beliefs vis-à-vis some global human rights regimes. Likewise, IGOs whose decision-making procedures are dominated by a single state (the United States) have been found to attract lower legitimacy perceptions (Johnson 2011). Meanwhile, *fair performance* could be judged in terms of institutional features that secure human dignity (i.e. the outcomes uphold norms of basic humanity for all) and distributive justice (i.e. the benefits are equitably shared among those concerned). For example, global justice protests have often targeted global economic institutions as a cause of unacceptable socioeconomic inequalities (Della Porta and Tarrow 2005; Scholte et al. 2016).

Thus, the schema proposed here includes a larger range of sources of legitimacy than earlier typologies and also specifies them more systematically and precisely. Moreover, the matrix allows for cultural variation in what audiences might understand by "democratic," "technocratic," and "fair" procedure and performance. The classification has the further merit of being applicable both broadly (to a GGI as a whole) and narrowly (to certain of a GGI's institutional parts, policies, or programs). Finally, the typology pertains both positively (when the relevant institutional sources of legitimacy are present) and negatively (when they are absent).

Of course, like any typology, this conceptualization of the institutional sources of GGI legitimacy involves simplifications, exclusions, and imposed priorities which need to be explicitly acknowledged. For example, alternative approaches might wish to give greater distinctive attention to legal grounds of GGI legitimacy (cf. Bernstein 2005: 152–6; Brunnée and Toope 2010; Pauwelyn et al. 2014). In contrast, the present categorization suggests that legal sources can be sufficiently covered by technocratic and fair procedure.

In addition, the proposed typology could be criticized for inadequately capturing what might be termed "substance-grounded" legitimacy beliefs. That is, legitimacy may derive primarily from "societal evaluations of organizational goals" (Scott 1991: 169; also Lenz and Viola 2017). Hence, some audiences might make judgments about the legitimacy of a GGI on the basis of its issue of concern, while having limited knowledge about its decision-making procedures or its policy outcomes. For example, people might regard the International Criminal Court (ICC) as legitimate because it addresses a perceived good cause of human rights; or people might consider the World Health Organization (WHO) legitimate since it pursues a perceived laudable aim of disease control. Possibly such beliefs could be classed amongst perceptions of technocratic effectiveness (whether or not the institution is actually successful in achieving its advertised aims). However, some critics might argue that the logics of this source of legitimacy are sufficiently distinct as to warrant separate treatment outside the typology.

The matrix could also in principle be expanded with a fourth column to cover potential charismatic sources of GGI legitimacy (cf. Scholte 2011b). Perhaps Weber's category is relevant in relation to certain GGI executives such as Dag Hammarskjöld as UN Secretary-General in 1953–61 or Fadi Chehadé as President/CEO of the Internet Corporation for Assigned Names and Numbers (ICANN) in 2012–16. Maybe high-profile celebrity involvement in certain IGOs has generated popular legitimacy perceptions rooted in charisma (Cooper 2008). Yet, these possibilities duly noted, our judgment remains that charismatic leadership does not figure as an institutional source of GGI legitimacy on a par with the six features highlighted here.

Likewise, the matrix excludes religious rationales as a further possible source of legitimacy beliefs vis-à-vis GGIs. Critics could note that religion is a major political force in much of the contemporary world and that large audiences might judge a GGI on the basis of a faith-based morality. For example, Catholics worldwide lend the Holy See legitimacy on mainly religious grounds, and religion has figured as a major legitimating rationale for the Organization of Islamic Cooperation (OIC) (Ameli 2011). Meanwhile, some revivalist movements have challenged existing GGIs on faith grounds (Sivaraksa 1999; El-Ghazali 2001: 368–78). That said, religious beliefs could arguably be encompassed within the 2×3 matrix as a type of fairness and justice perception.

So, as with any analytical classification, there are certainly potential limitations to the typology of institutional sources of GGI legitimacy offered here. Still, the 2×3 matrix set out above offers greater breadth and specificity than existing alternatives, while also focusing on generic sources in a way that facilitates systematic and nuanced empirical research. This promise gives ample reason to take the typology forward.

Applying the Typology: Exploring Variation

Having elaborated a conceptual framework regarding institutional sources of GGI legitimacy, how could this scheme be employed to explore variation in actor perceptions of legitimacy in global governance? Does the relative weight of the six posited core institutional bases of GGI legitimacy shift between contexts? For example, are there some circumstances where democratic procedure is most important and others where technocratic performance is most important for perceptions of GGI legitimacy? This is mainly a question for future empirical research. However, to guide such inquiries, the following discussion develops a set of plausible expectations about variation in the relative importance of these institutional sources of legitimacy. The subsections focus in turn on four overarching dimensions of variation: across GGIs, across countries, across societal groups, and over time.

Preliminarily we need to confront the broader issue of why we would expect to see variation at all. The answer to this question lies in the social embeddedness of legitimacy beliefs. Perceptions of legitimacy are formed in a context of social norms about the appropriate exercise of authority. In this vein Mark Suchman regards legitimacy as the "generalized perception or assumption that the actions of an entity are desirable, proper, or appropriate *within some socially constructed system of norms, values, beliefs, and definitions*" (1995: 547, emphasis added).

The six institutional sources of legitimacy beliefs highlighted here relate to norms in modern society about governance as good and desirable when it is democratic, technocratic, and fair in its organization and consequences. Yet these norms have not always been as relevant, nor are they everywhere of equal strength. Rather, their salience can be expected to vary across time and space, depending on contextual circumstances. The following discussion explores the potential significance of a number of these variations. The expectations developed should be read with an *all-else-equal* clause in mind, since they specify relationships that could hold were other determinants of legitimacy beliefs to be held constant.

Variation across GGIs

To start with, the institutional sources of legitimacy may vary in importance across GGIs, because of specific features of the authority of the governing body in question. A GGI possesses authority when it enjoys a recognized competence to make binding decisions in the name of the collective interest (Weber 1922/1978; Raz 2009; Hooghe and Marks 2015). It is plausible that the relative importance of different sources of legitimacy may vary depending on the nature of a GGI's political authority. Four dimensions of this authority could be particularly relevant: namely, level, issue orientation, functional orientation, and constitutional form.

First, the six institutional sources of legitimacy may vary in importance depending on the *level of authority* enjoyed by a GGI. The expectation is that higher authority for GGIs is related to greater emphasis on democratic procedure as a source of legitimacy. This expectation is based on a historical shift from technocratic performance to democratic procedure as the primary driver of legitimacy, in the wake of growing authority for GGIs (Lindberg and Scheingold 1970; Hooghe and Marks 2009; Zürn et al. 2012). This expectation is also supported by the observation that GGIs which possess the highest authority—such as the EU, the International Monetary Fund (IMF), and the World Bank—are typically among the institutions which public opinion most often evaluates on democratic criteria (Hooghe and Marks 2015). While it is vigorously debated whether or not these institutions suffer from "democratic deficits," similar debates do not arise in relation to low-authority GGIs, such as the Nordic Council and the Asia-Pacific Economic Cooperation (APEC) (Koopmans and Statham 2010; Nullmeier et al. 2010; Hobolt 2012).

Second, the salience of different institutional sources of legitimacy may vary depending on a GGI's *issue orientation*. Partly, this is a question of policy scope, where existing literature differentiates between task-specific and general-purpose GGIs (Lenz et al. 2015.). It is also a matter of issue area, where analysis commonly distinguishes between policy realms such as economic affairs, sustainable development, and human security (Rittberger et al. 2012).

Task-specific GGIs, such as the International Atomic Energy Agency (IAEA) and the FSC, address societal problems in discrete, functional pieces. These institutions have a narrow policy scope and are often not based on a shared sense of community. Technocratic and fairness criteria are likely to be particularly prominent when audiences evaluate the legitimacy of this type of authority (Tallberg and Zürn 2017). In contrast, general purpose GGIs, such as the EU and the Association of South East Asian Nations (ASEAN), are umbrella governance apparatuses, not unlike national governments, covering a full spectrum of problems. These institutions have a broad policy mandate and are often rooted in a sense of (regional) community. Audiences are more likely to evaluate such general purpose GGIs on democratic standards (Tallberg and Zürn 2017).

In terms of issue focus, the theory of basic needs suggests that people first and foremost seek to secure first-order requirements of survival and safety, before they aspire to "higher" needs (Maslow 1943). Extending this logic to problem solving in global governance, actors could be expected to privilege technocratic delivery, the more that a GGI serves to secure basic needs, which might include disease control, food security, and peace. In contrast, democratic procedure could be a more prominent determinant of audience legitimacy perceptions in respect of "higher" needs, which might include the regulation of product standards and the allocation of Internet domain names.

Third, the *functional orientation* of a GGI's authority may influence the relative importance of different institutional sources of legitimacy. Functional orientation relates here to whether GGIs primarily perform executive, legislative, or judicial roles. For example, it is reasonable to expect that legitimacy beliefs vis-à-vis international courts stem mainly from procedural criteria, such as independence, impartiality, fairness, and legal expertise, rather than from the substantive outcomes that courts generate (Franck 1990; Chayes and Chayes 1995: 133–4; Alter 2014: 8–10). Conversely, executive institutions, such as development banks, are probably more likely to attract public legitimacy through their contributions to collective welfare and fair outcomes, rather than through conformance to specific procedural criteria. It can also be expected that suprastate parliamentary assemblies and multistakeholder forums, which approximate the domestic legislative branch, are likely to have their legitimacy assessed more on democratic procedural criteria than on performance standards (Raymond and DeNardis 2015; Rocabert et al. 2016).

Fourth, and finally, the *constitutional form* of a GGI's authority may influence the relative salience of different institutional sources of legitimacy. As indicated in Chapter 1, GGIs come in four major constitutive formats: IGOs, transgovernmental networks (TGNs), hybrid institutions that combine public and private actors, and purely private bodies. While all possess authority, the ways in which it has been established, and is exercised by the GGI, vary across the four types and may affect the institutional sources of legitimacy. For their part, IGOs derive authority from treaty-based state consent and are principally governed by member governments. In contrast, TGNs are informal institutions linking regulators, legislators, judges, or other actors across national boundaries. TGNs have developed through frequent interaction and memoranda of understanding rather than from formal treaties (Slaughter and Hale 2011). Hybrid institutions are based on the notion that various state and non-state actors should be involved together in global policymaking that affects them. Finally, private governance bodies develop and monitor regulation without the participation of state and intergovernmental actors. Such differences in the constitutive nature of GGIs could suggest that technocratic procedure (e.g. legality) figures more prominently as a source of legitimacy for IGOs, while technocratic performance (e.g. expertise) matters more extensively for TGNs and private bodies, and democratic procedure (e.g. participation) stands out for hybrid institutions.

Variation across Countries

A second dimension of variation in the relative importance of the six institutional sources of GGI legitimacy relates to differences of perceptions across countries. Such variation is plausible since countries differ in a number of ways (political, economic, and cultural) that could influence domestic actors' views of GGIs.

First, the *political regimes* of countries may influence the relative weight of the different institutional sources of GGI legitimacy. Citizens and elites in democracies may be more prone to form legitimacy beliefs vis-à-vis GGIs on the basis of democratic procedure than audiences in countries with autocratic rule. Social norms of appropriate institutional design are engrained in political systems, leading actors in domestic democracies to formulate different expectations of GGIs than actors in domestic autocracies. For audiences in democracies, the expectation that GGIs should be democratic involves the extension of a familiar procedural standard—democracy—from national to global institutions. This is one reason why GGIs with more democratic memberships tend to be more transparent, accountable, and open to civil society involvement (Grigorescu 2007, 2010; Tallberg et al. 2016a). For audiences in autocracies, democratic procedure is not the same holy grail of legitimacy, even if the country's citizens may strive to achieve democracy, and even if autocratic governments may use the term "democracy" to legitimize or delegitimize institutions. For instance, it has been shown that representatives of authoritarian states often use democratic rhetoric in the General Assembly when challenging Western dominance in the UN (Eisentraut 2013; Binder and Heupel 2015).

Second, it is plausible to expect that differences in countries' level of *economic development* shape the relative importance attached to different institutional sources of legitimacy. Building on the hierarchy of needs (Maslow 1943), actors in more affluent countries can "afford" to base their legitimacy assessments on democratic procedural criteria, while their counterparts in less developed countries are more likely to base their evaluations on the technocratic performance of GGIs, as well as the fairness of their procedures and performances, especially in terms of securing impartial treatment relative to more developed countries. This expectation is consistent with the observation that developing democracies, such as India and Brazil, are generally less enthusiastic about democratic procedures in GGIs than developed democracies (Zürn and Stephen 2010). It is also consistent with demands from emerging powers that the IMF, the World Bank, and WTO adjust their decision-making procedures to take account of the increased economic role of these countries (Zangl et al. 2016).

Third, variation across countries in *cultural values* may shape the criteria used to evaluate the legitimacy of GGIs. Inglehart and Welzel's (2005) cultural map, based on data from the World Values Survey (WVS), shows that there is systematic cross-country variation in culture across two dimensions: traditional versus secular-rational values; and survival versus self-expression values (see also WVS 2016). Some world regions, notably the more Protestant parts of Europe, are characterized by greater emphasis on secular-rational and self-expression values, while other world regions, notably Africa and the Middle East world, are characterized more by traditional and survival values. Such patterns suggest that democratic and fair procedure could play a greater role in countries characterized by self-expression values, while technocratic and fair performance would be of greater importance in countries with a greater emphasis on survival values.

Variation across Social Groups

A third dimension on which institutional sources of legitimacy perceptions may vary relates to societal cleavages such as gender, age, education, socio-economic status, and ethnicity, as well as across the citizen-elite divide. Societies are heterogeneous. A range of social theories expect such differences to matter for people's attitudes, and public opinion research offers some support for these propositions. The following paragraphs discuss potential expectations related to age, education, and the citizen-elite divide, based on the assumption that differences across social groups could matter for legitimacy perceptions vis-à-vis GGIs.

First, expectations of *age* variation may be derived from research on attitudes toward politics in general. The dominant finding in existing literature is that individuals develop core political predispositions in childhood, adolescence, and early adulthood, and that these predispositions gradually become more stable as people age (Sears and Funk 1999; Norris 2011: 133–4). This means that generational cohorts typically carry with them the imprint of their early political experiences, and that general societal values change through generational replacement. This pattern has two implications. To begin with, it suggests that variation in institutional sources of GGI legitimacy is not tied to age per se, such as the widespread assumption that individuals become less liberal and more conservative as they get older (Crittendon 1962), for which there is little evidence (Sears and Funk 1999). In addition, the process of societal modernization entails that younger generations should put relatively greater emphasis on self-expression values than older generations. This should make democratic procedures and performances, most closely related to self-expression values, relatively more important for the formation of legitimacy beliefs towards GGIs among younger people.

Second, *education*, which is closely related to socioeconomic status or class, is associated with particular values in regard to political institutions. Greater education develops cognitive skills and affects civic engagement (Delli Karpini and Keeter 1996; Campbell 2006). In the words of Pippa Norris, "More educated citizens typically display far greater political interest, civic knowledge, internal efficacy, and activism in public affairs" (2011: 130; see also Verba et al. 1995). This translates into an expectation, borne out in empirical research, that more well-educated citizens put greater emphasis on democratic values in political life. Not only do these circles generally have higher aspirations as regards the realization of democracy, but they are also more critical when political decision making fails to live up to these standards (Norris 2011: 131–3). This pattern suggests that more educated individuals are more likely to evaluate the legitimacy of GGIs based on democratic procedure criteria.

Third, the relative priority given to different institutional sources of GGI legitimacy may vary across the *citizen-elite divide*. "Elites" are here understood as leaders in academic, business, civil society, government, media, and party-political circles, with significant influence on public policy. While the citizen-elite distinction might overlap with education and socioeconomic status, it is explicitly based on the formal positions of persons as leaders of central organizations in society, rather than their attributes as individuals. One potential expectation is that citizens in general are relatively more concerned with the performance of GGIs, while elites put greater emphasis on procedural features.

Variation over Time

A fourth and final dimension considered here is variation over time in the relative importance of different institutional sources of GGI legitimacy. Does the relative priority of "democratic performance," "technocratic procedure," "fair performance," and so on alter from one period to another? The central question here is whether the contexts that actors draw upon to formulate their legitimacy beliefs shift with time. This is plausible, considering how some of the factors highlighted in earlier sub-sections have changed over time. The following discussion focuses on how political authority, domestic democracy, and economic development may help to explain variation not only across institutions and countries, but also over time. However, it should be noted that also generational replacement and generally improving levels of education may translate into over-time variation in the relative salience of different institutional sources of GGI legitimacy.

In one important historical shift, the past few decades have witnessed an unprecedented growth in authority for GGIs that may have contributed to changing how these institutions are evaluated. This development is a result both of growing delegation of authority to GGIs and of increased pooling of authority within GGIs (Hooghe and Marks 2015; Zürn et al. 2015). It is frequently argued that this shift has changed the relative importance of different sources of legitimacy, away from technocratic performance and toward democratic procedure. In this view, GGIs historically earned their legitimacy through the collective benefits they produced for states and societies (Buchanan and Keohane 2006). In this regard Leon Lindberg and Stuart Scheingold (1970) spoke of a "permissive consensus" in Europe, where populations enjoyed the fruits of cooperation and supported its broad goals, while taking little concrete interest in the process of integration. However, as GGIs have gained greater authority, often at the expense of domestic governments, producing collective benefits is no longer sufficient to be regarded as legitimate (Scharpf 1999). Instead, being perceived to satisfy democratic criteria of decision making has also become central. Existing scholarship offers support for this claim by pointing to patterns of politicization and contestation of GGIs (O'Brien et al. 2000; Della Porta and Tarrow 2005; Hooghe and Marks 2009; Koopmans and Statham 2010; de Wilde and Zürn 2012; Zürn et al. 2012). While the term "democratic deficit" hardly existed in the 1980s, it emerged as a prominent way of characterizing and criticizing the EU in the early 1990s, and subsequently spread to public debates concerning other GGIs. In addition, GGIs tend to act as if the standards have changed in this direction, strengthening their democratic procedural practices and making greater reference to democratic criteria in their external communications (Tallberg et al. 2013; Rocabert et al. 2016; Dingwerth et al. 2016).

With another key historical shift, domestic democratization may have strengthened social norms privileging democratic procedure and performance as institutional sources of GGI legitimacy. The end of the Cold War brought widespread democratization of former authoritarian states in Central and Eastern Europe as well as other areas of the world (Gleditsch and Ward 2008). Illustrating the general burst of optimism about liberal democracy at that time, Francis Fukuyama spoke of "the end point of mankind's ideological evolution and the universalization of Western liberal democracy as the final form of human governance" (1992: 3). This expansion in domestic democracy is likely to have boosted the importance of democratic standards for popular legitimacy beliefs towards GGIs. Domestic democratization has led to more democratic procedures within GGIs and more attention to democracy promotion in the policies of GGIs (Pevehouse 2005; Grigorescu 2015; Tallberg et al. 2016a). It could also contribute to a general elevation of democracy as a source of GGI legitimacy perceptions. Several observers of global governance suggest that democracy has gained such a special status (Held 1995; Bodansky 1999; Archibugi et al. 2012).

Recent decades of economic development in the world may also have shifted the relative importance of the different sources of GGI legitimacy explored in this chapter. The trend is evident from the UN's Human Development Index (HDI), which measures wellbeing in terms of the three dimensions of health, education, and standard of living, rather than economic growth alone (UNDP 2016). The index shows that the world as a whole over the past twenty-five years has seen a notable increase on the index from 0.597 to 0.711. If the world had been a country, it would have transitioned from the category of "medium human development" to "high human development." The improvements are particularly notable in the least developed countries, which have seen a collective HDI increase from 0.348 to 0.502. As countries have transitioned to higher levels of development, basic needs such as food, water, and security are fulfilled to a greater extent. One implication may be that the importance attached to technocratic performance declines relative to other institutional sources of legitimacy. Instead, procedural standards that meet citizens' growing demands for self-expression through autonomy, participation, and free choice may gain in prominence. As the WVS findings put it, "When basic physiological and safety needs are fulfilled there is a growing emphasis on self-expression values" (WVS 2016; see also Inglehart and Welzel 2005).

Conclusion

This chapter has: (a) reviewed existing literature on the institutional sources of sociological legitimacy in global governance; (b) developed a new and richer typology of such sources; and (c) discussed why and how these sources may vary in salience across time, space, social group, and governance organization. The following conclusion expands on implications of this novel typology for future research.

The typology offers a useful basis for empirically testing if, when, and how different institutional features of GGIs, singularly or in combination, shape actors' legitimacy perceptions. Compared to previous conceptualizations, the classification elaborated in this chapter is richer: covering democratic, technocratic, and fairness qualities of both procedure and performance. The typology arguably encapsulates the main institutional sources of GGI legitimacy in play today. In addition, the categorization is more precise, by ordering specific features of GGIs (e.g. transparency, expertise, distributive outcomes) into the six alternative institutional sources of legitimacy. This makes the typology amenable to nuanced analysis of the circumstances which shape legitimacy perceptions. Finally, the typology comes with a range of theoretically grounded expectations of variation in the salience of these sources. These expectations offer starting points for systematic empirical testing of the conditions under which the six sources are particularly powerful determinants of audience evaluations of GGIs.

In moving towards testing of the institutional sources of GGI legitimacy, devising an empirical strategy is the central challenge. How can legitimacy and its institutional sources be operationalized in empirical research? What data are available to systematically map and analyze the relative prominence of different institutional sources of legitimacy? What methods are most suitable for careful and comprehensive empirical analysis? As this research agenda moves forward, it needs to consider the strategies for measuring legitimacy discussed by Lisa Dellmuth in Chapter 3, as well as promising ways for systematically evaluating the impact of institutional qualities of GGIs. In the first case, focus group interviews might provide a solution, while in the latter case, recent research suggests that survey experiments may be particularly useful (Bernauer and Gampfer 2013; Dellmuth et al. 2017).

This chapter also has implications for themes explored in subsequent chapters of this volume. The present chapter has examined sources of legitimacy in terms of actor perceptions of institutional features of GGIs; it has left unspoken the relationship between those actor-level dynamics and deeper structures of world politics. An array of macrotheories—including realism, liberalism, constructivism, and a variety of critical approaches—suggest various understandings of how larger social structures relate to legitimacy in global governance. Chapter 5 complements the current chapter by examining how legitimacy perceptions may be shaped by societal structures related to, for instance, norms, hegemonic states, capitalism, discourse, (post)modernity, and social stratifications.

In addition, this chapter speaks to processes of legitimation and delegitimation—the focus of Part III of this volume. Legitimation and delegitimation shape audiences' beliefs about GGIs' legitimacy through discursive, institutional, and behavioral practices (see Bäckstrand and Söderbaum, this volume). These practices typically invoke the standards identified in this chapter to justify or challenge the authority of GGIs. For instance, opponents of GGIs often present discursive narratives that criticize these institutions as being undemocratic and unfair. GGIs themselves engage in institutional reforms that aim to shore up legitimacy through greater efficiency and increased participation. Behavioral protests target GGIs' shortcomings in terms of solving urgent policy problems, such as poverty and climate change. Identifying the institutional sources of legitimacy is therefore essential—not only in its own right, but also for understanding the dynamics of legitimation and delegitimation in global governance.

5

Social Structure and Global Governance Legitimacy

Jan Aart Scholte

This volume develops a research agenda on the sociological legitimacy of global governance. Sociological explanations generally encompass both actor circumstances (i.e. features of the behavioral units involved) and structural circumstances (i.e. features of the social order in which the studied phenomenon is situated). Chapters 3 and 4 have highlighted actor-centered (in the sense of both individual and institutional) sources of legitimacy in global governance. The present chapter rounds off a sociological picture with a focus on social-structural sources (also taken up in the concluding overview of Chapters 11 and 12). A structural analysis expects that forms and degrees of legitimacy beliefs around global governance emanate (at least in part) from characteristics of the prevailing social order.

It should be immediately underlined that actor sources and structural sources of legitimacy are interrelated. Thus, Chapter 3 in its exploration of individual sources of global governance legitimacy also referred to matters such as identity and values which are partly embedded in the societal framework. Likewise, Chapter 4 expected that institutional (in the sense of organizational) sources of legitimacy vis-à-vis global governance would vary inter alia across countries and social groups. By the same token, the present chapter, while focusing on social-structural sources of legitimacy in global governance, also links these societal ordering principles to the features of individuals and institutions. In this way Chapters 3–5 can be seen as a package.

The task of this chapter is to consider how social structure can shape legitimacy beliefs vis-à-vis global governance. To be sure, legitimacy perceptions are held by individuals and refer to regulatory institutions; however, this interplay of subjects and their governing bodies unfolds amidst a social architecture. The issue is how that societal organization influences forms and extents of legitimacy in global governance.

The rest of the chapter explores this question in two parts: the first metatheoretical and the second theoretical. The metatheoretical part examines broad ontological, epistemological, and methodological issues regarding social structure, its power, its changes, and its spaces—all as these matters relate to legitimacy dynamics around global governance. The second part then explores a range of possible specific social-structural sources of legitimacy vis-à-vis global governance institutions (GGIs). These postulated world-ordering forces include norms, hegemonic states, capitalism, discourses, modernity/postmodernity, and social stratifications. Throughout, the chapter assesses promises as well as challenges of incorporating social-structural sources into empirical research on legitimacy in global governance.

Metatheoretical Concerns

Structural explanations involve certain broad ontological, epistemological, and methodological issues that want examination before one addresses the specific features of social structure that might be relevant to legitimacy in global governance. The following discussion considers four such metatheoretical concerns. The first sub-section below elaborates on the character of social structure as a source of legitimacy. The second discusses the power of social structure: that is, its capacity to affect outcomes. In particular, this sub-section examines, with reference to the dynamics of legitimacy, different sociological understandings of the causal relations between actor circumstances and structural circumstances. The third sub-section addresses structural change, a crucial question since such transformations alter the larger societal framings of legitimacy beliefs. The fourth sub-section considers the arena of social structure, highlighting in particular a distinction between territorial, global, and transscalar conceptions of "society." A crucial question here is how far, in respect of global issues and their governance, social structure maps onto territorial units such as countries—or whether structural patterns operate across transborder spaces.

Social Structure

Part II of this book explores why people may believe that GGIs exercise appropriate authority (or not). The three chapters approach the sources of legitimacy from different angles: individual, institutional, and structural. Some analysts regard these three types of explanation as rival, while others (including the present author) see them as complementary.

Chapter 3 suggested that important sources of GGI legitimacy (or its absence) lie with the circumstances of the individual. For example, a person might ascribe rightful authority to a GGI as a function of their particular political knowledge, their self-interest calculations, their feelings of social trust, their self-identity constructions, and their reception of political communications. In these different ways, legitimacy beliefs would arise from the cognitive workings of the believer's mind (Tyler 2006).

Chapter 4 proposed that legitimacy perceptions towards a GGI result from institutional features of the GGI itself. The focus of attention thereby shifted from the perceiver to that which is perceived. From an institutional angle, legitimacy beliefs vis-à-vis global regulation emanate from the agenda, the procedures, and/or the performance of the GGI, such as the International Monetary Fund (IMF) or the African Union (AU). As proposed in Chapter 4, the qualities of institutional operations and outcomes which could elicit legitimacy beliefs include democracy, technocracy, and fairness.

Now Chapter 5 considers that, alongside individual and institutional sources, legitimacy in global governance also has deeper structural sources. Indeed, why do individuals formulate their interests and construct their identities in the particular ways that they do? Why are institutional sources of legitimacy such as "democracy," "effectiveness," and "fairness" today generally understood in certain ways (e.g. along Western-modern lines) rather than others (e.g. with indigenous-traditional perspectives)? Such questions cannot be fully answered with reference to the characteristics of individuals and institutions. Structural explanations suggest that actor perceptions and behaviors are (at least partly) a function of the social order of the day.

"Social structures" are patterns that arrange a population's collective life (Parsons 1937; Merton 1949/1968). This ordering is "deep," in the sense of being embedded in the underlying fabric of social relations. As such, deeper "social" structures (such as capitalist production or rationalist knowledge) are distinct from surface "institutional" structures (such as a government, a firm, or a civil society association). Thus, for example, the United Nations (UN) and the Forest Stewardship Council (FSC) are institutional structures, whereas caste and gender are social structures. True, some scholarship uses the term "social institution" in a deeper structural sense, speaking for instance of science as an "institution" (Buhari-Gulmez 2010). However, to avoid a confusing conflation, the present discussion invokes "institution" to mean a tangible organization and "structure" to mean an underlying societal ordering principle.

Structural analysis anticipates that, for example, a subsistence black Islamic female caregiver for disabled persons in rural Uganda is very unlikely to see the legitimacy of global governance in the same way as an urban white secular able-bodied male banking executive in Canada. That in any event was this author's impression from interviewing both individuals about the same GGIs (Scholte 2004b). The two persons have the same cognitive processes of perception and evaluate the same organizations, so the difference in their perspectives on global governance legitimacy would appear to result from their contrasting social-structural positions. Which particular structural features make the difference is a matter for further investigation, as discussed in the second half of this chapter. The prior point to make here is that such research is needed. An explanation of legitimacy beliefs which omits the social-structural dimension would be incomplete.

Structural ordering is a deeper intangible governance of society which manifests itself in the tangible governance of concrete rules (such as statutes) and concrete regulatory agencies (such as states). Thus, for example, although there is no concrete "World Patriarchy Organization," a social-structural "rule" of masculine domination is nevertheless evident as a prevailing feature across individual behaviors and institutional arrangements in contemporary global governance. Likewise, world politics knows no formal "Global Modernity Agency," but current GGIs are for the most part instances of modern social structure, with organizing features (elaborated later) such as capitalist production, state-centric governance, nation-centric identity, territorial geopolitics, and rationalist knowledge.

Sociological literature on legitimacy has often drawn attention to structural sources of subject beliefs in rightful rule. For example, Max Weber (1922/1978) emphasizes the different workings of legitimacy between traditional and modern societies. Jürgen Habermas (1973/1976) understands "legitimation crisis" as a function of late capitalism. Mark Suchman's oft-cited definition situates legitimacy "within some socially constructed system of norms, values, beliefs, and definitions" (1995: 574). David Beetham (2013) underlines the role of capitalism and socialization through the family in shaping legitimacy perceptions. That said, these theorists have normally discussed social structure and legitimacy *in respect of the modern state*.

In contrast, the study of sociological legitimacy in *global* governance has to date largely underplayed social-structural sources of these beliefs. As ever, there are certain exceptions. For instance, Steven Bernstein has underscored the importance for GGIs of "broader legitimating norms and discourses—or social structure" (2011: 17; see also Chapter 11, this volume). The so-called "practice turn" in International Relations theory has likewise emphasized the role of "socially organized and meaningful activities" (Adler and Pouliot 2011a: 4; also Bueger and Gadinger 2015). In addition, as this chapter will later elaborate, some other research has explored structural sources of legitimacy in world politics with regard to hegemonic states, a capitalist order, and (post) modernity. However, on the whole, structural analysis of legitimacy vis-à-vis GGIs is a minority strand in the existing literature relative to studies on individual and institutional sources. Arguably, this imbalance wants rectification.

To summarize the discussion so far, a sociological explanation normally affirms that legitimacy beliefs arise in some measure from the societal order. Legitimacy perceptions have the forms and strengths that they do owing (at least partly) to prevailing organizing principles of social relations. On the whole, actors are more likely to perceive legitimacy when a GGI's features and behaviors conform to the predominant social structures of the day and to perceive illegitimacy when the GGI deviates from those frameworks. Moreover, actors' legitimacy beliefs are generally affected by their position in relation to social divisions and hierarchies.

Structural Power

As the preceding section has already intimated, social structure is not a passive feature of society: i.e. merely an outcome of other forces. Structure is also a shaping influence in its own right. Hence to speak of structural *sources* of legitimacy in global governance is to acknowledge their causal significance. Social structures have a distinct power of their own, apart from the impacts of actors (Lukes 2005).

Structural power induces most actor perceptions and behaviors to "fall into line" with a given societal organizing principle. For example, it is not that each person and each collective actor in global governance decides—autonomously and deliberately—to conduct capitalist transactions or to express security discourses. Rather, social structure sets patterns with which most actions around global governance conform. Thus, although social structure may be intangible, its impacts are very substantial.

Indeed, the force of social structure often makes transgression of these ordering principles difficult, costly, or even unimaginable. Deviation from, and resistance to, established social structure therefore tends to be exceptional and, in most cases, of limited consequence, at least in the short run. With regard to gender hierarchies, for instance, the current government of Sweden is unique for expressly affirming a "feminist foreign policy" in global governance and tends to raise eyebrows or even ridicule for doing so (Government of Sweden 2017). Likewise, few actors in today's world politics dare—or even consider—to challenge reigning social-ecological structures of anthropocentrism and extractivism, in spite of their potentially far-reaching harmful implications for the biosphere and even the human species itself (Boddice 2012; Acosta 2013). Thus actors normally "comply" with social structure, much as they usually comply with the institutional governance of explicit laws and standards.

The question of compliance with, and resistance to, social-structural power brings into focus the question of agency: i.e. how much scope subjects have to self-determine their destiny in world politics. Put another way, is there an ontological hierarchy between individual, institutional, and structural sources of legitimacy in global governance, where one has causal primacy over the other two? This question generally elicits three types of answers.

First, what may be termed individual*ist* and institutional*ist* accounts of legitimacy in global governance place all causality respectively in human psychology and in organizational qualities. These approaches thereby affirm that actor-based forces are determining in world politics and accord no autonomous significance to social structure in generating legitimacy beliefs. From methodologically individualist and institutionalist perspectives, societal patterns (if they are considered at all) are only outcomes (i.e. an aggregation of actor initiatives) with no causal impact of their own (Elster 1982). Such "actorist" explanations have a maximal view of agency, where behavioral units are completely self-directing subjects with full scope to determine whether and on what grounds they regard a given global governance arrangement to be legitimate.

Second, and conversely, what can be called structural*ist* accounts of world politics place all causality in forces of the social order. From this perspective, all of the individual and institutional sources of legitimacy discussed in Chapters 3 and 4 are outcomes of social structure and have no distinct impact of their own. For example, certain liberal theories of "development" have postulated an unstoppable singular linear course of societal "progress" towards a universal Western-modern condition (Rostow 1960; Fukuyama 1992). For their part, certain Marxist arguments have suggested that individuals and institutions have no choice but to enact sociohistorically prescribed class roles in an unfolding capitalist mode of production (Poulantzas 1973). Structuralist analyses of legitimacy in global governance accord no role to agency: GGIs and their audiences have no choice but to play out preset scripts laid down by the social order.

In practice, few analyses of global governance adopt an absolute actorist or structuralist position. A third "in-between" line of approach treats the question of agency in terms of co-constituting actors and social structures. In this ontology, individual, institutional, and structural sources of legitimacy in global governance are mutually determining. That is, each of the three is simultaneously cause and effect of the other two. Theorists have variously dubbed such a perspective "structuration" (Giddens 1984), "field theory" (Bourdieu 1993), "relationalism" (McCourt 2016), and "practice theory" (Adler and Pouliot 2011a, 2011b). All share the position that individuals, institutions, and social structures are not discrete forces (and thus cannot be separately measured). Rather, the three are interrelated, fused, co-producing dimensions of a social moment. In this view, legitimacy in global governance happens (or not) through co-creating individual, institutional, and structural sources, where none can be disentangled from the others, since they coexist as a systemic whole.

Following a structuration principle, actors have delimited agency in their views of GGIs. Ernest Mandel called this condition "parametric determinism": i.e. choice within parameters (1989: 118). On such an account, actors do take deliberate decisions (in the present context regarding legitimacy and legitimation in global governance); however, those choices are made from a structurally configured range of possible options. Thus, for example, in a secularly ordered society actors might "reasonably" choose between democracy, technocracy, and fairness as institutional sources of GGI legitimacy, but structural forces would tend to exclude the will of God as a "normal" criterion for rightful rule.

Structuration analyses are spread across a spectrum, between a pole of actor reductionism on one end and a pole of structural reductionism on the other. Thus some structuration arguments lean more in the direction of structuralism, by positing harder and tighter structural parameters of actor choice. Other versions of structuration lean more towards actorism, suggesting that structural boundaries of agency are looser and wider. Yet the principle of actor-structure co-determination prevails in all of these cases.

Structural Change

Actorism, structuralism, and structuration analyses offer different accounts of the dynamics which generate change in social structures. According to the first approach, reconstruction of the social order happens due to individual and collective actors. From an actorist perspective, it is the visions, determination, tactics, and resources of social movements and other change makers that provide the engine of structural transformation in global politics (Della Porta and Tarrow 2005; Della Porta 2016; Gregoratti and Uhlin, this volume). In contrast, from a structuralist perspective, change of the social order results from forces within the structures themselves: e.g. from class dialectics or from a self-propelling modernization process. For a structuration analysis, meanwhile, new societal patterns arise out of agent-structure interrelations.

Yet, whichever of these modes of explanation is adopted, structural analysis of the sources of legitimacy in global governance raises questions about social change. Although structures are deeply embedded in the fabric of society, they are not forever fixed. On the contrary, the structural bases of legitimacy (for global and other governance) can and do periodically undergo major reconstruction. Given that structural transformation shifts the overall framing of legitimacy beliefs, it is important to track these changes and to understand how they transpire.

The lifecycles of social structures are usually quite extended. Changes in individuals and institutions generally unfold over the short and medium term, whereas structural sources of GGI legitimacy normally shift slowly over what historian Fernand Braudel (1958) dubbed the *longue durée*. Occasionally, in a revolutionary situation, structural transformation may come quickly; however, more often these deeper changes unfold at rates that are imperceptible from one year to the next.

Research on structural sources of legitimacy in global governance therefore benefits from a long-term perspective. While the effects of individual and institutional circumstances are often immediately visible, structural impacts only come into sharper focus over a period of decades, if not centuries. For example, it took several hundred years for the discourse of human rights to become a legitimating structure of contemporary global governance (Ishay 2004). Meanwhile, *Pax Americana* rose for half a century from the 1890s to become a structural source of legitimate global governance in the 1940s, and it now looks to be taking multiple decades for hegemony of the United States government to recede (Agnew 2005).

A further methodological consideration regarding change in structural sources of legitimacy concerns the agency of the researcher. Put another way, what is the relationship between academic knowledge and political practice in respect of legitimacy in global governance? Does the researcher merely record social structures and their changes; or is professional knowledge production part of the processes of continuity and transformation in the social order? In the latter case, where scholars are among the agents who shape structures, what are the consequences of academic research and teaching for maintaining or changing those patterns? Indeed, what are the normative implications of a researcher's choice—however (sub)conscious—to direct their scholarship towards reproduction or reconstruction of social structure?

On the one hand, some accounts take the social structure that they study as given and normatively good. In this vein, certain analyses of US hegemony, liberal norms, and Western modernity in world politics have (openly or tacitly) reinforced and endorsed these structures, finding them (explicitly or implicitly) worthy of legitimacy beliefs (cf. Ikenberry 2004). In contrast, so-called "critical" theories of global governance identify social structures with a purpose to question, subvert, and transform the prevailing world order (Cox 1981; Edkins and Vaughan-Williams 2009; Worth 2015). Critical perspectives presume that current social structures harbor repressive power relations which scholarship should help to expose, dismantle, and replace. Different critical theories highlight different kinds of purported structural harms: e.g. capitalist exploitations, gender-based injustices, discursive oppressions, or the ecological damages of anthropocentrism. Across these diverse diagnoses, however, critical theories share an epistemological position that academic structural analysis is an important tool in struggles to change social structure. Critical research on legitimacy in global governance is in this sense concurrently sociological and explicitly normative.

Spaces of Structure

Having established that social structure can significantly shape legitimacy in global governance, including with changes over time, a key further question arises concerning the form of "society" to which these ordering principles apply. Here a basic distinction exists between methodological territorialism (which defines "society" as a bounded container, usually a country), methodological globalism (which conceives of a single universal human society), and methodological worldism (which locates society in fluid transborder spaces with variable structures).

Modern social science (including most political-sociological research on legitimacy) has generally adopted a premise of methodological territorialism (and related presumptions of methodological nationalism and methodological statism) (Scholte 1993). These notions affirm that "society" takes form as a bounded country-nation-state unit. So everyday language speaks of "Brazilian society," "Russian society," "Vietnamese society," and so on. In this perspective, humanity is distributed between discrete territorial parcels (countries), each with a distinct population (nation) and a distinct governance apparatus (state). On this basis, social structure maps onto territorial spaces, with a resulting "Canadian social structure," "Lebanese social structure," "Nigerian social structure," and so on. Comparative analysis then proceeds to identify and measure similarities and differences between these territorially contained "societies."

Applied to the study of legitimacy in global governance, methodological nationalism looks for social-structural sources of these beliefs in the organization of the country-nation-state. Thus, for instance, territorialist analysis might posit that legitimacy perceptions vis-à-vis global governance vary as a function of a country's economic structure (e.g. whether it is low, middle, or high income). Methodological territorialism also underpins structural arguments that legitimacy in global governance varies depending on the political order of a country (e.g. whether it is authoritarian or liberal-democratic) (Eisentraut 2013). Another territorialist formulation might suggest that a country's cultural structure (e.g. as traditional, industrial, or post-materialist) would shape legitimacy perceptions towards GGIs.

Most empirical research in modern social science has rested (explicitly or implicitly) on methodological territorialism. Societal data are then collected and analyzed in relation to country-nation-state units. Indeed, *statistics* has methodological statism built into its very name, reflecting the modern assumption that societal numbers are necessarily and suitably calculated about and for the project of the territorial nation-state (Poovey 1998). Even most "global" data sets—such as the Human Development Index (HDI) and the World Values Survey (WVS)—are broken down into country-based figures.

Hence available data tend to push quantitative studies of structural sources of global governance legitimacy into a methodologically nationalist frame of analysis. There are few "globistics" and "regionistics" alongside the masses of "statistics." Veritably transborder data—such as recent calculations of a global (as distinct from a country-based) Gini coefficient—are rare (Milanovic 2016). Sometimes national numbers can be aggregated into larger units, for example, by assembling figures from countries in different world regions to get a proxy for global data. However, it would require a complete overhaul of data-collection practices in order to document social structures in other arenas with the same detail and rigor that has been applied to national statistics.

Yet, since the 1970s many theorists have questioned the assumption that social relations and their structures fall into territorial containers (Taylor et al. 1996). Critiques of methodological nationalism have spawned studies of "transnationalism," "world systems," "globalization," "world society," "world polity," and more (Robertson 1992; Buzan 2004; Wallerstein 2004; Khagram and Levitt 2008; Krücken and Drori 2009). These new research directions share a premise that social relations (and thus also legitimacy beliefs) unfold as much across as within countries, to the point that treating territories as discrete units of social analysis is not viable.

Some such work has tended towards a methodological globalism that "lifts" social structure and structural power from the national-territorial sphere to the planetary level. Thus, for example, dependency theory has asserted the primacy of a global core-periphery structure (Frank 1966; Amin 1973). On this thesis, legitimacy beliefs vis-à-vis GGIs would be strongly conditioned by a person's location in the core or in the periphery of the global political economy. Similarly, some contemporary sociology posits modernity to be a global social structure (Robertson 1992); some feminist theory has suggested that patriarchy operates as a global structure (Mies 2014); some Marxist analysis has affirmed a globalization of capitalist social structure (Sklair 2002); and some poststructuralist thinking regards neoliberalism as a global discursive structure (Larner and Walters 2004). From these perspectives, the social-structural sources of legitimacy beliefs are planetary rather than country-bound.

While such methodological globalism has the advantage of recognizing the transborder character of social structure, these accounts can slip into a universalism that fails to appreciate variations in the expressions of global-scale structures at different regional, national, and sub-national locations. For instance, modernity (with structural features such as rationalist knowledge, national community, and the territorial state) takes varying forms across "glocalities" (Featherstone et al. 1995; Eisenstadt 2000). Likewise, literature on varieties of capitalism highlights contrasting expressions across the planet of an overarching structure of surplus accumulation (Crouch and Streeck 1997). Similarly, post-war hegemony of the United States did not operate on the same lines in Africa, Asia, Europe, and Latin America. Thus the social structures which shape legitimacy beliefs cannot be isolated at the global level any more than at the national level.

A more viable alternative methodology could be one that conceives of "transscalar" structures within "world society" (Scholte 2016: 216–18). In this conception, "world" is not equivalent to "global," but rather refers to the whole social space that people inhabit. Hence for some persons in certain settings the "world" might be a village. In ancient times the "world" was the Mediterranean for some people and the Middle Kingdom for others. Meanwhile, contemporary history has seen the increasing significance of a global world (to such an extent that many people today understand "world" to mean "global").

A world society perspective on social-structural sources of legitimacy contrasts with both methodological nationalism and methodological globalism (Scholte 1993: ch. 2). This third approach supposes neither that all people fall under the same social structures nor that social structures are tied to any bounded territory. Thus, a given world society could encompass coexistent premodern, modern, and postmodern structures. A world society could also contain multiple types of capitalism, plural gender norms, different kinds of racialization, diverse discourses of "development," and so on. However, in contrast to methodological nationalism, a world society perspective would not expect such variations to map onto any bounded territorial unit, whether it be a locality, a country, or a region. Rather, different structures "flow" in irregular transborder fashion across world spaces. As a result, different sites in a world society—including within a single country—can have their legitimacy beliefs shaped by quite variable combinations of structural forces.

To be sure, a world society perspective on social-structural sources of global governance legitimacy is challenging to execute in empirical investigations. The researcher must trace complex variation as multiple social structures interrelate both with each other and through a plethora of diverse transscalar sites. With a world society approach one cannot treat social structure as a single and fixed dependent variable whose effects are tested across a large-N sample of situations. The more intricate conceptualization rather points towards fine-grained qualitative research.

What Structure(s)?

Having addressed metatheoretical concerns about social structure as a source of legitimacy in global governance, the second half of this chapter shifts focus to the more specific character of relevant world-ordering principles. In this regard different theories advance a variety of propositions about the main feature(s) of social structure that can shape legitimacy beliefs, including norms, hegemonic states, capitalism, discourses, modernity, and social stratifications. These notions have already surfaced earlier in the chapter, when illustrating the metatheoretical points. Below, these different accounts of the structural sources of global governance legitimacy are examined more systematically, albeit still only summarily.

As the range of perspectives indicates, conceptions of social-structural sources of legitimacy in global governance can highlight material as well as ideational qualities. On the one hand, methodologically materialist approaches (such as Marxist theories) suggest that the social order has a primarily physical character involving, for example, ecological and economic forces. On the other hand, methodologically idealist approaches (such as poststructuralist theories) deem that deeper social patterns have a primarily mental character involving, for example, linguistic and cultural forces. In addition, some other conceptions see social structure in terms of interrelated material and ideational qualities, as when Weberian theories of world-scale modernity posit the centrality of co-constituting capitalism, industrialism, nationalism, and rationalism.

The following survey covers six possible types of social-structural sources of legitimacy in global governance. The general logic is to move from more immediately apparent conceptions to more complex notions of social structure, without meaning thereby to favor one or the other approach. The overview begins with embedded norms as a commonly cited and more immediately visible type of social structure. Subsequent consideration of hegemonic states, capitalism, and discourses examines three propositions about deeper but also unidimensional conceptions of social structure. The discussion then proceeds to modernity/postmodernity and intersectional stratifications as more multifaceted and complex conceptions of social structure that could shape legitimacy beliefs vis-à-vis global governance.

To be sure, the six categories overlap at points, as when neo-Gramscian theories highlight class stratification, and when discursive theories address norms. Indeed, certain empirical analyses might decide to combine several conceptions of social structure. Moreover, the classification is neither exhaustive (e.g. omitting ecological and theological conceptions) nor incontestable (e.g. treating gender and race among a range of social stratifications rather than with separate headings of their own). However, the aim here is not to provide a complete and definitive account, but to identify key distinctions of approach and suggest lines for further development and debate.

Norms

One major type of structural explanation for legitimacy in global governance highlights the power of embedded norms. On these lines Ian Clark has suggested, in relation to world society, that "the multiplicity of norms constitutes the reservoir from which claims to legitimacy can be drawn" (2007: 182). This perspective argues that certain conventions, principles, standards, and values come to set key contours of expected and accepted behavior in world politics. Constructivist theories in particular have sought to explain how, why, and with what consequence certain ideas become reigning norms for global governance, as well as for world society more generally (Keck and Sikkink 1998; Bernstein 2001; Barnett and Finnemore 2004; Lechner and Boli 2005; Clark 2007; Barnett 2013).

Examples of structurally embedded norms in contemporary world politics include gender equality, human rights, humanitarian assistance, liberal democracy, national security, peaceful dispute resolution, sovereignty, sustainable development, and transparency. As discussed in Chapter 4, such principles provide touchstones for what audiences today normally regard to be "democratic," "effective," and "fair" in GGI procedure and performance. Thus, so this line of argument goes, a GGI's legitimacy is generally enhanced to the extent that the organization conforms to embedded norms of world politics and is weakened to the extent that it deviates from them.

Norms exert structural power in the sense that GGIs and their audiences are constrained to invoke these standards when making legitimacy claims. Thus GGIs are substantially obliged to justify their policies and actions in relation to embedded norms: e.g. to proclaim that they respect sovereignty, promote sustainable development, advance gender equality, and so on. Likewise, opponents of GGIs are structurally pushed to articulate their critiques with reference to prevailing norms: e.g. to allege transgressions of human rights, threats to national security, violations of transparency, and so on.

While affirming this structural power of norms, constructivist explanations of norm creation and change also tend to include strong elements of agency. These accounts generally highlight the role of social movements and other so-called "norm entrepreneurs" (Sunstein 1996) in embedding the various standards in global governance practice. The relevant literature often explores actors' use, when promoting one or the other norm, of opportunity structures, resource mobilization, boomerang effects, and narratives. With such emphases, constructivist theories usually lean more towards the actor-centric pole on the spectrum of structuration thinking.

In contrast, perspectives that lean more towards the structuralist pole of this spectrum would explain norm changes with reference to other world-order forces, such as hegemonic states, capitalism, discourses, modernity, and social stratifications. On these other accounts (discussed below), norms are not themselves the main structural source of legitimacy in global governance. Rather, these conventions and values are seen as products of other, more primary, social structures. One may indeed ask whether other structural forces help to determine which norms become prominent in global governance and which do not. What deeper power relations lie behind the norms of global governance, and what interests are served by the adoption of certain norms rather than others?

Hegemonic State(s)

A second prominent set of arguments about structural sources of legitimacy in global governance has put a spotlight on hegemonic states. This line of thinking suggests that, in the absence of a centralized world government, global governance often depends on sponsorship from a dominant territorial state or group of states. Different states (e.g. Britain, USA, etc.) might fulfil this structural role at different moments in time, and each hegemon may exercise leadership on global governance in its own particular way. However, so goes this proposition, a hegemonic state (or group of states) is an important— perhaps even indispensable—structural condition for effective global governance in an anarchical world order.

This state leadership is moreover characterized as "hegemony" owing to the sociologically *legitimate* character of the dominance. Hegemonic states generate global governance not only with their preponderance of resources (economic, military, and ideological), but also with widespread audience endorsement of their supremacy. Thus, significant ranges of subjects (e.g. other states, elites, and/or general publics) regard the hegemonic state(s) to be exercising appropriate global authority. In this vein, certain scholarship has argued that subordinated states endorsed US supremacy in constructing global regimes in the mid-twentieth century (Gilpin 1988). With this quality of legitimacy, hegemony is different from coercive empire (Agnew 2005: ch. 2).

Proponents of this thesis point to various historical instances where global governance has rested substantially on hegemonic states. For example, Henry Kissinger (1957) argues that a Concert of Europe among leading states of the day provided a legitimate international order in the early nineteenth century. Niall Ferguson (2002) affirms a purported pivotal role of the British state as the hegemonic promoter of a liberal-imperial world order in the late nineteenth century. Charles Kindleberger (1973) blames the absence of a hegemonic state for weak international governance between the world wars of the early twentieth century. Many other scholars claim that United States hegemony was a crucial underpinning for legitimacy beliefs towards global governance after the 1940s (Keohane 1984; Gilpin 1987; Agnew and Corbridge 1995). Some wonder whether China could emerge as the main sponsoring state of future global governance (Robinson 2011). Others speculate whether the Group of Seven/Eight (G7/G8) or the Group of Twenty (G20) could constitute a new multipolar concert for global governance of the twenty-first century (Kirton et al. 2001; Postel-Vinay 2011). All of this literature suggests that legitimacy in global governance prevails when a leading state or states promote GGIs which most other parties endorse.

Certain accounts have gone beyond merely describing a historical succession of hegemonic states and seek also to explain the rise and fall of these legitimacy-generating sponsors of global governance. In particular, several theorists have proposed that a cycle of hegemony constitutes a—if not the—core *longue durée* of world order. On this interpretation, different leading states in turn rise to dominance, use that position to underwrite global governance arrangements which enjoy broad legitimacy, and then at some point decline, most often owing to overstretched resources (Wallerstein 1983; Gilpin 1987; Modelski 1987; Desai 2013).

Propositions about hegemonic states as a structural source of legitimacy in global governance have merit insofar as much international and global governance in modern history has involved major initiative and support from a dominant state or group of states. Yet claims that such dominance has also entailed legitimacy may want more careful scrutiny: how much audience endorsement has actually underpinned *Pax Britannica* and *Pax Americana*? How broadly has legitimacy for these leading states extended: that is, beyond certain governments and certain elites to states and society at large? Little detailed empirical research has examined whether, how far, in what circles, and for what reasons hegemonic states have in practice attracted legitimacy for GGIs.

Structural arguments about hegemonic states also do not explain why rationales for legitimacy in global governance take the specific forms that they do at different times and among different audiences. For example, the fact of hegemony per se cannot explain why development promotion has figured more prominently in legitimacy beliefs towards global governance under US leadership than under the Concert of Europe. Likewise, state hegemony as such does not explain why colonial empire could attract considerable legitimacy perceptions under *Pax Britannica* but not under the G7. To untangle these more specific dynamics of legitimacy in global governance, analysis must look beyond the structural power of state hegemony to examine also individual, institutional, and/or other structural sources.

Capitalism

Among those possible other social-structural sources of legitimacy beliefs in GGIs is capitalism. Marxist theories in particular identify surplus accumulation as the foremost ordering pattern of international relations and world society. Some Marxists might acknowledge a role for norms and hegemonic states as sources of legitimacy in global governance (Gill 1992; Rupert 1995, 2005), but then these other structures are viewed as subordinate to a primary structure of capitalism. Thus, for example, human rights standards and *Pax Americana* would serve accumulation processes, without an autonomous dynamic of their own.

In Marxist conceptions, global governance exists to provide a regulatory framework for capitalism on a world scale. Some of the rules (e.g. concerning contracts, finance, investment, labor, money, property, and trade) serve directly to enable accumulation processes. Other global regulations are not themselves necessary for capitalism, but are set in ways that further surplus accumulation. For instance, current global Internet governance promotes virtual capitalism, and much global environmental governance champions market-based responses to ecological problems. Still other global rules (e.g. regarding cultural heritage or meteorology) may have little if any relevance to surplus accumulation; however, under a capitalist order these measures are at least formulated so as not to hamper accumulation. Indeed, on Marxist accounts the structural power of capitalism normally excludes from global governance alternative political-economic logics (e.g. of a care-based society, shariah, or social ecology).

In these analyses, legitimacy involves the legitimation of (global) capitalism (Slaughter 2015). Legitimacy issues figure most explicitly in Gramscian variants of Marxism, including neo-Gramscian theories of world politics (Cox 1987; Mittelman 2004, 2011; Bieler et al. 2006). These approaches highlight how "ideology" operates to generate legitimacy perceptions towards capitalism and its governance. A capitalist order, on this account, requires a general consciousness across society that embraces existing rules and regulatory institutions, including GGIs. Such ideological knowledge is produced through school curricula, mass media, government propaganda, political-party rhetoric, corporate communications, academic research, think tanks, and more. Key legitimating ideas in contemporary global capitalism could include "economic growth," "free trade," "market efficiency," "consumer power," and "corporate social responsibility." Collectively, such notions are frequently labelled "neoliberalism" (Harvey 2005).

Neo-Gramscians characterize capitalist ideology as "hegemonic" in the sense that it legitimates dominant power (Cox 1983; Worth 2015). Whereas the previously discussed conception linked hegemony with dominant rule-sponsoring states, neo-Gramscian theory understands hegemony in terms of the supremacy of global capitalism and an associated transnational ruling class (Van der Pijl 1998; Sklair 2001). In both cases hegemony involves beliefs on the part of subordinated subjects that forces which dominate them are legitimate. Marxists sometimes portray this condition as "false consciousness," alleging that hegemonic ideology blinds exploited classes to their subjugation. Neo-Gramscians also invoke the concept of "counter-hegemony" to designate forces of social movements which seek to delegitimate global capitalism with critiques and alternative ideological programs (Gill 2008; Paterson 2010).

Propositions concerning capitalism as a structural force shaping legitimacy in global governance warrant serious attention inasmuch as surplus accumulation figures pervasively and deeply across contemporary society. The neglect of material-economic forces in constructivist and other "cultural" theories of world politics seems indefensible in the shadow of global corporations, digital networks, finance capital, and labor migrations. Legitimacy beliefs surely cannot be isolated in ideational realms, with no connection to economic structure.

At the same time, Marxist notions that capitalism constitutes the exclusive primary social structure behind legitimacy dynamics in global governance seem unsustainable as well. Other theories argue—and much evidence would seem to confirm—that norms, hegemonic states, and other world-ordering patterns still to be discussed below are substantially not reducible to logics of surplus accumulation. Capitalism is important, but not all-important. Indeed, to temper methodological materialism some recent theorizations of capitalism have taken a "cultural turn" in order to integrate material and ideational forces (Best and Paterson 2010; Sum and Jessop 2013).

Discourses

Shifting to more methodologically idealist perspectives, discourse analyses explore structural sources of legitimacy beliefs in terms of the social construction of meaning, as expressed through language and associated communication (Bell 2002; Van Leeuwen 2008). "Discourse" here involves an ordered arrangement of verbal expressions: patterns of text and conversation which set a framework for knowing the world. Where investigations of capitalism focus on production, distribution, and consumption of resources, explorations of discourse concentrate on the creation, exchange, and reception of linguistic signifiers. While Marxist theories subordinate knowledge structures to economic structures, discursive approaches reverse this ontological hierarchy, so that the architecture of linguistic practices underpins the wider social order and its power relationships. In this vein one might apply to world politics Ludwig Wittgenstein's thesis that social relations are "language games" (Wigen 2015).

The social-structural power of discourse entails that certain forms of meaning are embedded as the "conventional wisdom" in a given societal context—and marginalize or exclude alternative understandings of the world. As expressed by Michel Foucault (1969/1989), the dominant knowledge/power disciplines subjects to rationalize—and consequently act upon—their situations in certain structurally prescribed ways. In relation to world politics, too, poststructuralist theories posit that certain knowledge orderings define the reigning truths of the day and relegate other meanings to the realm of myth and abnormality (Larner and Walters 2004; Edkins 2008; Bonditti et al. 2017).

For example, considerable poststructuralist research has examined the role of security discourses in shaping contemporary world politics. This line of argument affirms that a pervasive language of "threat," "risk," "terror," "instability," "crisis," "violence," and "uncertainty" generates a key mindset that subjects bring to their engagement with world politics (Williams 2003). Other poststructuralist theorizing has focused on the power of neoliberal discourse concerning market freedom, business efficiency, customer satisfaction, and the like. (NB: where Marxism treats neoliberalism as an ideological buttress for capitalist structure, poststructuralism regards neoliberalism as a primary discursive structure in its own right.) Other poststructuralist research on world politics has dissected reigning discourses of "sovereignty" (Walker 1993), "accountability" (Ebrahim and Weisband 2007), "resilience" (Chandler 2014), and more.

Discursive structures become sources of legitimacy in global governance when they set the linguistic terms and knowledge frames for assessments of appropriate authority vis-à-vis GGIs. From a poststructuralist perspective, subjects tend to regard a GGI as more legitimate when its language and related behavior conform to reigning discourses. Conversely, the GGI becomes less legitimate when its texts and associated activities do not resonate of the dominant knowledge/power. As elaborated further in Chapter 6 of this volume, GGIs can use discursive strategies—manipulations of language and meaning—to bolster legitimacy beliefs, while their opponents can deploy linguistic tactics to undermine legitimacy perceptions.

Hegemony also has a place in poststructuralist theories, albeit in a different form than with state- and class-centered approaches. As in the other interpretations, hegemony is a situation where subordinated parties endorse their subordination; however, in this case subjects embrace dominant discourse, even when this way of knowing the world may oppress them. For example, critical readings suggest that security discourses can support authoritarian rule, that neoliberal discourses may perpetuate avoidable poverty, and that resilience discourses can burden individuals with responsibilities that could otherwise be held collectively.

Resisting these alleged harms, critical discourse analysts often expressly promote counter-hegemony. Their research undertakes "deconstruction" to reveal the social production (as distinct from ahistorical fixedness) of know-ledge, as well as to identify the arbitrary and exclusionary power that emanates from dominant discourse. Meanwhile, counter-hegemonic social movements actively promote alternative discourses and the allegedly better societal orders that these different structures of meaning could generate. Counter-hegemonic forces use different kinds of language (e.g. discourses of care, emancipation, Mother Earth, and peace) to oppose hegemonic knowledge/power and instead advance other realities (Bandy and Smith 2005).

Propositions concerning discursive structures in global governance are com-pelling to the extent that language and meaning fall into broad socially constructed patterns which substantially shape political power. Legitimacy arguments around global governance clearly have different formulations with, say, discourses of security relative to discourses of solidarity. Imperialist discourses about race plainly imply different kinds of legitimacy perceptions towards world order than egalitarian discourses. Language matters.

However, it is something else to say that language is everything. Linguistic-discursive determinism would seem no less reductionist than the statist and economic determinisms discussed earlier. Thus a "material turn" has attempted to bring correctives in poststructuralism not unlike the "cultural turn" in Marxism. Matter matters also (Carlile et al. 2013). Taken together, these two "turns" suggest that structural sources of legitimacy in global gov-ernance have both ideational and material qualities.

Modernity

A further stream of structural thinking which combines ideational and mater-ial qualities of social order relates to modernity. These perspectives on legit-imacy in global governance might be characterized as "Weberian" inasmuch as they follow Max Weber's attention to both cultural and economic struc-tures of modern society (Weber 1922/1978; Parsons 1960). Weberian argu-ments generally identify several interconnected deeper ordering principles of governance, in contrast to the focus in previously covered theories on a single primary dimension of structure.

Different Weberian historical sociologists ascribe different combinations of structures to a world order of modernity. For example, Anthony Giddens (1985) regards modern society as an interplay of capitalism, industrialism, and the state system, with additional forces of nationalism and the military. Michael Mann (1986: ch. 1; 1993: ch. 20) highlights four "sources of social power": ideological, economic, military, and political. John Meyer analyzes a modern world society structured by rationalization and the nation-state (Krücken and Drori 2009).

Relatedly, some sociological thinking has linked contemporary globalization (including an unprecedented expansion of global governance) to a shift from modernity to postmodernity. For example, on these lines Martin Albrow (1996) describes a "global age" where social structure transforms "beyond modernity" of the nation-state and territorial, rational, industrial society. Similarly, the present author has elsewhere linked "globalization" to shifts from territorialist to supraterritorial geography, from physical to virtual capitalism, from statist to polycentric governance, from nationalist to plural identities, and from rationalist to reflexive knowledge (Scholte 2005).

These various accounts all suggest that GGIs are expressions of—and channels to spread and reinforce—(post)modern social orders. From such a perspective, social structures of (post)modernity generate legitimacy beliefs for global governance inasmuch as GGIs and their audiences tend to regard these patterns as suitable ways to organize society. Thus, for instance, the UN could enhance its legitimacy by—in line with the modern nationality principle—promoting decolonization. The World Bank could attract legitimacy by furthering policies of "sustainable development" which—in contrast to more radical ecological programs—conform to modern structures of anthropocentrism and capitalism. The Internet Corporation for Assigned Names and Numbers (ICANN) could bolster its legitimacy by—in line with a modern rationalist focus on techno-scientific problem solving—advancing a working global digital communications network. Private GGIs like ICANN could also struggle to obtain legitimacy among modernists insofar as these regimes marginalize states, but not have this problem among postmodernists who embrace regulation beyond the state.

Indeed, various contemporary social movements challenge the legitimacy of modernist global governance. They include anti-industrialist indigenous mobilizations, anti-secularist religious revivalisms, anti-nationalist identity politics, anti-capitalist protests, and strivings for ecological justice. Similarly, in academic quarters theories of postcolonialism have critiqued an "orientalist" modern world order (and its global governance institutions) for being Eurocentric and racist (Krishna 2009; Anievas et al. 2015). For such critics, structures of modernity as expressed through global governance tend to generate perceptions of *il*legitimacy towards GGIs.

The illustrations just given suggest that legitimacy in global governance can have important structural sources in modernity (and perhaps also shifts towards postmodernity). This line of theory has the attraction of encompassing multiple facets of social structure in fluctuating combinations. The approach thereby arguably reflects (better than more unidimensional conceptions) the complexity of actual social orders and their transformations.

Yet this very complexity can generate lengthy, messy, and (for many tastes) overly complicated and variable explanations of global governance. Other notions of social structure (such as those covered above) are more parsimonious and more readily manageable, both conceptually and empirically. Indeed, many propositions around (post-) modernity are difficult to operationalize in empirical research: what kind of indicators and evidence can adequately capture capitalism, nationalism, rationalism, etc. as sources of legitimacy beliefs, let alone their interrelations? Given such challenges it is perhaps not surprising that no detailed empirical research linking legitimacy in global governance to (post)modernity is yet available.

Social Stratifications

Finally, in this survey of possible social-structural sources of (il)legitimacy in global governance come social stratifications: that is, embedded inequalities between group categories. Some such hierarchies (e.g. involving class, gender, and race) have had earlier mention in this chapter. Other structural stratifications fall on lines of age, caste, (dis)ability, faith, geography, language, nationality, sexual orientation, and species (i.e. *homo sapiens* over others). Whatever the axis of hierarchy, these social structures generate inequalities: of resources, of political access and influence, of legal protection, of ecological vulnerability, of cultural expression, of historical recognition, and of exposure to physical and psychological violence. In short, social stratifications increase and reduce life chances based on embedded group identifications.

Different theories of world politics highlight different lines of social stratification. For example, liberalism takes general aim at the ways that structural hierarchy violates principles of equal opportunity and meritocracy. Among critical theories, Marxism puts emphasis on class strata (Sklair 2001), feminism on gender (Runyan and Peterson 2014), dependency theory on geographical core and periphery (Frank 1966), queer theory on sexuality (Picq and Thiel 2015), posthumanism on species (Cudworth and Hobden 2018), and so on. Postcolonial theories furthermore stress "intersectionality," where social relations involve complex interplays of various stratifications that sometimes reinforce and sometimes counteract one another (Grzanka 2014). Normatively, all of these theories regard disempowerment that flows from structurally embedded social inequality to be profoundly unjust.

Given these widespread critiques of social stratifications—in political programs as well as academic theories—the legitimacy of GGIs can be fragile to the extent that they are perceived to create or sustain these inequalities. Indeed, arbitrary social hierarchies go against all of the institutional sources of legitimacy discussed in Chapter 4. These stratifications are generally regarded to be unfair (i.e. partial and discriminatory), undemocratic (i.e.

denying due voice and control), and ineffective (i.e. inefficient and irrational). GGIs are especially vulnerable to critiques concerning structural inequalities inasmuch as these attacks resonate not only with many counter-hegemonic social movements, but also with many liberal cosmopolitans who could normally be expected to embrace established forms of global governance.

Not surprisingly, then, issues of structural stratification figure in many legitimation and delegitimation struggles around contemporary global governance. For example, most GGIs in one way or another affirm their promotion of, and compliance with, "human rights" as a principle of equality for all people. Similarly, supporters often seek to legitimate global governance with assertions that it serves "the international community" and "universal humankind" rather than particular countries or social groups. GGIs likewise regularly legitimate themselves with claims to further "development" for structurally disadvantaged populations (global south, underclasses, women, etc.).

Conversely, opponents frequently invoke social stratifications as grounds to delegitimate GGIs. For instance, many so-called "anti-globalization" protesters have charged global economic institutions with reinforcing structurally arbitrary privileges of the global north and "the 1%" of wealthy classes across the planet. In addition, many advocacy groups have pressed GGIs to attend more to marginalized quarters such as Dalits, disabled persons, indigenous peoples, linguistic and religious diversity, Mother Earth, sexual minorities, and youth. Tensions between rhetorics of equality and practices of stratification indeed suffuse the politics of legitimacy in global governance.

Conclusion

This chapter has supplemented the preceding two with an examination of possible social-structural sources of legitimacy beliefs in global governance. The general proposition has been that explanations of these beliefs do well to consider three dimensions—individual, institutional, and structural—including how these three aspects of causality may be interrelated and co-determining.

As this chapter has indicated, structural accounts of legitimacy vis-à-vis GGIs involve a range of challenging metatheoretical issues and analytical choices. As seen in the first part, none of the key ontological questions—i.e. regarding definitions, powers, changes and spaces of social structure—is straightforward. As seen in the second part, theories of world politics offer many contrasting interpretations of the main social structures that are at play in legitimacy dynamics around global governance. Different arguments spotlight the purported structural power of norms, hegemonic states, capitalism, discourses, (post)modernity, and social stratifications.

Selecting among the various possible approaches—or ignoring structural sources of legitimacy altogether—is a matter for each researcher to decide. All of the theories about social structure in world politics covered above are logically coherent in their own terms. In addition, each conception can be corroborated with ample empirical evidence, depending on where and how the researcher looks. Thus choice of approach comes down in good part to the researcher's positionality: i.e. where they themselves are socially located, and what they personally find interesting and compelling. Meanwhile, critical theory propositions about knowledge-practice interconnections (as discussed above in relation to structural change) would furthermore suggest that the adoption of one or the other conception of social structure (or neglecting its role) is a political matter. In this light, choice of theory is also a choice (perhaps unconscious) of what kinds of social power relations the research will expose and interrogate—or alternatively leave unspoken and unchallenged. To this extent theoretical preferences are normatively charged.

Whatever one's theoretical choices, a large field is open for empirical research of social-structural sources of legitimacy in global governance. Relatively few detailed case studies have examined structural aspects of GGI legitimacy (Gill 1992; Bernstein 2001; Barnett 2011). Global ethnography of GGIs is in its infancy (Niezen and Sapignoli 2017). Structural sources have also figured little in interviews, surveys, and textual analysis regarding legitimacy in global governance. Hopefully the present chapter has provided conceptual clarifications that will spur more empirical work on these issues.

Part III
Processes of Legitimation and Delegitimation

6

Legitimation and Delegitimation in Global Governance

Discursive, Institutional, and Behavioral Practices

Karin Bäckstrand and Fredrik Söderbaum

In 2011, the Obama Administration withdrew funding from the United Nations Educational, Scientific and Cultural Organization (UNESCO) following the decision to make Palestine a member of the organization.[1] In 2017, President Trump announced that the US will withdraw as a member from UNESCO as well as pull out of the 2015 Paris Agreement negotiated under the auspices of the United Nations Framework Convention on Climate Change (UNFCCC). These are all instances of delegitimation of global governance institutions (GGIs) by a powerful member state. They illustrate the growing importance of delegitimation as well as legitimation in today's global governance. This chapter shifts focus from the sources of legitimacy dealt with in Part II of this book to processes of legitimation and delegitimation.

Our point of departure is that previous research has paid too little attention to the many and varied practices, strategies, and tactics that GGIs and their members employ in order to justify or contest the authority of these organizations vis-à-vis different target audiences (Zaum 2013a). Even less work has considered how legitimacy claims are supported or contested by social movements, non-governmental organizations (NGOs), and citizens at large. In response to these gaps and the fragmentation of the literature on (de)legitimation, this chapter synthesizes research on legitimation in order to develop an empirically applicable framework for conceptualizing how GGIs and other

[1] This chapter has benefitted from the many constructive comments by the editors and other contributors of this volume. We are also grateful for the constructive comments by Linnéa Gelot, Johan Karlsson Schaffer, Nora Stappert, and Sören Stapel.

agents (both states and non-state actors) justify and communicate their legitimacy claims and counter-claims. This framework enables us not only to classify different types of legitimation and delegitimation, but also helps to clarify variation of different practices and their potential impact on legitimacy.

The study makes three important original contributions beyond existing knowledge on (de)legitimation in global governance. First, while previous research has primarily focused on legitimation, we suggest that legitimation and delegitimation often shape each other and therefore need to be integrated within a single framework. As Rittberger and Schroeder note, "Legitimacy claims and practices destined to enhance or reinforce legitimacy of an institution are rarely uncontested; institutions face oppositions and are confronted with attempts geared towards their de-legitimation" (2016: 586). Such delegitimation is frequently carried out by civil society actors and social movements that contest the norms, values, and policies of GGIs (Gregoratti and Uhlin, this volume; O'Brien et al. 2000). Moreover, while previous research has emphasized delegitimation performed by non-state actors, our research indicates that member states and even GGI staff can also engage in delegitimation activities, for instance, by withdrawing funding or articulating public criticism.

Second, and closely related to our first contribution, while previous literature is predominantly state-centered and views GGIs and their member states as the primary legitimation agents, our framework acknowledges that a range of wider societal actors are not simply target audiences, but also (de)legitimation agents in their own right (Bernstein 2011). The framework therefore integrates insights on social movements and civil society into the debate about legitimation in global governance (Bandy and Smith 2005; Della Porta and Tarrow 2005).

Third, although research on (de)legitimation of GGIs is expanding, most previous work has been rather selective about the types of practices studied. Considerable scholarly attention has been directed to discursive practices and to a lesser extent institutional practices of legitimation and delegitimation. In contrast, the framework advanced in this chapter aims to capture and integrate the whole spectrum of legitimation and delegitimation practices, which we classify as discursive, institutional, and behavioral.

The legitimation and delegitimation practices in focus in this chapter link to both of the two other substantive concerns of this book. To begin with, legitimation and delegitimation practices typically invoke the type of institutional sources of legitimacy elaborated by Scholte and Tallberg in Chapter 4. For instance, institutional legitimation may involve measures to boost democratic procedure in a GGI, while discursive delegitimation may involve criticism of the fairness of GGI performance. In addition, legitimation and delegitimation practices carry implications for the consequences of legitimacy explored in

Part IV of this book. Depending on the success of legitimation and delegitimation in shaping audience perceptions, such practices contribute to the legitimacy whose effects are analyzed in Chapters 9 and 10. In sum, a focus on legitimation and delegitimation helps to bridge analyses of the sources and consequences of legitimacy in global governance.

The chapter proceeds as follows. In the next section, we further elaborate how the framework is embedded in previous research on processes of legitimation in global governance. The third section advances a typology for conceptualizing different legitimation and delegitimation practices employed by GGIs, member states as well as other agents. The fourth section sketches the contours of a research agenda that explores variation in different types of legitimation and delegitimation.

Starting Points

In this section, we elaborate how our framework on legitimation and delegitimation of GGIs builds on previous research. Three starting points are essential: approaching (de)legitimation as social practice; going beyond state-centrism to acknowledge the full range of agents; and distinguishing the main types of legitimation and delegitimation practices. The following discussion elaborates on these three elements in turn.

(De)legitimation as Social Practice

Legitimation is an "activity which can be observed . . . it is something people do" (Barker 2001: 24). Rather than making theoretical-normative judgments about legitimacy and the right to rule, the empirical-sociological approach employed in this volume focuses on the political *process* through which legitimacy is obtained, maintained, contested, and withdrawn. This process-oriented perspective brings attention to the role of agents, practices, and strategies in the acquisition, maintenance, contestation, and transformation of legitimacy (cf. Barker 2007; Beetham 2013). Hence, (de)legitimation is a contested political process involving both supporters and opponents of an authority (Barker 2001: 24–8). It furthermore entails an *interaction* between rulers (GGIs) and audiences (actors who perceive that they are subjects of a GGI) (Hurrelmann et al. 2007: 9; Bexell and Jönsson, this volume).

Legitimation *practices* and legitimation *claims* are closely related. Legitimation claims occur when actors seek to justify their norms, principles, identities, interests, and behaviors. These acts of justification are the lifeblood of the *politics* of legitimacy (Reus-Smit 2007: 159; Clark 2005: 2–3). The growing literature on this topic emphasizes that legitimacy claims are often matched by counter-claims (Hurrelmann and Schneider 2014). Thus, we need to know why and how legitimacy claims are supported, validated, or contested by GGIs as well as states, societal actors, and citizens (Steffek 2009; Zaum 2013a). This again underlines the relevance of the interactive process perspective as well as why legitimation and delegitimation need to be integrated within the same framework.

There is a long social science tradition, especially within sociology, to study social practice (Van Leeuwen 2008). While a more specific form of practice theory currently attracts considerable attention in the field of international relations (IR), we adopt a more generic understanding of social practice. We approach (de)legitimation as social practice, rather than as strategy more narrowly. Practices include—but go beyond—strategies. While strategies involve "goal-oriented or intentional activities" (cf. Gronau and Schmidtke 2016: 41), social practice entails "what people do" within a broader societal context (Van Leeuwen 2008: 5). The advantage of studying (de)legitimation as social practice, rather than as strategy alone, is thus intended to transcend intention-based notions of (de)legitimation and to approach activities as they are socially embedded. So, while practices certainly include conscious and strategic acts of political performance, they also encompass "dynamic material and ideational processes that enable structures to be stable or to evolve, and agents to reproduce or transform structures" (Adler and Pouliot 2011a: 4–5; also Slaughter 2015).

Agents of Legitimation and Delegitimation

Previous literature on legitimacy beyond the state has often focused on what GGIs do in order to secure confidence among different target audiences, ranging from member states, the GGI's own staff, non-state actors, other GGIs, as well as the wider public (Gronau and Schmidtke 2016; Symons 2011). Recently, scholarly work has shifted focus from the GGIs themselves towards their member states. According to Zaum, the most "important actors engaging in legitimation efforts are not the supranational bureaucracies, but member states" (2016: 1). That said, we need also to go beyond GGIs and their member states to consider a range of non-state agents as well.

The distinction between *top-down* and *bottom-up legitimation* is relevant in this regard (Gronau and Schmidtke 2016: 38; Gronau 2016; Zaum 2013b). Top-down legitimation is manifested in actions, speeches, policies, rituals, rhetorical devices, and displays through which GGIs justify their own activities (Zaum 2013b: 11; Gronau 2016). Bottom-up legitimation occurs when those who are subject to a GGI's authority recognize and validate its authority claims (Zaum 2013b: 10). The form of bottom-up legitimation most commonly addressed in previous literature occurs when GGIs are legitimated through the expressed confidence of their member states, for instance, by joining a GGI and accepting its rules and regulations (Zaum 2013b: 11).

Other legitimation "from below" happens through non-state actors. Past scholarship has predominantly considered these actors as audiences and constituencies, on the receiving end of the legitimation activities carried out by GGIs and their member states (Bexell and Jönsson, this volume). In this perspective, the importance of non-state actors rests first and foremost with their capacity to provide consent and support. Previous research has rarely treated them as genuine legitimating agents in their own right. Here we argue for looking beyond the hierarchical relationships between GGIs and member states, acknowledging that (de)legitimation involves a broader set of agents in world society (cf. Bernstein 2011; Clark 2005; Scholte 2007; Slaughter 2015; Symons 2011; Zaum 2013b).

By distinguishing between a state-centered and a society-centered approach to legitimacy, Rittberger and Schroeder illustrate the plurality of legitimation agents (2016: 582). The state-centered approach focuses on states and national communities, whereas the society-centered approach posits that other agents and individuals can also be bearers of rights and political order. In line with the society-centered approach, our framework transcends "methodological nationalism" and maintains that non-state actors play an increasingly important role not only as actors providing confidence in GGIs, but also as agents performing legitimation and delegitimation practices in global governance. From this perspective, an agent of (de)legitimation can be defined as any actor who engages in (de)legitimation practices in relation to a particular GGI. For example, as elaborated by Gregoratti and Uhlin (this volume), since the late 1990s there is a significant amount of research about social movement protests against GGIs (cf. Bandy and Smith 2005; Della Porta and Tarrow 2005). Although these studies are seldom explicitly framed as studies of legitimacy, they examine how societal actors engage in practices of legitimation and delegitimation (Haunss 2007; Riggirozzi 2014a). A focus on the dynamic interplay between GGIs, their member states, and a range of other societal agents enables us to bridge the hitherto separated literatures on legitimation and on social movements.

Steffek (2009: 316) distinguishes between different categories of agents involved in the legitimation of global governance. They include state representatives (politicians, civil servants/diplomats), experts, activists and lobbyists, NGOs and social movements, journalists, and citizens at large. While Steffek's categorization is detailed, it defines agents in relation to discourse or as "speakers" of (de)legitimation. For instance, journalists are included, since they can be understood as "multipliers and gatekeepers of political discourse" (Steffek 2009: 316). Although this point is relevant, it is open for discussion whether it makes journalists legitimating agents in their own right. Furthermore, Steffek's categorization has some limitations. In response, we propose a categorization based on GGIs (including their staff), GGI member states, non-member states, civil society actors (i.e. NGOs and social movements), market actors, and individuals (citizens, general public).

Types of Legitimation and Delegitimation

Although there is growing literature on different forms of legitimation and delegitimation vis-à-vis GGIs, studies tend to focus on rather specific legitimation agents, strategies, organizations, and cases. This results in a fragmented research agenda and a range of competing conceptualizations.

As mentioned in the previous section, one common way to classify (de) legitimation practices is according to the relationship between the legitimating agent and the target audience. For instance, Gronau and Schmidtke (2016) distinguish between governmental, bureaucratic, and societal legitimation strategies. These distinctions highlight that GGIs try to persuade member states (governmental audiences), their own staff (bureaucratic audiences), as well as non-state actors and the wider public (societal audiences). The distinction mentioned above, between top-down and bottom-up legitimation, is also largely defined according to the relationship between agents and audiences, in particular between GGIs and their members.

Although such distinctions can be analytically useful, (de)legitimation practices are, more often than not, directed simultaneously towards multiple audiences (see Bexell and Jönsson, this volume; also Zaum 2013b). As a result, we need categories that highlight types of practice rather than types of audience. Another reason for avoiding a focus on agent-audience relationships is that they tend to be dynamic and complex. In fact, GGIs and their members are often simultaneously both producers and audiences of legitimation. Similarly, non-state actors may also be both agents and audiences.

Already some scholarly work on legitimation practices has focused on what "agents do" rather than on relationships between agents and audiences. In particular, this research has examined discursive legitimation. In fact, many scholars argue that establishing, maintaining, and countering legitimacy is to a large extent a discursive phenomenon (Reus-Smit 2007: 163; cf. Steffek 2003, 2009; Halliday et al. 2010). In addition, institutional (de)legitimation has received growing scholarly attention. For example, Zaum (2013a) in the book *Legitimating International Organizations* identifies a range of institutional practices by GGIs, directed primarily at their member states. GGIs have also pursued institutional legitimation by "opening up" to civil society actors (Scholte 2011a; Tallberg et al. 2013). So, it is evident that both discursive and institutional dimensions are relevant for constructing a typology of (de) legitimation practices.

In addition, our approach identifies a third and usually overlooked type of (de)legitimation practice, which we refer to as "behavioral" (Tallberg and Zürn 2017). This category covers a range of other actions which affect audiences' perceptions of GGIs, such as protest demonstrations, opinion polls, ranking exercises, and performance reviews. Although some of these behavioral practices are included in social movement research, they are seldom taken into account in legitimacy research.

A Typology of Legitimation and Delegitimation

In sum, the classification of (de)legitimation practices developed in this chapter is built around three fundamental components (Table 6.1). First, we integrate legitimation and delegitimation practices within a single framework. Second, we distinguish between GGIs and other agents of legitimation and delegitimation, such as member states, civil society organizations, market actors, and citizens. Third, we seek to cover the whole spectrum of legitimation and delegitimation by identifying discursive, institutional, and behavioral practices. Such a typology encompasses all agents and all practices.

The following section now elaborates further on types of (de)legitimation practices. The three sub-sections below respectively outline discursive, institutional, and behavioral practices, as enacted by both GGI representatives and other agents. Admittedly this typology excludes practices whereby a GGI delegitimizes itself (although it includes when a GGI delegitimizes another GGI). This is not to deny the fact that individual staff and bureaus within

Table 6.1. Types of legitimation and delegitimation

Agent	Legitimation		Delegitimation
	GGIs	Other agents (states, non-state actors, individuals, other GGIs)	Other agents (states, non-state actors, individuals, other GGIs)
Type			
Discursive	Public information	Public information	Public information
	Self-legitimation	Endorsement	Criticism
	Narrative construction	Rhetorical repertoires	Rhetorical repertoires
Institutional	Constitutional reform	Participation	Exit from organization
	Institutional emulation	Consent	Non-payment of fees
	Broadened participation	Supportive voting	Oppositional voting
Behavioral	Performance review	Financial aid	Protest
	Campaigning	Supportive lobbying	Oppositional Campaining
	Opinion polls	Positive rankings	Repertoires of contention

a GGI may sometimes engage in shaming and delegitimation of their own GGI. One prominent example is the ousting of Paul Wolfowitz as World Bank president in 2007 against a backdrop of internal staff revolt. However, on the whole, self-delegitimation by GGIs is too rare to warrant frontline attention in our typology.

Discursive Legitimation and Delegitimation

Steffek (2003) argues that modern modes of legitimation make extensive use of argument and reason. Inasmuch as legitimation involves explicit rationalization—i.e. articulating reasons why an authority has a right to rule—language is often core to the politics of legitimacy (Reyes 2011). With discursive practices, governors establish their legitimacy through public self-justification of their actions and/or through the construction in rhetoric and other messages of positive impressions of their rule. The governed in turn draw on language and other communications to endorse or challenge these justifications and images. These discursive practices are manifested in a wide range of texts and speech acts, such as mission statements, constitutional documents, speeches, policy papers, press releases, public relations communications, social media, straplines, protest slogans, spontaneous talk in negotiations, and so forth (Schneider et al. 2007; Steffek 2003). The importance of discursive and communicative dimensions of legitimation has methodological implications. Hence, discourse analysis and text-analytical approaches have become increasingly important for the empirical study of (de)legitimation of GGIs (Gronau 2016; Halliday et al. 2010).

Discursive practices operate in various ways. In many cases, legitimating agents make explicit associations between themselves and commonly perceived sources of legitimacy, such as the purported democratic credentials, technocratic standards, and fairness of a governing institution (Scholte and Tallberg, this volume). From another angle, literature around legitimacy crises has suggested that discursive practices may be intensified and take on new patterns when unexpected disruptive events challenge previous conceptions of normality. For instance, during the Eurozone crisis after 2008, a range of discourses concerning "financial capitalism, humanism, nationalism and Europeanism played a central role in legitimation, delegitimation and relegitimation" (Vaara 2014: 500). Vaara shows that both the European Union (EU) and other agents engaged in a variety of discursive practices, making reference to "authority," "knowledge," "rationalization," "moral evaluations" (such as unfairness), and what is referred to as "mythopoiesis" (which implies legitimation through narrative structures about the past or future) (Vaara 2014: 500; also Van Leeuwen 2007, 2008).

Additional insights can be gained from discursive legitimation around the African Union (AU). African ruling elites, especially in the context of the AU, deploy a range of discursive legitimation strategies directed at different audiences inside as well as beyond Africa. Both in official texts and in many speeches, African heads of state and senior AU officials invoke legitimating ideas of African culture, indigenous values, and specific historical African traditions such as consensus politics (Gelot and Tieku 2017; Gelot 2012). These practices are well illustrated by the AU's Agenda 2063, which seeks to stir the collective political imagination with a narrative concerning the "African people" and the need for "a united Africa" through the AU (Gelot and Tieku 2017). Thus Agenda 2063 and similar texts are framed to boost perceptions of the AU and other state-led regional governance mechanisms in Africa as legitimate authorities (cf. Lotze 2013; Rittberger and Schroeder 2016).

There is also a growing literature about how GGIs and their members engage in delegitimation. For example, the AU and a number of African governments (especially Kenya, Rwanda, and South Africa) have strongly criticized the International Criminal Court (ICC) for allegedly failing to resolve conflicts, for imposing "double standards," and for being inconsistent with domestic laws (Caldwell 2015). Other agents, such as civil society organizations and social movements, are also deeply involved in discursive delegitimation. Taking another illustration from Africa, the Southern African People's Solidarity Network (SAPSN) has emerged as a key civil society alliance for alternative regionalism in southern Africa (Godsäter 2016; Söderbaum 2016). SAPSN considers itself to be part of a worldwide anti-globalization movement, and the network relies first and foremost on a variety of discursive delegitimation practices. In one of its most widely distributed documents, SAPSN claims that the general neoliberal insistence upon the benefits of "free trade" and "market forces" does not serve the interests of the people of southern Africa and "runs counter to the potential for full and effective, internally-generated and rooted national and regional development" (SAPSN 2000: 2). SAPSN furthermore demands that:

> the Governments of SADC [the Southern African Development Community] desist from their collaboration and collusion with national and international political and economic forces and neo-liberal agencies, particularly the IMF [International Monetary Fund] and World Bank, to turn SADC into an "open region" of free trade, free capital movements and investment rights, to the benefit of international traders, transnational corporations and financial speculators.
>
> (SAPSN 2000: 2)

In a similar fashion, the global climate justice movement has employed a range of discursive delegitimation practices targeting the UNFCCC. These performances were manifest in for instance rhetorical repertoires by Climate

Justice Now! (CJN!) in the lead-up to the 2015 climate summit in Paris. These activists also maintain that the resulting Paris Agreement fails to promote necessary deeper structural changes. CJN! demands not only an equitable and democratic representation of vulnerable communities in the UNFCCC bodies, but also a radical overhaul of the multilateral system (Bäckstrand and Lövbrand 2016). As is elaborated below, speech acts and verbal critiques can be closely related to behavioral practices such as protests and demonstrations. Key member states frequently engage in major discursive delegitimation practices, as illustrated by the aforementioned announcement in June 2017 by the Trump Administration to withdraw from the Paris Climate Agreement.

Institutional Legitimation and Delegitimation

Institutional legitimation by GGIs has received growing attention among scholars. According to Zaum, institutional reform has emerged as one of the most prominent GGI legitimation practices during recent decades. It "prioritizes form over function, signaling to important and powerful audiences to encourage their continued material and political support" (Zaum 2016: 1). Examples of such practices include constitutional reforms, administrative reorganizations, transparency initiatives, civil society engagement programs, policy adjustments in response to critiques, and so on.

In pursuing institutional legitimation practices, GGIs sometimes model other organizations. Emulation and isomorphism can also occur for reasons other than legitimacy (DiMaggio and Powell 1983). However, more recent discussions have considered whether GGIs can gain legitimacy by copying other governance mechanisms which are perceived as legitimate. The EU has featured strongly in this research on emulation (Lenz and Burilkov 2017). For instance, Jetschke shows that: 'By mimicking the European integration process, ASEAN [the Association of South East Asian Nations] member states have effectively created an isomorphic organization. The Association's institutional development reflects a concern for international legitimacy and less an objective functional demand arising from the specific interactions of member states' (Jetschke 2009: 407). Several other scholars have drawn attention to emulation and mimicking of the EU in Africa, where the incentives for seeking legitimacy through institutional isomorphism are higher than in other regions (Piccolino 2016). Several scholars have argued that local actors and GGIs are not really appropriating these EU-sponsored models, but rather follow them as a way to boost their international legitimacy and obtain financial support from the EU (Rittberger and Schroeder 2016; Söderbaum 2016; Lenz 2012).

A rich existing literature examines how different GGIs have sought to enhance their legitimacy by promoting participation by civil society and market actors in their policy processes (Tallberg et al. 2013). Most GGIs have designed mechanisms to facilitate involvement by non-state actors, including accreditation schemes, board and committee membership, various consultation forums, and sub-contracting of policy implementation.

One example of such institutional legitimation is the UNFCCC's Global Climate Action Agenda that was established in advance of the 2015 Paris climate summit to encourage commitments by non-state and sub-state actors to reduce greenhouse gases. It was launched by the secretariat of the UNFCCC, the executive office of the UN secretary-general, and the French and Peruvian presidencies of the Conference of the Parties (COP). This joint initiative by GGI bureaucracies and member states seeks to mobilize coordinated transnational climate action by non-state actors to promote the Paris Agreement, limit global warming, foster climate resilience, and decarbonize the world economy. As a multistakeholder process involving climate commitments from more than 12,000 non-state actors, the Global Climate Action Agenda represents an institutional legitimation practice by the UNFCCC secretariat to gain legitimacy for the 2015 Paris climate agreement among business, civil society, and sub-state actors (Bäckstrand et al. 2017; Hale 2016).

Growing literature also problematizes the institutional legitimation efforts by GGIs. For example, research suggests that many attempts to ensure civil society participation within regional governance institutions in the Global South have been rather superficial. For instance, the Southern Common Market (Mercosur) is state-centric and presidentially led. Civil society plays only a minor role in spite of its inclusion in certain committees. While the Union of South American Nations (UNASUR) may be more inclusive, especially in the field of health, research concludes that there is still a "lack of participation of civil society organizations in the definition of UNASUR social policies, agendas, and institutions" (Riggirozzi 2014b: 144). In Southeast Asia, ASEAN has constructed an institutional framework for collaboration with civil society (Gerard 2015); however, these mechanisms, too, offer only limited inclusion of civil society (Uhlin 2016). Civil society participation has been widely discussed in Africa as well. The example of SADC reveals that virtually all of its interactions with civil society associations take place at lower levels within the secretariat and in technical committees (Godsäter and Söderbaum 2017). The prevailing top-down approach at SADC prevents civil society from challenging prevailing policies, proposing alternatives, and contributing to more participatory and accountable policy development. In these circumstances one influential civil society organization, the Anti-Privatization Forum (APF), refuses to join the "NGO crowd" and participate in state-led regional schemes like the AU and SADC, arguing that civil society is only being used to gain a veneer of public legitimacy. According to one APF representative, the SADC NGO Council "is a joke and we don't take it very seriously ... It is a classic example of institutionalized co-option" (quoted in Godsäter 2016: 123).

111

Those subject to an institutional authority are particularly important for legitimation as well as delegitimation. Zaum underlines that the practice of consent is one of the most prominent forms of legitimation in global govern-ance. As he notes, "[i]nternational organizations are legitimated from below through the consent that states express by joining an institution, and accept-ing its rules and regulations" (2013b: 11). Consent is also practiced through voting to support an institution's policies and programs. At the same time, lack of consent can be a powerful delegitimation practice. For instance, the UNFCCC received a major blow when the Bush Administration in 2001 pulled out of the Kyoto Protocol, deeming it "fundamentally flawed" (Bäckstrand 2011). Failure to pay membership fees or obstructive voting are other delegit-imation practices. Perhaps the most powerful delegitimation tool is to exit from an organization, as illustrated by the UK's withdrawal from the EU. As noted above, other agents and civil society actors may also try to avoid or counteract a GGI's institutional legitimation strategies, for instance, by non-participation or lack of consent.

Behavioral Legitimation and Delegitimation

Behavioral practices are a third type of (de)legitimation. Here, the emphasis is on *actions* that may affect audiences' legitimacy perceptions, rather than discursive speech acts or institutional reforms and challenges. Examples include performance reviews, visual representations, opinion polls, external validation, street protest, and campaigns. Often, behavioral (de)legitimation goes hand in hand with discursive (e.g. protests invoking a specific narrative) or institutional (e.g. funding for an organizational reform).

Many GGIs try to boost their legitimacy by conducting public relations, performance reviews, and opinion polls. For instance, the EU attempts to boost its own legitimacy through symbols and rituals, such as the EU flag, the European anthem, and a rich variety of EU funding instruments. Similar legitimating symbolic and financial behaviors can be seen in other GGIs with a pronounced normative and ethical content, such as the UN.

Some GGIs can be legitimated through receiving outside funding—and delegitimated through having such funding withdrawn. For example, EU funding and institutional capacity building legitimizes other regional organ-izations in other parts of the world, not least in Africa (Lenz and Burilkov 2017). However, the fact that many regional organizations in Africa are so extremely dependent on outside funding has also become a legitimacy prob-lem (African Union 2017; Rittberger and Schroeder 2016). The withdrawal of US funding to UNESCO, due to the acceptance of Palestine as a member, not only put the organization in a vulnerable financial situation but was also a deliberative attempt to undermine its legitimacy.

Although GGI staff only exceptionally delegitimate their own institution, its member states may certainly engage in a range of delegitimation practices, either unilaterally or jointly with civil society actors and social movements (Zaum 2013a). For example, actors can delegitimize the organization by campaigns, street protests, or walking out of its meetings. A prominent example of behavioral delegitimation is that undertaken by the global climate justice movement, which questions the market-driven approach to multilateral climate diplomacy embedded in certain GGIs, such as the UNFCCC. This rejection of the prevailing global climate regime has been expressed in large-scale protests in conjunction with the annual COPs under the slogan "system change not climate change" (Bond 2012; Hadden 2015).

In a similar fashion, the SAPSN has engaged in direct resistance during SADC's high-level summits, where activists shout slogans against neoliberal free trade and economic partnership agreements with the EU (Godsäter 2016). The construction of SADC as an enemy has consolidated the SAPSN movement itself, but ridicule and insults against political leaders have also scared off mainstream politicians and SADC officials (Godsäter 2016).

There are many types of behavioral delegitimation. Gregoratti and Uhlin (this volume) draw attention to broad "repertoires of contention" in the literature on social movements, ranging "from peaceful petitions, demonstrations and strikes to more disruptive blockades and occupations, as well as the destruction of property and physical violence targeting opponents." These repertoires of contention go beyond traditional protest activities mentioned above and also include walkouts from meetings with GGI representatives, cyber-protests, critical action research, monitoring of GGI activities, and other forms of everyday resistance. As noted previously, discursive and behavioral practices can overlap and interrelate, and several studies have shown that discursive delegitimation often spills over into behavioral delegitimation (Derman 2014; Orr 2016).

Accounting for Variation

The typology developed in the previous section may be used for several purposes. In the first place, it provides a general conceptual framework that is relevant for and applicable across a range of empirical contexts. In this respect, the typology can promote a more systematic and comparative research agenda for mapping legitimation and delegitimation practices across various types of GGIs, as well as for assessing the impact of such practices on audiences' legitimacy perceptions.

A more ambitious aim is to use the typology in research that accounts for variation of legitimation and delegitimation practices. In such work, the typology can be used for (at least) two main purposes. On the one hand, the typology can be employed to categorize legitimation practices as the dependent variable. In this case, we try to identify the factors that help to explain why some legitimation practices are used more frequently than others. On the other hand, the typology may also be used to categorize legitimation practices as the independent variable. In this case, we seek to understand what factors account for variation in the impact of legitimation and delegitimation practices on audience perceptions of GGIs.

The section below sketches a preliminary research agenda that identifies some of the factors that can account for both types of variation. The discussion particularly emphasizes four factors which have been highlighted in previous research: namely, the occurrence of a legitimacy crisis, the nature of the issue area, the type of organization, and the geographic scope of the organization (cf. Zaum 2013c).

External Shocks and Legitimacy Crises

A rich literature has explored how various types of external shocks and legitimacy crises can shape patterns of legitimation and delegitimation, as well as the impact of these practices on legitimacy beliefs (Vaara 2014; Zaum 2013a; Zelli, this volume). Legitimacy crises of many GGIs—including the EU, the UNFCCC, the Group of Eight (G8), the IMF, the World Bank, the Internet Corporation for Assigned Names and Numbers (ICANN), and more—have precipitated efforts to maintain and regain legitimacy among elites as well as societal stakeholders (Bäckstrand 2011; Reus-Smith 2007). For example, the financial crisis of 2008 spurred the G8 to engage in both discursive and institutional legitimation practices, targeting member states and the public (Gronau 2016). The Group of Twenty (G20) also suffered a legitimacy crisis as a result of the financial shocks and engaged in various legitimation practices to reach a range of audiences (Slaughter 2015). Similarly, the Asia financial crisis in 1997 triggered a legitimacy crisis for the IMF, which led the organization to employ a variety of discursive as well as institutional practices to counter heavy criticism from member states, civil society, the media, and the broader public (Seabrooke 2007). In the field of health, pandemics around AIDS and Ebola have triggered institutional and discursive legitimation strategies at the World Health Organization (WHO) (McInnes 2015). The failure of the 2009 Copenhagen climate summit to produce a successor agreement to the Kyoto Protocol represented a legitimacy crisis for the UNFCCC. With the 2015 Paris Agreement the UNFCCC regained legitimacy as the key GGI of climate change governance, but this was subsequently challenged again in June 2017 by President Trump's announcement to withdraw the US from the treaty.

As these examples indicate, crises often spark a flurry of delegitimation efforts by various agents. Sometimes a legitimacy crisis may even result from delegitimation practices. For example, the critique by the so-called anti-globalization movement against the Bretton Woods institutions and the "Battle of Seattle" against the World Trade Organization (WTO) in 1999 are important instances when comprehensive discursive and behavioral delegitimation practices (protest, campaigning, and direct action) have created legitimacy deficits (Gregoratti and Uhlin, this volume). In times of crisis, delegitimation can also be carried out by state actors. For instance, the G8 was delegitimated when President Obama denounced the group as an inadequate forum for dealing with the 2008 financial crisis (Gronau 2016; Slaughter 2015).

The preceding examples point to a rich research agenda. What similarities and differences in (de)legitimation practices can be detected across different crises? Does variation depend on the nature of the crisis? What types of practices (discursive, institutional, behavioral) are most common and most effective in changing legitimacy beliefs among different audiences during crises? How do (de)legitimation practices undertaken in times of crises compare to those pursued in non-crisis situations?

Nature of the Issue Area

Along with crisis situations, we may also expect legitimation and delegitimation practices and their impacts to vary depending on the issue area. Different policy fields can involve different dominant agents, different modes of governance, and different distributions of audiences. So far, however, little empirical research has systematically explored variation of (de)legitimation practices by issue area.

In the security realm, for instance, GGIs and member states tend to be the main producers as well as targets of legitimation/delegitimation practices, and non-state actors play a much less significant role. Although discursive legitimation in the field of security may target non-state actors, institutional legitimation practices designed to open up access for civil society participation are conspicuously absent in this field (Binder and Heupel 2015). The so-called "Arria Formula" for NGO consultations at the UN Security Council is a rare exception in this regard.

In contrast, a richer variety and more complex interplay of agents and practices marks issue areas such as the environment, development, and health, with their widespread use of multistakeholder diplomacy. In these issue areas, we hypothesize that it is possible to detect a greater combination of discursive, institutional, and behavioral practices employed by a broader set of agents.

The area of economic affairs (encompassing communications, finance, investment, and trade) generally falls between the more state-centric pattern in the security realm and the more diverse pattern in the social-environmental domain. In addition, economic governance issues may tend to involve business audiences more prominently than the security and social-environmental fields.

Type of Organization

As noted throughout this book, GGIs come in many varieties, ranging from comprehensive supranational authorities (such as the EU), intergovernmental organizations with a sizable secretariat (such as the WTO), intergovernmental bodies with a weak secretariat (Mercosur), treaty negotiation processes with coordinating secretariats (UNFCCC), informal "club models" of GGIs with rotating chairs (such as the G8 and the G20), multistakeholder institutions (such as the World Commission on Dams (WCD)), and private governance mechanisms where corporate and civil society representation are generally stronger (such as the Forest Stewardship Council (FSC)). Although previous research clearly underlines that we can expect the type of organization to impact on the variation and impact of different legitimation practices (Bernstein 2011), there is still a deficit of systematic and cross-regional studies.

Several organizational characteristics are relevant to consider in this regard. One aspect is that financial resources and staff size of GGIs may explain both the variation and impact of different legitimation strategies. For example, the WHO has a staff ten times larger than the United Nations Development Programme (UNDP) and twice as big as the United Nations Environment Programme (UNEP) (van der Lugt and Dingwerth 2015).

Some GGIs are bureaucracies with a relatively large degree of autonomy and supranational authority, such as the WTO and the World Bank (Barnett and Finnemore 2004; Steffek 2003). Such bodies may also embody a Weberian rational-legal authority which encourages their legitimation efforts to empha-size technocratic sources of legitimacy. However, GGIs may also be arenas for intergovernmental cooperation and bargaining in which states seek to advance legitimacy claims. For example, most observers view the EU and other multipurpose regional organizations such as the AU and ASEAN as political projects. The UN Security Council is also politicized and dominated by a few powerful states (Welsh and Zaum 2013).

Another relevant distinction is between task-specific and general purpose GGIs (Lenz et al. 2015). The former is concerned with a particular type of activity, usually within a given sector such as trade or transport, while the latter spans several themes or sectors. In spite of a rapidly growing literature about different types of institutional designs in global governance, there is still a lack of systematic research about how these variations shape patterns and impacts of legitimation and delegitimation.

Geographic Scope

A further question arises concerning variation in the employment and impact of legitimation and delegitimation practices of worldwide as compared to regional GGIs. Although considerable research has addressed certain GGIs (such as the EU, the WTO, and the UNFCCC), global and regional organizations are seldom compared (for an exception see Williams 2013). In this chapter, we have tried to bridge this gap by consistently drawing upon illustrations from both global and regional GGIs while developing our typology. However, much more systematic global-regional comparative research is needed with regard to variation in patterns and impacts of legitimation and delegitimation practices.

For instance, some GGIs with worldwide membership, especially within the UN family, have institutionalized accreditation and relatively generous access for a range of non-state actors. As a result, the UN-led negotiation of the Sustainable Development Goals (SDGs) involved 196 states and a rich variety of societal stakeholders from business, local governments, and indigenous movements (Abbott and Bernstein 2015). Even if regionally based GGIs have a more limited membership composition, many of them also have patterns of legitimation and delegitimation shaped by dense interactions between their representatives, member states, and civil society actors (Söderbaum 2016).

Most (multipurpose) regional organizations around the world, such as ASEAN, AU, EU, MERCOSUR, and SADC, have established a range of mechanisms to promote access and participation by civil society and private actors in policymaking and project implementation. Yet beyond the EU, the ability of civil society actors to have a real impact in regional GGIs is limited by the fact that virtually all interaction takes place within lower levels of secretariats and technical committees (Söderbaum 2016). Hence these institutional mechanisms for producing democratic legitimacy in regional GGIs do not appear to work. It is worth exploring whether these conclusions also hold in respect of globally based GGIs.

It is equally relevant to explore variation in the delegitimation of regional as opposed to worldwide GGIs. For instance, there is very little systematic knowledge regarding whether protests and other delegitimation practices against global GGIs (such as the WTO) are more or less effective compared to regional GGIs (such as ASEAN). This matter is further elaborated by Gregoratti and Uhlin (this volume).

Conclusion

This chapter has explored the plethora of practices that GGIs, states, and societal agents employ in processes of legitimation and delegitimation.

Responding to the fragmented nature of the research field on legitimation and its tendency to focus on specific strategies and cases, we have developed a general framework which is designed to be applicable to different agents, cases, and contexts. Through illustrative examples, we have also demonstrated the diversity of legitimation and delegitimation practices across regional and global GGIs.

The typology advanced in this chapter is exhaustive to the extent that it covers a full spectrum of practices (discursive, institutional, and behavioral) among all relevant agents (GGIs, member states, and various societal actors). Designed in this way, the typology can provide a general and empirically applicable conceptual framework for future research which spans specific agents, cases, and contexts.

The framework can be used in multiple ways. First and foremost, it allows us to map and compare different types of legitimation and delegitimation practices. Second, it can be employed to identify which institutional sources of legitimacy (e.g. democratic procedure or fair performance) that legitimation and delegitimation practices invoke. Third, it offers a starting point for evaluating the effects of various legitimation and delegitimation practices on the perceived legitimacy of GGIs among core audiences.

The typology can also be further developed and nuanced. For example, the empirical illustrations provided above are by no means exhaustive. Additional sub-types of discursive, institutional, and behavioral practices could be identified. Similarly, it is both possible to unpack the typology's category of "other agents" and make more nuanced distinctions between GGI member states, other states, various types of non-state groupings, and individual agents.

After developing and illustrating the typology, the final section of the chapter considered factors that can explain variation in legitimation and delegitimation practices across different GGIs. We argue that the typology can be used to categorize (de)legitimation practices as both dependent and independent variable. The former implies identification of factors that explain why some practices are used more frequently than others. The latter implies the identification of the factors that account for variation in the relative impact of different practices on different audiences' legitimacy perceptions vis-à-vis GGIs. These two purposes are complementary. We have proposed a preliminary research agenda that has highlighted a number of potential factors affecting variation in the use of (de)legitimation practices, such as the occurrence of a legitimacy crisis, the nature of the issue area, the type of organization, and the geographic scope of the GGI. Although we are confident that all these factors are relevant, we do not claim that the list is complete, and future research can identify additional factors.

7

Audiences of (De)Legitimation in Global Governance

Magdalena Bexell and Kristina Jönsson

Chapter 6 distinguished different practices (discursive, institutional, and behavioral) through which legitimation and delegitimation of global governance institutions (GGIs) are pursued. Now the present chapter turns attention to actors who are at the receiving end of legitimation and delegitimation efforts, namely, the audiences. As indicated in Chapter 1, an audience can be understood as a set of actors who hold or withhold legitimacy beliefs vis-à-vis GGIs.

Research on audiences of GGI (de)legitimation remains underdeveloped in the study of world politics (cf. Goddard and Krebs 2015). Existing investigations of legitimation and delegitimation primarily examine the *practices* employed by agents in attempts to boost or undermine the legitimacy beliefs of others (see Bäckstrand and Söderbaum, this volume; Zaum 2013b; Halliday et al. 2010). Far less is known about the nature, the construction, and the reactions of the *audiences* of (de)legitimation efforts. (Reasons for preferring the term "audience" to related notions, such as stakeholder or subjects, are elaborated later in this chapter.)

The issue of audience encompasses a number of key questions for research on legitimacy and legitimation in global governance. For example, who in society holds legitimacy beliefs about GGIs? How might the different audiences of a GGI be classified? How are audiences constructed through political practices? How and why do agents of (de)legitimation target different audiences with different kinds of practices? How do audiences respond to various legitimation and delegitimation strategies? What grounds for legitimacy are most convincing to certain audiences? This chapter develops two key analytical distinctions to advance the empirical study of audiences: namely, between "constituencies" and "observers" of GGIs; and between "targeted" and "self-appointed" audiences.

Constituencies are audiences with institutionalized political bonds to a governing authority, while observers lack such a connection. Yet, audiences of (de)legitimation do not exist a priori, but rather are constructed through political processes. Another key distinction for studying the above questions is therefore between targeted audiences (i.e. those constructed by agents of (de) legitimation strategies) and self-appointed audiences (i.e. those constructed by respondents themselves). So far, systematic knowledge is lacking on how, when, and why agents of (de)legitimation target certain audiences and the conditions under which audiences are instead self-appointed reactors to legitimation attempts.

Prior legitimacy research has mainly concerned constituencies, while observers are becoming increasingly important as GGIs have opened up for broader direct engagement. Many GGIs today provide channels to involve not only states, but also a diverse set of non-state actors, including civil society organizations (CSOs), political parties, academic institutions, business enterprises, foundations, and more. Thus one cannot today presuppose that a GGI's audience is composed of any particular range of actors. Moreover, the same actors who form audiences of (de)legitimation can also be agents of these processes when they themselves attempt to shape the legitimacy beliefs of others. To this extent the line between agents and audiences of GGI (de) legitimation can be blurred in practice.

The rest of the chapter proceeds as follows. The first section reviews previous research on actors who hold legitimacy beliefs vis-à-vis GGIs. The discussion highlights the large variety of actors that might be relevant, as well as the large variety of terms and conceptualizations that researchers have invoked in their analyses. The second section distinguishes categories of audiences for the purpose of studying patterns and variation across different actors who hold perceptions of GGI legitimacy. Particular attention is given here to the distinction between "constituency" and "observer." The third section asks how audiences come into being, arguing that audiences do not exist a priori, but are constituted either by being targeted by GGIs or by being self-appointed. The conclusion identifies future research to explore these propositions further. Throughout the chapter points are illustrated with examples from different types of GGIs, in order to show that questions about audiences in global governance apply across issue areas and across institutional types.

Audience: an Emergent Concept in Legitimacy Research

This section reviews existing literature concerning actors whose legitimacy beliefs are implicated in processes of legitimation and delegitimation. The survey has two parts, the first empirical and the second conceptual. The empirical considerations describe the broad range of actors that can be at the receiving end of initiatives to (de)legitimate GGIs. The conceptual considerations assess the disparate notions and terms that are used with respect to targets of and respondents to (de)legitimation practices.

Empirical Considerations

As already suggested in the introduction to this chapter, many types of actors can today be the subject of and/or react to (de)legitimation strategies in respect of GGIs. Indeed, it is questionable whether the term "audience" is suitably used in the singular when referring to the entirety of actors who engage with a specific GGI. Rather, "audiences" in the plural better reflects the diversity of actors who are today involved in the legitimation and delegitimation of GGIs (Bexell 2015a). Thus, for instance, audiences of the International Criminal Court (ICC) can include state parties, states that are not ICC parties, legal professionals, civil society associations, victims of war crimes, defendants, the media, and the public at large.

As the ICC example indicates, receivers of (de)legitimation strategies concerning GGIs can extend beyond elite circles to citizens at large. For instance, the World Health Organization (WHO) faces a range of elite audiences, such as governments, experts, and pharmaceutical and other companies, as well as general public audiences such as patients and health-care workers. As the WHO expands its agenda to, for example, non-communicable diseases, this GGI also increasingly addresses consumers with their nutritional and other health-related lifestyle choices (Jönsson 2014).

The increasing diversity of audiences of GGIs is part of a broader trend towards increased politicization of global governance, leading to more public discussion, political mobilization, and contestation of the institutions involved (Zürn 2014). This trend has been particularly manifest in the realm of global economic governance, with GGIs such as the Group of Eight (G8), the Group of Twenty (G20), the World Trade Organization (WTO), the International Monetary Fund (IMF), and the World Bank (O'Brien et al. 2000; Gronau 2016).

Empirical studies to date have mostly examined either member states or citizens as the primary audiences of GGIs (cf. Quack 2010; Symons 2011). David Beetham argues that citizens are the ultimate audience of legitimacy claims within nation-states, while political elites form the prime audience for legitimacy in international society (2013: 271). Terence Halliday et al. distinguish three key legitimation audiences for GGIs: state policymakers, domestic interest groups affected by GGI policies, and other GGIs (2010: 109). Jennifer Gronau and Henning Schmidtke (2016) study three types of constituencies of intergovernmental organizations (IGOs): member states, civil servants of the

GGI, and the wider public. In the area of environmental governance, Steven Bernstein (2011) has demonstrated that the more variable set-up of audiences for hybrid GGIs invites more potential for normative contestation of their legitimacy, as compared with IGOs and their generally narrower focus on state audiences.

In a key contribution on discerning different legitimation audiences for GGIs, Dominik Zaum distinguishes between internal audiences (member states and their publics) and external audiences (non-member states and their citizens). He acknowledges that non-governmental organizations (NGOs) and civil society do not always fall easily into one or the other category (Zaum 2013b). An IGO that lacks legitimacy in the eyes of its internal audiences will have weak authority and ensuing problems to secure compliance with its decisions (Ba 2013: 134). The internal-external distinction overlaps with the differentiation of constituencies and observers in the study of GGI audiences (Tallberg and Zürn 2017). However, as discussed further later, we prefer the constituency-observer distinction, as it puts the quality of the political relationship between participants in legitimation processes center stage.

Clearly, the interests, expectations, and normative reference frames can differ greatly among GGI audiences. As a result, audiences do not react in the same way to legitimacy claims. Indeed, audiences may base their legitimacy beliefs on quite different sources. As indicated earlier in this volume by Scholte and Tallberg, legitimacy sources may vary significantly between elites and the general public. Audience dynamics may also differ across societal cleavages based on class, gender, and age.

It is a matter of empirical inquiry to determine which audiences are relevant in a given (de)legitimation process and to explain how these audiences vary between different (de)legitimation settings. To date only limited empirical research has examined this issue. Little evidence has been collected concerning, for example, to what extent the targets of GGI legitimation practices vary in relation to the institutional form or the policy area of global governance. Likewise, little work has examined when GGIs strategically select specific audiences and when they direct legitimation practices at multiple audiences simultaneously.

Conceptual and Terminological Considerations

The concept of "audience" first appeared in legitimacy research with the work of Mark Suchman (1995). Suchman uses the notion in a generic sense, stressing the role of a "social audience" in legitimation processes. Suchman emphasizes that, rather than being a quality of an organization itself, legitimacy involves a relationship between an organization and its audiences (1995: 594).

Other influential authors on legitimacy came to the concept of audience more gradually. For example, Beetham in the first edition of *The Legitimation of Power* (1991) only employed the terms "dominant groups" and "subordinate groups" when discussing the holders of legitimacy beliefs. Twenty years later the second edition of the book added the concept of "audience" to speak about those who might react to legitimacy claims (Beetham 2013: 271). In research on legitimacy in global governance more specifically, Ian Hurd in his initial work described those who hold perceptions on the legitimacy of a rule or institution as "actors" (Hurd 1999: 381). A decade later he invoked the term "audience" to refer to those who held legitimacy beliefs regarding the United Nations Security Council, albeit that this study only considered an audience of states (Hurd 2008: 204).

Many investigations of legitimacy in global governance have used the term "audience" interchangeably with related vocabulary. For example, Ian Clark's study of international legitimacy uses the words "audience" and "constituency" interchangeably, in terms of a "world-society constituency" and "a world audience" (2007: 97, 147, 205). Halliday et al. primarily use the term "audience," but at times they replace it with the phrases "regulatory subject" and "set of constituencies" (2010: 80, 82, 110). Jens Steffek (2007) depicts a "turn to citizens," using the phrases "rule addressee" and a "transnational constituency of citizens." Jonathan Symons (2011) speaks of "communities" and "social constituencies." Sigrid Quack (2010) describes the actors who respond to legitimacy claims in transnational economic governance variously as "addressees," "communities," "constituencies," "participants," "publics" and "stakeholders." None of these authors elaborates on their choice of terms, despite the quite different connotations of "constituency" and "addressee" in the context of political bonds, which lie at the heart of legitimacy.

Selection of vocabulary in regard to holders of legitimacy perceptions is significant. Terminological decisions guide research in certain directions rather than others. The choice of words influences how the role of participants in (de) legitimation processes is conceptualized and theorized. For instance, the term "constituency" tends to direct more attention to those who are formally bound by a GGI's authority and rules, while downplaying or excluding actors who become involved in GGI legitimation processes on other grounds. Meanwhile, the term "addressee" tends to highlight actors who are directly targeted by legitimation practices, while neglecting the rest. The term "stakeholder" tends to emphasize parties who are materially affected by GGI policies and to sideline those who react, say, primarily on ethical grounds. Thus different terms can have significantly different implications regarding whose legitimacy beliefs are seen to matter for GGI legitimacy, and in what way (cf. Meine 2016).

Loose and sometimes inconsistent terminology in respect of the holders of legitimacy beliefs can also hamper cumulative research on the sociological legitimacy of GGIs. Interchangeable use of potentially discrete terms can dilute concepts and neglect nuances of meaning, which reduces analytical leverage in relation to both theory development and empirical study. Tighter and shared terminology would moreover facilitate comparative research that seeks to map and explain variation with regard to audiences of (de)legitimation.

Here we prefer the concept of "audience" on several grounds. First, the term provides a generic notion to distinguish between initiators (agents) and receivers (audiences) of legitimation practices. Second, the concept does not presuppose what kind of actor is agent and/or audience in a legitimation scenario. Third, "audience" conveys a notion of interaction, where receivers not only take in legitimation efforts, but also respond to them, which can then in turn influence the shape of the next attempts at legitimation. The following section discusses how further to categorize the concept of audience in order to make it applicable in empirical research.

Categorizing Audiences: Constituencies and Observers

Having settled on the concept of audience to characterize those who are on the receiving end of legitimation, a next issue is to refine the notion by identifying categories of audience. The distinction of audience types can help to capture patterns of GGI legitimacy perceptions and variations in responses to legitimation practices. The aim is to arrive at categories which: (a) are mutually exclusive; (b) encompass the full range of audiences; (c) apply to all types of GGIs, including IGOs, transgovernmental networks, private and hybrid governance arrangements; and (d) direct attention to the political-institutional bonds between governors and governed, a relationship which lies at the heart of legitimacy.

The typology of "constituencies" and "observers," proposed by Jonas Tallberg and Michael Zürn (2017), best fulfills these four criteria, as it highlights the political bonds between governors and governed while also providing a residual category for studying audiences which fall outside such bonds and still have an active engagement with GGIs. Yet, as discussed below, the distinction also raises two important challenges when employed in the study of global governance. The first is its application to private and hybrid GGIs. The second involves difficulties to distinguish active audiences from agents of legitimation.

Constituencies

A constituent is the subject from whom a constitutional order originates (Oates 2017). This broad concept of constituency has historically related to national politics. In that context "constituency" refers to the electoral base of a politician. That base is a group of people who vote the politician into public office. In some constitutional orders the term constituency also refers to a geographical district where the electorate resides (Bradbury 2009). The legitimacy of the government then lies substantially in this voluntary delegation of power by the constituency to its elected representatives in executive, legislative, or judicial office.

The notion of constituency translates reasonably well from national to global governance in the case of IGOs (Tallberg and Zürn 2017). In this case the territorial scope of the constituency is the country, the popular base of the constituency is the citizens of that country, and the representative of the respective countries at the IGO is their government. In this perspective the constituencies of an IGO are its member states and their citizens, and the IGO would seek its legitimacy in relation to national governments and their peoples.

Yet this conventional conception of constituency does not translate well to hybrid and private GGIs, where territorial states play only a limited and sometimes even no role in making and implementing the rules. For example, government representatives work in tandem with delegates from civil society and business in the Extractive Industries Transparency Initiative (EITI). States figure even more on the sidelines of the Internet Corporation for Assigned Names and Numbers (ICANN), through its Government Advisory Committee (GAC). Meanwhile, states have no formal place at all in wholly private GGIs such as the Forest Stewardship Council (FSC) and the International Accounting Standards Board (IASB). In the case of hybrid and private GGIs, some or all participants in the formal decision-making process answer to a non-territorial support base, for example, of company shareholders or civil society activists.

Broadening the concept of constituency to cover this larger variety of relationships in global governance raises problematic issues about the nature of "the people" who grant authority to GGIs. There may be multiple and diverse types of constituencies for GGIs, some of them territorial and others not. Moreover, a single individual may be part of several GGI constituencies: e.g. as a citizen of a state; as a shareholder in a company; as an activist supporting an NGO; as a consumer of the resources being governed; and so on. Further thorny issues arise about how to give institutional form to "representation" of these diverse constituencies in a GGI: e.g. in a board of directors, in advisory councils, in review panels, etc. Also, how are representatives to such bodies to be selected, and to whom are they to be held accountable (Kuyper and Bäckstrand 2016)? Despite these questions, hybrid and private GGIs are today involved in political relationships of rule-making authority that merit application of the term "constituency" in the study of their (il)legitimacy and (de)legitimation.

Ambiguity also arises regarding the position of GGI staff in relation to the concept of constituency in global governance. Research has demonstrated that the bureaucracy of an IGO often holds a degree of autonomy, an influence in policy processes which is separate from the member states (e.g. Bauer and Ege 2016). For example, the WHO bureaucracy—spread across global headquarters, regional offices, and national bureaus—takes notable initiatives in formulating, implementing, and reviewing rules. Similar autonomy would seem to prevail for the staff of hybrid and private GGIs, even if this subject has not yet been systematically studied. Still, even if GGI staff are in practice not merely servants of authoritative representatives in the GGI, the bureaucracy may be included in the category of constituencies rather than observers, since the staff's mandate is derived from the constituent parties of a GGI.

In sum, preference is given here to the audience category of "constituency" because it puts the spotlight on delegated representative authority as a key aspect of legitimacy and legitimation processes. That said, the conceptualization of constituency needs some important adjustments when its application is shifted from national to global governance, particularly in the case of hybrid and private GGIs.

Observers

The counterpart to constituencies is the category of observers. In global governance literature, the term observer is primarily used in connection with "observer status" in multilateral fora. This label usually implies that non-members of a GGI get the possibility to attend and listen to deliberations, but not to vote or obtain other decision-making competences. The degree of access of observers varies between GGIs and has raised considerable debate about transparency in global governance (cf. Nanz and Steffek 2004). The term observer provides a useful contrast to the term constituency in the key sense that observers of a GGI are not bound by its authority. The notion is also broad enough to invite empirical study of the expanding range of groups that today engage with and hold beliefs on the legitimacy of GGIs. As a dichotomy, the constituency-observer distinction meets the four criteria for a helpful classification set out at the start of this section.

The observer category can include both active and passive non-constituent audiences. At first sight the notion of observer may convey a sense of passivity: i.e. that of being an onlooker, spectator, listener, reader. Such an audience is likely to be interested in what they see and hear (cf. Oxford English Dictionary entry for "audience"); however, it is generally presumed that onlookers do not intervene into that which they are observing. Yet, the conceptualization of audience deployed here includes a possibility of active observation. For example, the audience at a theater might initially appear to be a passive onlooker which lacks influence on the performance. However, observers evaluate a performance and communicate through applause, booing, or critical reviews. Observers can call bluffs and expose performers to embarrassment. Feedback from observers can prompt performers to change their acts, resulting in an interactive process where performer and observer influence each other. Hence audiences are not merely passive recipients for imposed meanings, but actively participate in the making of performative practices (Livingstone 2015; Park-Fuller 2003; Rigney 2001: 149).

Such a process is mirrored in contemporary world politics, where many actors who are not constituents still actively engage with GGIs. For instance, a government that is not a member of the North Atlantic Treaty Organization (NATO) might issue a critical statement about that institution. Or a CSO that is not party to the FSC might oppose that scheme. Or business enterprises based outside the Organisation for Economic Co-operation and Development (OECD) countries might endorse and follow its Guidelines for Multinational Enterprises. In such cases being a non-constituent does not preclude active involvement in a global governance arrangement.

This diversity of audiences brings diverging expectations on GGIs. For example, even if the WHO followed protocol during the 2014 Ebola crisis, it received harsh criticism for its belated and ineffective response. Expectations that the WHO should prevent Ebola did not primarily come from its constituency audience of member states, but from its observer audiences of civil society, foundations, and the media, who particularly criticized the WHO Africa Regional Office for lacking competence in the crisis (McInnes 2015). In the case of the Association of South East Asian Nations (ASEAN), observer audiences include powerful non-member governments whose judgments greatly impact on ASEAN's standing in international politics. Internally, from constituents, ASEAN continues to enjoy substantive and procedural legitimacy; however, externally, from observers, it faces major criticism (Ba 2013).

The activation of GGI observers may become all the more pronounced in today's thoroughly mediatized and digitalized society (Livingstone 2015). New information and communication technologies provide transnational advocacy groups with greatly enhanced means to shape the communicative aspects of legitimation practices around global governance. Social media networks such as Facebook and Twitter can make even the individual observer of a GGI an active participant in legitimation processes. Meanwhile, new means of communication also enable GGIs to reach more audiences than before.

Of course constituencies, which have a formal authority relationship with a GGI, may also adopt active or passive stances towards the institution. Whether observers and constituencies are active or passive is an empirical question whose answer will vary over time and across different instances of (de)legitimation processes. A key difference, however, is that constituencies have formal institutionalized channels to participate in decision making at a GGI, whereas observers must influence the GGI through other means, such as informal lobbying, media communications, and street demonstrations.

These considerations raise the analytical challenge of where to set the boundary between an active observer of (de)legitimation and an agent of (de)legitimation. What level of activity must an audience (whether constituency or observer) reach to become an agent of (de)legitimation? What degree of passivity must an agent reach to become an observer? Drawing the line between agency and passivity in an audience is difficult both conceptually and empirically. Hence it is advisable not to make this matter a core distinction for a typology of GGI audiences.

Next to the role of agency and passivity, another concern with regard to observers is how to capture power relations among them in empirical studies. Legitimation processes are embedded within broader power structures of world politics, and accordingly resources are unequally distributed among observer audiences in legitimation processes. Obviously this is also the case for constituent audiences. Observers usually lack the formal entry points to GGIs that constituents have, even if observers at times gain consultative status or become involved in state delegations. Actors that lack formal authority relations with GGIs can have power and resources which make GGIs target them for support. For instance, in global economic governance, a large business alliance can get more attention than a small low-income country. Hence the legitimacy of GGIs is often dependent on obtaining confidence and support of actors beyond formal constituents (Bruen et al. 2014). Studying who, among the broad observer category, are selected as recipients of legitimacy claims or for participation in GGI consultation procedures, sheds light on deeper issues related to inclusion and exclusion in global governance and on what kind of power resources count.

An illustration of these power dynamics is the consultations which preceded the adoption by the United Nations (UN) of the Sustainable Development Goals (SDGs) in September 2015. These consultations during 2012–15 constituted a major legitimation attempt by the UN. They involved both constituencies and observers of the UN, following the typology above, and extended to CSOs, academics, and the business sector as well as states. However, power relations meant that some parties obtained more consultation than others. The face-to-face format biased participation to actors from the Global North who were more able to access UN headquarters in New York. Only when consultations occurred online was there larger engagement from the Global South, albeit that the majority of respondents came from a limited number of countries (Sénit et al. 2017). Moreover, online consultations privileged those with Internet access. For example, over half of the respondents to the online MYWorld survey questionnaire, the largest UN consultation survey ever, were aged between 16 and 30 (Fox and Stoett 2016). In addition, the (only loosely accountable) UN staff who drafted the reports on these consultations had much power in describing the results and thereby influencing the SDG agenda.

This example well illustrates that, in global governance, "observer" is an open-ended category that does not in itself say anything about power relationships among observers. Yet empirical observation shows these power relations to be ubiquitous. For example, while Twitter may at first glance seem to be a tool of horizontal politics, hierarchy intrudes as some tweeters become more influential than others due to the platform's technical architecture as well as the users' active steering strategies (van Dijck 2013). Likewise, while multistakeholder dialogues are enveloped in narratives of inclusion, in practice they are often only accessible to those in positions of structural power. In this vein, Carl Death (2011) sees "political theater" at play at global summits, where "consultations" aim to persuade global audiences that political elites are responding to citizens. Extending the theater metaphor, in global governance the "frontstage" may be open to public view, but "backstage" power disparities are less transparent.

In sum, the concepts of constituency and observer are useful to map audiences of GGIs. The categories lend themselves well to answering research questions on what kinds of actors are or might be holding beliefs regarding GGI legitimacy. On a note of caution, however, both concepts may conceal differences between active and passive audiences. Moreover, both concepts may draw insufficient attention to power relations as a significant factor shaping the effects of (de)legitimation practices on audience perceptions of GGIs. Therefore, the next section introduces a distinction related to questions of how audiences are produced in the first place.

Constructing Audiences: Targeted and Self-Appointed

Audiences are not fully formed in advance of (de)legitimation processes, but rather are generated in the course of those processes and shaped by patterns of inclusion and exclusion. To study such power-imbued construction processes another important distinction divides the universe of audiences: namely, that between targeted and self-appointed groups. This categorization highlights how legitimation and delegitimation practices themselves constitute audiences. On the one hand, GGIs and other agents may construct *target audiences* by aiming their (de)legitimation strategies at groups that they deem relevant. On the other hand, other groups may constitute themselves as *self-appointed* audiences, even when they are not recognized as an audience by the agents of (de)legitimation. For example, sexual orientation and gender identity movements have over recent years formed themselves as an audience of the UN even though few among the UN staff and member states may have (certainly initially) viewed them as such. An audience is either self-appointed or targeted in a given concrete instance of (de)legitimation. Over time and across (de)legitimation attempts the status may shift back and forth.

The production of audiences as target groups or self-appointed groups is a rich vein for research, particularly using constructivist theory. So far systematic knowledge is lacking on how, when, and why GGIs target different audiences. Likewise, studies have not examined how audiences may create themselves, separately from the intentions of those who execute (de)legitimation efforts. Indeed, self-appointed audiences might affect legitimation processes in unexpected ways, ultimately affecting the relative success of a legitimation attempt. Needless to say, research of such issues must be grounded in careful conceptualization.

Targeted audiences are those which are directly and explicitly addressed by agents of (de)legitimation, either through institutional, discursive, or behavioral legitimation practices (see Bäckstrand and Söderbaum, this volume). In fact, new audiences can be purposefully created by being repeatedly and deliberately targeted in legitimation practices. In this regard, Suchman notes that:

> Roughly, legitimacy-building strategies fall into three clusters: (a) efforts to *conform* to the dictates of preexisting audiences within the organization's current environment, (b) efforts to *select* among multiple environments in pursuit of an audience that will support current practices, and (c) efforts to *manipulate* environmental structure by creating new audiences and new legitimating beliefs.
>
> (1995: 587)

The SDG consultations is an example of an attempt to combine strategies (a) and (c). This is done by targeting both pre-existing audiences of states and UN major groups, and by creating new audiences through Internet surveys and country-based consultations with groups not normally consulted in global policymaking. Examples of the latter are vulnerable groups in low-income countries (Sénit et al. 2017). This shows that the reasons for targeting different actors in legitimation attempts can range from a wish to draw on their power resources to the more symbolic value of increased participation.

In contrast to targeted groups, other audiences can appear when self-appointed groups claim the status of being a legitimation audience and act accordingly. Self-appointed audiences are those who are not targeted by agents' legitimation practices, but who nevertheless respond to them, whether positively or negatively. They may do so because they are materially affected by GGI policies or because they have broader normative concerns about the GGI. The emergence of self-appointed audiences is facilitated by a mediatized public sphere that provides the information needed for groups beyond constituencies to engage in legitimation or delegitimation of GGIs (cf. Michailidou and Trenz 2013). The public availability of information on GGIs clearly plays a key role in the formation of self-appointed audiences in legitimation processes (Chapman 2009; Steffek 2009; Dellmuth, this volume).

It is an empirical question whether constituencies and observers are targeted, self-appointed, or not involved at all in specific (de)legitimation processes regarding GGIs. Historically, the main targeted audience in legitimation practices by IGOs has been government policymakers in member states. Today, most GGIs in addition target a range of observers, particularly with outreach to civil society and business circles (Tallberg et al. 2013). For example, UN secretary-general Kofi Annan actively invited business corporations into cooperative relations through a win-win legitimation claim in the context of the UN's Global Compact initiative. However, targeting business in this new way also created tensions between the UN and civil society, showing that increased GGI focus on one audience might reduce the trust of another (Sethi and Schepers 2014).

In some cases, it is harder to distinguish empirically which audiences are targeted and which are self-appointed. For instance, the UN's global consultations preceding the adoption of the SDGs were quite open in terms of who was invited to provide input through the World We Want homepage and other digital channels. It is therefore hard to determine whether these online respondents were "targeted" or "self-appointed" audiences. Clearly, developments in information and communications technology are changing the contours of audiences and how they become involved in (de)legitimation of GGIs.

In sum, the differentiation of targeted and self-appointed audiences is helpful in studying how audiences of legitimation and delegitimation are constituted in global governance processes. This distinction shows how (de)legitimation processes can expand accountability relationships in global governance beyond their traditional state-centered parameters. Attention to self-appointed as well as targeted audiences moreover highlights that the contours of GGI audiences are far from given, and on the contrary are constantly evolving. Indeed, the distinction indicates that who is recognized as an audience of GGI legitimation is itself a contested question (cf. Meine 2016; Oates 2017).

Conclusions

This chapter has explored a range of questions concerning audiences of legitimacy and legitimation in respect of GGIs. The discussion has reviewed the as yet limited academic literature on the subject, concluding that the concept of audience has considerable potential to advance knowledge about who receives and responds to (de)legitimation practices around global governance, how they do so, and why. The analytical benefits of the concept were then further advanced by underlining a distinction between "constituency" and "observer" qualities of audiences, as well as a distinction between "targeted" and "self-appointed" audiences.

These distinctions between different kinds of audiences can underpin future comparative empirical research on GGI legitimacy and legitimation. Such studies can investigate, for example, variation across types of GGIs (e.g. in terms of how audiences for legitimacy and legitimation differ depending on the issue area or the institutional design). In addition, future research can consider variation in GGI strategies towards audiences (e.g. who the GGIs identify as relevant audiences and how far the GGIs adjust legitimation practices depending on the targeted audience). On the side of audiences, research can examine variation across different reception groups (e.g. in terms of the kinds of legitimacy beliefs that different audiences hold and the kinds of reactions that they have towards different legitimation practices). Do legitimacy beliefs differ between general publics and political elites; and are the legitimacy beliefs of some audiences more affected by certain kinds of legitimation and delegitimation practices than others? In-depth case studies of specific (de)legitimation processes can contribute to more nuanced findings on the role and significance of different types of audiences in (de)legitimation. Exploring such issues would greatly advance knowledge about the dynamics of (de)legitimation in global governance.

Conducting such research raises methodological questions about data sources. Three types of evidence may be highlighted. One important source of data concerning agent-audience relationships in (de)legitimation processes is provided by political communication material. Most of the actors involved (GGIs, states, CSOs, etc.) produce a wealth of texts, including self-descriptions, press releases, speeches, policy statements, annual reports, websites, social media messages, as well as audio-visual outputs. These materials can be explored through a range of methods such as quantitative content analysis and qualitative discourse analysis. Longitudinal studies of these kinds of documentation can indicate whether there has been change over time in the contours of GGI audiences, the strategies pursued to influence their legitimacy beliefs, and their responses to those strategies.

Surveys can provide a second major source of data for investigations of legitimacy and legitimation in GGI audiences. Opinion questionnaires can identify and measure legitimacy beliefs in different audiences and in addition suggest how far those perceptions are affected by one or the other (de)legitimation practice. In addition, survey experiments can present sample audiences with scenarios that reveal how far their legitimacy beliefs are shaped by one or the other (de)legitimation practice. To explore patterns of variation among audiences, opinion surveys and survey experiments can highlight distinctions between elites and general populations, between audiences in different world regions, and between audiences of different GGIs.

Yet documentary analysis and survey data often do not reveal much about the detailed thinking behind legitimacy and legitimation in global governance. Interviews with representatives of audiences in legitimation processes can therefore be used, for example, to tease out more precisely: (a) the grounds on which audiences form legitimacy beliefs about GGIs; (b) the strategies that active audiences adopt in their efforts to (de)legitimate GGIs; and (c) the reception of political communications that shape audiences' legitimacy beliefs about GGIs.

A final note in this chapter may acknowledge that the foregoing discussion has said relatively little concerning general theories of world politics. The analysis has clearly contradicted realist approaches to international relations by positing that both non-state and state actors can be relevant audiences with regard to legitimacy and legitimation in global governance. In a liberalist vein, the chapter has emphasized the institutionalized authority of governors in relation to the governed as a key element of legitimacy, justifying the study of strategies and practices of global governance bodies, as well as the views and reactions of their audiences. The approach in this chapter has been constructivist with its attention to the mutual constitution of agents (with their legitimacy-claiming practices) and audiences (with their legitimacy-granting practices). Further ventures into critical theories, not undertaken in this chapter, could explore how agent-audience relations in legitimation processes of global governance relate to possible underlying structures of world politics, such as capitalism or gender hierarchies. Yet, even if such avenues have not been explored here, the conceptual distinctions offered in this chapter could be taken to, and further developed in, a full spectrum of macrotheories of world politics.

8

Civil Society Protest and the (De)Legitimation of Global Governance Institutions

Catia Gregoratti and Anders Uhlin

As this volume attests, research on the social legitimacy of global governance institutions (GGIs) is growing. This chapter follows Chapters 6 and 7 in focusing on less well-researched *processes* of legitimation and delegitimation. Whereas Bäckstrand and Söderbaum provided a general conceptualization of such processes, and Bexell and Jönsson elaborated on the audiences of (de)legitimation, this chapter focuses on the (de)legitimizing aspects of a particular type of political activity—protest. Protest often indicates that people believe that an institution's authority is not exercised appropriately. Since the late 1990s, large protests challenging the legitimacy of some of the major GGIs have received much media attention, making the study of protest an important, but so far relatively neglected, focus of research on GGI legitimacy.

Protest is conceptualized here as a public and overt expression of opposition, signaling disagreement with institutions, policies, elites, or an entire political regime. Protests against GGIs may come from many different types of actors and take many different forms. When states hold back funding, ignore GGI policies, or even terminate their membership in a GGI, this might be interpreted as acts of protest. Establishing a new, competing GGI might also be seen as an implicit protest against existing GGIs in the field—what Morse and Keohane (2014) label "competitive regime creation" in the context of "contested multilateralism." A notable example of this is the China-led establishment of the Asian Infrastructure Investment Bank (AIIB). Citizens of a country might also protest against a GGI by voting against membership, as in the recent referendum on British membership of the European Union. Although businesses may not be commonly associated with protest, they can resist a GGI, as witnessed, for example, in the hunger strike of the chairman of the Rapaport Group against the Kimberley Process (KP) (Rapaport Press Release 2010).

While acknowledging this diversity of actors and actions in this broader understanding of protest, the present chapter focuses on protests by civil society activists targeting GGIs. Civil society is commonly defined as a political space comprised by "nonofficial and nonprofit bodies that share an interest to reinforce, reform, or radically transform the rules that govern one or the other aspect of social life" (Scholte 2002: 3). However, there is much debate concerning: the dividing lines and overlaps between the state, the market, and civil society; what counts as a civil society organization (CSO); and even how much organization is required to qualify as belonging to civil society (Van Rooy 2004: 7–8). As the first part of the chapter elaborates, protest against GGIs have commonly featured sustained activism carried out by particular CSOs and social movements. The chapter focuses on civil society protests not because much of the literature conflates protest with CSO activities, but to examine if and how such analysis can advance research on (de)-legitimation in global governance.

Civil society protest against GGIs goes back at least to the 1970s. At that time anti-nuclear movements demonstrated against the European Community (EC) and the International Atomic Energy Agency (IAEA) (Meyer 2014). Likewise, protests against certain GGIs such as the World Bank and the International Monetary Fund (IMF) have occurred in different parts of the Global South at least since the 1970s (Walton and Ragin 1990).

While civil society protests against GGIs have this long history, scholarly attention to the legitimacy of GGIs grew precisely when civil society protests in the Global North began to target prominent GGIs around the turn of the millennium. Such protests have often been conceived as disruptive, in the sense of being explicitly contentious and confrontational, either physically or symbolically (Death 2015). Early research noted that some of these protests had particular effects. For example, civil society resistance against the Multilateral Agreement on Investment (MAI) in the late 1990s interfered with neoliberal designs for global governance. In other cases protest was found to trigger a variety of institutional and discursive responses through which legitimacy is seemingly restored (Steffek 2003; Zürn 2004: 279–83).

More recent scholarship has addressed cyber-protests, street protests taking place directly outside GGI conferences and summits, and other demonstrations in cities and squares around the world (Della Porta et al. 2006; Daase and Deitelhoff 2014; Dauvergne and LeBaron 2014; Suliman 2014). Violent and non-violent protests have occurred outside the United Nations Climate Change Conferences and the United Nations Conference on Sustainable Development, the Group of Eight (G8) and the Group of Twenty (G20), and the Association of South East Asian Nations (ASEAN). In contrast, recent protests outside ministerial conferences of the World Trade Organization (WTO) or the annual meetings of the IMF and World Bank look rather pale in comparison to protest events of the 1990s and early 2000s (Gill 2015). Possibly the spaces of protest against GGIs have changed, as considerable resistance of the 2010s has implicated the IMF and European Central Bank (ECB) as "architects and advocates of austerity" (Burke 2014: 29).

However, growing research attention to protest events, spaces, and actors has not been matched by advanced theorization on the relationship between civil society protest and GGI legitimacy. This chapter addresses this gap in the literature on global governance, suggesting a novel analytical model to answer the question: When and how does civil society protest matter for the legitimacy of GGIs?

The first part of this chapter reviews extant research on civil society protest against GGIs, aiming at identifying key arguments and significant gaps when it comes to understanding the relations between protests and the legitimacy of GGIs. The section also interrogates how existing literature on legitimacy and (de)legitimation in global governance has treated civil society protest. It is suggested that these two strands of literature can benefit from sustained dialogue. That said, neither the protest literature nor the legitimacy and (de)legitimation literature provide adequate theory of how protest relates to GGI legitimacy.

The second part of the chapter then clarifies how protests can be linked to legitimacy. It develops a novel analytical model which explains when and how protest is likely to influence the legitimacy of GGIs. The model highlights (a) whether or not protesters are recognized by the GGI as significant actors for its legitimacy; and (b) whether protests are directed at the GGI as a whole or at certain of its practices or policies. The model seeks to deepen and nuance previous writing on legitimacy, which tends to view all civil society protest as delegitimizing or, to use a more common formulation, "challenging" the legitimacy of GGIs. Yet which protests, more particularly, constitute a legitimacy challenge? The chapter argues that protests which do not fundamentally question the basic existence, values, and ideology of a GGI might even be considered acts of legitimation rather than delegitimation. Moreover, some protests provoke responses from the GGI which defer legitimacy challenges or enhance the institution's legitimacy. And some protests fail to have any impact because the targeted GGI does not recognize the protesters as significant for its legitimacy.

In order to clarify our model and substantiate our claims we provide empirical illustrations of different ways in which civil society protests matter for the legitimacy of GGIs. While the model is developed as a reaction to literature on civil society protest against GGIs, it is possible that our formulations could also apply to protesting actors beyond civil society. Finally, the chapter conclusion offers suggestions for future research on protest and (de)legitim-ation of global governance.

Civil Society Protest, Global Governance, and Legitimacy

In a first step, this section of the chapter reviews extant research on civil society protests against GGIs, highlighting key conceptual, empirical, and methodological arguments. The discussion also asks whether, in what ways, and to what extent this literature has examined questions of legitimacy. In a second step, this section surveys research on legitimacy in global governance, probing how this literature has treated issues of protest. It is argued that these two strands of literature—one on civil society and the other on legitimacy—can be fruitfully brought into closer conversation with each other. Yet this rapprochement also provokes further theoretical and analytical queries.

Civil Society Protest against GGIs

What contemporary activists do has been variously conceptualized as resistance, dissent, contestation, and protest. Disentangling these terms—and appreciating the analytical purchase of each—is by no means straightforward. In a seminal review of the concept of resistance, Hollander and Einwohner (2004) under-stand protest as a particular "mode of resistance." Coleman and Tucker regard the notion of dissent as coterminous with protest, resistance, campaigning, advocacy, and quotidian forms of contestation. In this expansive conceptual-ization, protests are understood as a sub-category of dissent, more specifically as a "recognized form of dissent." However, the question who recognizes protesters as such is left open (Coleman and Tucker 2011: 399).

Large-scale protests are commonly understood as dramatic public confron-tations in which protesters directly and openly challenge authorities through bodies and/or material objects (Suliman 2014; Hollander and Einwohner 2004). In this vein, Haunss (2007: 171) conceptualizes protests as manifest and performed through, for example, demonstrations, marches, blockades, strikes, and other forms of collective mobilization. However, like others Haunss also recognizes that forms of protest change over time and vary depending on their social, cultural, and political context. A recent glossary of protest forms charts 200 types of protest and related actions (Hanna et al. 2016).

Building on these various conceptual accounts, protest is conceptualized here as a public and overt expression of opposition, signaling disagreement with policies, institutions, elites, or an entire political regime (cf. Kalm and Uhlin 2015: 7). Our definition is admittedly broad and places an exclusive emphasis on the political act of opposing, which may range from "loyal opposition" to full-scale rejectionism (Clark 2003: 76; cf. Kalm and Uhlin 2015: 61). Much protest movement literature focuses on political activity that takes place in cyberspace and/or "on the streets" (O'Neill 2004). Yet protest and lobbying are not mutually exclusive activities either (Kalm and Uhlin 2015: 55). Thus, when understood as oppositional action, protest cannot be easily confined to a single space, as many protesting actors cross the boundaries between the street and the inner corridors of the GGI that they target.

In the past two decades, increasing research has addressed the "scaling-up" of protest activity to the international level. GGI summits have become prominent venues to protest against states, neoliberal globalization, and at times the GGIs themselves (Gill 2000; O'Neill 2004; Bandy and Smith 2005; Della Porta and Tarrow 2005; Death 2010). Protesting actors commonly include local, national, and international civil society associations, such as non-governmental organizations (NGOs), social movements, grassroots initiatives, faith-based groups, trade unions, and think tanks (Kalm and Uhlin 2015: 45–6). Civil society thus includes diverse organizational forms, divergent ideological orientations, multiple political purposes, and varying relationships with states, GGIs, and the market. Yet an exclusive focus on civil society *organizations* may still be restrictive inasmuch as it overlooks the widespread protest activity undertaken towards GGIs by non-affiliated, non-programmatic, disorganized protesters who contest gross inequalities in wealth and power (Tormey 2012).

Several insights of potential relevance for legitimacy can be garnered from extant research on protest against GGIs. For example, the afterlife of the anti-globalization protests of the 1990s has been subject to intense scrutiny. These protests have often been credited for encouraging a broad transformation of the "global public sphere," coinciding with the rise of multistakeholder initiatives, public-private partnerships, and private governance arrangements (Ruggie 2004). On their part, GGIs have variously responded to protests by creating points of interaction with civil society and moves to increase public accountability and transparency (O'Brien et al. 2000). As these institutional changes have unfolded, protests have become increasingly "corporatized," involving a deradicalization of claims and the adoption of corporate styles of fundraising and marketing strategies (Death 2010: 133; Dauvergne and LeBaron, 2014). Many NGOs have also "technocratized," with a stronger emphasis on expert knowledge concerning GGIs (Hopewell 2015).

Only a couple of studies have *explicitly* linked civil society protests to questions of GGI legitimacy. Alison Van Rooy's (2004) extensive study of the anti-globalization movement is mainly concerned with the legitimacy of civil society actors protesting against GGIs, but she also addresses the democratic crisis of global governance. Haunss (2007) explores social movement activism in relation to (de)legitimation processes. For Haunss, "repertoires of contention" involve a range of behavioral legitimation and delegitimation strategies, learnt, mimicked, chosen, or permitted in different contexts, while "collective action frames" provide useful evidence on the presence or absence of legitimating and delegitimating arguments. However, Haunss' approach offers few indications on when protest constitutes a legitimacy challenge vis-à-vis targets or on what counts as a (de)legitimating action or statement.

For its part, contemporary international relations (IR) research on protest, like much of social movement theory, has not deployed the vocabulary of "legitimacy" as such. Instead, related issues have been conceptualized in terms such as "politicization" (Zürn 2014), "a post-modern Prince" (Gill 2000), and "counter-conduct" (Death 2010). Perhaps protest research in IR has been reticent on the question of legitimacy since the concept often seems geared towards incremental institutional reform, unwittingly condoning or leaving unquestioned the ongoing normalization of largely Western and neoliberal global governance (Brassett and Tsingou 2011). However, sociological legitimacy has the potential to be a creative tool for critical theorizing, as it links critiques of power, of which civil society protest may be one expression, and increasingly complex governance practices. Our precise understanding of the relationship between civil society protest and (de)legitimation of GGIs will be elaborated later on, but first the chapter reviews treatments of civil society protest in extant research on legitimacy.

Legitimacy and Civil Society Protest

Recent research on legitimacy in global governance has shown increased interest in "claims made by the rulers," often inspired by Rodney Barker's (2001) argument to make the observable claims of power holders the starting point of an enquiry. In this vein studies have explored how institutions speak to various audiences (Zaum 2013a; Gronau and Schmidtke 2016). Other research has considered the legitimacy-enhancing strategies of GGIs (Guastaferro and Moschella 2012). Yet this work has not attempted to understand if and how far legitimation discourses and strategies are recognized and accepted by a GGI's various audiences, including protesters (cf. Beetham 2013: 255).

Arguably, it is precisely resistance to global governance which ignited greater engagement with the question of legitimacy in IR since the late 1990s (cf. Clark 2003). Such research has generally treated civil society protests as one-off high-profile events (Zürn 2004). Literature on the legitimacy of particular GGIs often mentions highly visible street protests as a (vaguely defined) legitimacy challenge particularly to intergovernmental organizations (IGOs), such as ASEAN and the IMF, and transgovernmental networks (TGNs), such as the G8 and the G20. In an extensive review on how existing legitimacy research has studied civil society protests, Peters (2013) also detects that protests have often been treated in abstract terms, most notably as evidence of a crisis of democratic legitimacy and as bearers of democratic claims.

Research on protest has seldom discussed hybrid private GGIs. Exceptionally, Bernstein (2011) has examined how civil society protests directed towards the Marine Stewardship Council (MSC) engendered an overhaul of that institution. The lack of attention to protest and legitimacy vis-à-vis non-governmental GGIs does not mean that protests within or against them have not been mounted and may rather imply an oversight by researchers.

Albeit only parenthetically, protest has also featured in methodological discussions on (de)legitimation practices. In literature on (de)legitimation a common distinction is drawn between discursive and institutional strategies (Gronau and Schmidtke 2016). Sometimes behavioral practices are added as a third category (Bäckstrand and Söderbaum, this volume). Alternatively, institutional practices are viewed as a sub-category of behavioral practices (Tallberg and Zürn 2017).

Protest may contain both behavioral and discursive elements (Haunss 2007). However, discursive (de)legitimation of GGIs has received more research attention to date. As argued by Steffek, "international organizations are contested by popular movements by means of making good arguments against their goals, means and principles" (2003: 250). Discursive delegitimation also occurs when critiques of climate governance stress its marketized and privatized character (Paterson 2010). Non-verbal acts (such as placard images, masquerades, and street art) have also been highlighted as an important means of discursive (de)legitimation (Gronau 2016). However, behavior and discourse are so entwined in protest that it is often difficult to disentangle them (Gronau and Schmidtke 2016: 7–8).

The above literature review may be summed up as follows. On the one hand, most research on protests against GGIs has not explicitly framed these acts as (de)legitimation practices, but this work can fruitfully be reinterpreted in terms of (de)legitimation. On the other hand, research on legitimacy in global governance has shown little interest in protests, and provides little analytical specificity about relations between protests and GGI legitimacy. The rest of this chapter seeks to fill this gap by developing an analytical framework that can help disentangle when and how civil society protest affects GGI legitimacy.

Protest and GGI Legitimacy: Significant Actors and Types of Protest

The few theoretical discussions on protest and legitimacy have taken place within wider attempts to theorize how power is legitimized. For example, David Beetham has alluded to how protest may relate to the constitutive dimensions of legitimacy. Beetham mainly relates protest to delegitimation, where the latter is defined as "a process whereby those whose consent is necessary to the legitimation of government act in a manner that indicates their withdrawal of consent" (2013: 209). This formulation broadly conforms to the conceptualization proposed in this volume, where delegitimation involves actions by opponents of GGIs. Such actions, as we will explain, express particular legitimacy beliefs and may also alter other audiences' beliefs in the legitimacy of these institutions (Tallberg et al., this volume). Of course this raises the further question of whose dissent may make the legitimacy of a GGI falter.

It is now widely acknowledged that actors or audiences other than states may matter for the legitimacy of GGIs (Zaum 2013a; Bexell and Jönsson, this volume). True, many conventional IGOs may be able to ignore negative legitimacy beliefs among non-state actors as long as these institutions have the consent of their member states. However, some IGOs such as multilateral development banks routinely consult with people affected by their projects, as well as with CSOs. Private and public-private governance institutions recognize civil society and business, often referred to as "stakeholders," as formal constituencies. Hence, some GGIs view societal actors as important legitimacy-granting audiences, whereas other GGIs can afford to ignore negative legitimacy beliefs among less influential but recalcitrant groups. Who is and is not regarded as a significant legitimacy-granting actor is one focal concern in the model developed below for studying *when* protests are likely to matter for the legitimacy of GGIs.

GGIs accord different degrees of recognition to civil society actors. In the case of public-private governance arrangements, CSOs can hold formal status as a constituent member of the GGI. Another form of recognition occurs, for example, when a GGI follows a policy of civil society consultation. In other cases a GGI may recognize the relevance of protest because of its capacity to influence general public opinion and/or particular constituencies. In certain circumstances, protests may in fact unsettle prevalent understandings of who grants legitimacy, potentially constituting new significant audiences (Symons 2011; Meine 2016). On the other hand, lack of recognition of protesting actors can occur when GGIs exclude, ignore, marginalize, or even criminalize them (Van Rooy 2004; Death 2015: 580).

The second focal concern for the model pertains to types of protest. As noted in the previous section, legitimacy research has tended to treat protests in very abstract and loose terms, but recent literature on legitimation suggests that a tighter conceptualization is wanted. David Easton's distinction between diffuse and specific support is widely used as a means to study the legitimation strategies of GGIs (Gronau and Schmidtke 2016). Diffuse support, or the general evaluation of what a GGI means to one or more actors, is contrasted with specific support, which pertains to the satisfaction resulting from the output and performance of political authorities. Our model applies the same distinction to protest, differentiating between protests which contest the overall authority of a GGI (diffuse protests) and protests which target aspects of the GGI, such as policies or particular institutional practices (specific protests). In practice, of course, certain protests may exhibit both diffuse and specific elements.

Diffuse and specific protests closely mirror the distinction between polity politicization and policy politicization. The overall authority of an institution can be challenged (polity politicization), but politicization can also be directed at specific policies of the institution (policy politicization) (Zürn et al. 2012: 98). Diffuse protest or polity politicization expresses negative legitimacy beliefs, as it is the overall authority of the GGI that is challenged. Specific protest, on the other hand, is a form of policy politicization, which does not explicitly challenge the rightfulness of political rule (cf. Hurrelmann 2017: 66). Diffuse and specific protest is a conceptual distinction that allows us to understand *how* protests matter for the legitimacy of GGIs.

Protest in relation to the legitimacy of GGIs can thus be redefined as an *oppositional act whereby actors indicate that they reject either the authority of the GGI as a whole, including its principles and structure, or the appropriateness of its specific policies and practices.* Importantly, this definition does not assume that all forms of protest are expressions of negative legitimacy beliefs. Protests focusing on specific policies or institutional practices, at least implicitly, reflect beliefs that overall authority of the GGI is legitimate.

Our conceptualization of different types of protest (diffuse and specific) and different types of protesting actors (recognized and unrecognized by the GGI) suggests that the relation between protest and GGI legitimacy might not be as straightforward as often assumed. Protests against a GGI might express negative legitimacy beliefs that the GGI has to account for; express negative legitimacy beliefs that can be ignored; or express positive legitimacy beliefs while politicizing specific practices and policies.

Thus far we have focused on protests as expressions of the protesting actors' legitimacy beliefs. However, it is important to note that protests may also influence other audiences' legitimacy beliefs. Different audiences are likely to react in different ways and the same protest event might damage the legitimacy of the targeted GGI in the eyes of some audiences while boosting its legitimacy from the perspective of other audiences. Moreover, the expression of negative legitimacy beliefs of protesters may provoke successful attempts at relegitimation by the GGI, positively affecting other audiences' legitimacy beliefs. Such consequences of protests for GGI legitimacy, however, cannot be predicted in any analytical model as they will always vary across an infinite number of audiences. How protest may lead to changes in other audiences' legitimacy beliefs must be analyzed in context-sensitive empirical studies.

Protest and the Legitimacy of GGIs: an Analytical Model

In order to further theorize when and how protest matters for GGI legitimacy, the chapter now sets out an analytical model that links forms of protest with the legitimacy of the GGI. This model, expressed in Table 8.1, combines the two factors discussed above as pertinent for explaining when and how protests are likely to matter for GGI legitimacy. First, the model stresses the distinction diffuse and specific protests. Second, the model distinguishes between two types of protesting actors: those recognized by the GGI as significant and those not recognized as significant. Interlinking these two dimensions results in four possible scenarios. It should be stressed that the expectations developed in the model involve an *all-else-equal* caveat which holds constant other possible determinants of GGI legitimacy.

This conceptualization of forms of protest and protesters prioritizes some aspects and excludes others. Indeed, some may argue that a distinction between behavioral, discursive, and institutional (de)legitimation practices (as by Bäckstrand and Söderbaum, this volume) is more important than a distinction between diffuse and specific protests. However, the diffuse/specific distinction might prove more promising when aiming at explaining when and how protests matter for GGI legitimacy. Unlike the behavioral/discursive/ institutional conceptualization, it comes with clear assumptions about likely reactions by a GGI targeted by protests. Moreover, as previously discussed,

Table 8.1. Protests and GGI legitimacy

	Protesters recognized by GGI as significant	Protesters not recognized by GGI as significant
Diffuse protest	Expressions of negative legitimacy beliefs likely to result in relegitimation attempts by the GGI	Expressions of negative legitimacy beliefs likely to be ignored by the GGI
Specific protest	Expressions of positive legitimacy beliefs; politicization of specific policies and practices likely to be taken seriously by the GGI	Expressions of positive legitimacy beliefs; politicization of specific policies and practices likely to be ignored by the GGI

most protests display both behavioral and discursive features, making that distinction less fruitful for empirical studies of relationships between protests and GGI legitimacy.

The model might also have distinguished between "inside" and "outside" protest activities. "Inside" protest is communicated through direct interaction with representatives of the GGI, for example, through established consultation processes. "Outside" protest features demonstrations around conference venues and GGI headquarters with a view to influencing public opinion. To some extent the inside/outside distinction mirrors the specific/diffuse distinction; however, it may be more useful to focus on the objects of protests (diffuse/specific) than on the venues of these activities (outside/inside), particularly since civil society activists often combine inside and outside strategies.

In addition, the model could be criticized for only emphasizing characteristics of protests and neglecting the nature of GGIs. For example, certain GGIs might be more sensitive to civil society protests than others. However, this feature is to some extent captured by the degree of recognition that a GGI confers upon protesters as (in)significant actors for its legitimacy. This relational attribute of a GGI might be more significant for explaining when and how protests matter for the legitimacy of GGIs than are GGI characteristics such as issue area, type of authority, or institutional design. Such factors need to be considered in detailed empirical studies, but in order to develop a parsimonious analytical model what are privileged are two important analytical dimensions, which are also two neglected dimensions in previous research.

A further important limitation is that the model assumes an unmediated relation between protesters and the GGI. In other words, it assumes that protests reflect legitimacy beliefs held by protesters and that GGIs may react (or not) to those beliefs. However, as suggested earlier, there may also be indirect relations at work through changes in other actors' (positive or negative) legitimacy beliefs. Who these other actors are, and what the indirect effects may be, cannot be determined with reference to the conceptual distinctions in the model, but must instead be assessed within the context of specific cases. This limitation of the analytical model is unavoidable, but it can be overcome through closer empirical analysis, as elaborated in the following examples.

To explore one scenario in greater detail, protest targeting a GGI as a whole by actors whom that GGI views as significant (upper-left cell of Table 8.1) implies an expression of negative legitimacy beliefs. When significant actors do not (or no longer) believe the authority of the GGI to be appropriate, their protest challenges the legitimacy of the GGI. Most likely it will trigger GGI attempts at relegitimation, directed against the protesting actors as well as other audiences. Diffuse protests as well as the accompanying attempts at relegitimation are also likely to influence legitimacy beliefs of other actors.

Protests against the G8 (G7 since 2014) illustrate this scenario. The G8 is one of the most contested GGIs in recent history. Most of its meetings have been accompanied by more or less violent street demonstrations and people's summits. While the G8 certainly has not recognized the protesters—instead trying to shield off the summit venues in order to avoid interactions with the activists—democratic member states were forced to acknowledge the significance of public contestation. Anti-G8 protests in the aftermath of the 2008 financial crisis have contributed to delegitimation of the institution, "culminating in a fundamental crisis of the G8 legitimacy" (Gronau 2016: 108). Of course, street protests did not singlehandedly ignite this crisis, and intersected with widespread perceptions that the G20 was becoming a more relevant and representative institution. Gronau and Schmidtke (2016) argue that the G8 navigated its way through the crisis with relegitimation strategies addressed at different audiences. In particular, it strengthened its commitments to promote the "global common good." Yet this strategy has in no way diminished protest activity. Hence, the anti-G8 protests demonstrated the negative legitimacy beliefs of the protesters while also influencing legitimacy beliefs of other audiences as critiques of irrelevance and unrepresentativeness resonated among member states. Moreover, the protests prompted relegitimation efforts, including attempts to recalibrate the overall identity and purpose of the G8.

Taking another scenario, protest targeting specific practices or policies of the GGI by actors recognized as significant (lower-left cell in Table 8.1) implicitly or explicitly recognizes the general appropriateness of the GGI's authority, while pointing out certain deficits. Hence, this type of protest expresses positive legitimacy beliefs vis-à-vis the GGI while politicizing specific practices or policies.

Civil society engagement of the Asian Development Bank (ADB) is a good example of this dynamic. The NGO Forum on ADB—a transnational civil society network monitoring the ADB—has since the 1990s been engaged in a number of campaigns challenging the transparency, accountability, and safeguard policies of the bank, as well as specific projects which are perceived to have negative consequences for affected communities. The ADB recognizes CSOs as an important audience, and even quite critical groups like the NGO Forum are invited to join consultation processes. Making use of this access to the ADB, while engaging in outside protest activities as well, the NGO Forum and other CSOs have contributed to the politicization of certain ADB policies and also influenced reform of these policies. Due to civil society protest, certain development projects have been severely critiqued and amended, and in some cases completely stopped (Uhlin 2016: ch. 6). Crucially, however, there is no indication that these specifically targeted protests have led to a delegitimation of ADB as a whole. On the contrary, by demonstrating that it recognizes and listens to CSOs—including some quite radical ones—the ADB has arguably strengthened its legitimacy in the eyes of the CSOs as well as other actors. Moreover, by participating in ADB consultation processes, the NGO Forum has implicitly recognized the ADB's general legitimacy, even if activists have been highly critical of specific ADB policies and projects. The fact that the ADB highlights its civil society connections in its public communications further indicates that the GGI considers this a legitimation strategy. Moreover, institutional reforms implemented by the ADB can be seen as a form of relegitimation response to civil society protests.

Turning to protest targeting a GGI as a whole by actors who are not recognized as significant (upper-right cell in Table 8.1), the model assumes that this kind of protest expresses negative legitimacy beliefs that are likely to be ignored by the GGI. Protesters show their negative legitimacy perceptions in relation to the GGI, but unless this rejection persuades other actors also to change their legitimacy beliefs, the consequences for the GGI are insignificant.

An illustration of this scenario might be the Occupy protests in 2011–12. Occupy circulated many manifestos which express a lack of diffuse support for major GGIs (Gregoratti 2014). However, these GGIs did not consider the Occupy protesters as a significant legitimacy audience. Hence, these protests were largely ignored by the targeted institutions. Nonetheless, Occupy's visions were endorsed and reformulated (and most certainly deradicalized) by an influential group of cosmopolitan intellectuals through the Manifesto for Global Democracy (Gregoratti 2014). Calling for an expanded and improved global governance, this statement has reached multiple centers of power, including the Italian Senate. Thus, rather than undermining the legitimacy beliefs of other audiences, Occupy's contestation of GGIs might actually have indirectly reinforced the legitimacy beliefs of a community of intellectuals.

Finally, protest targeting specific GGI practices or policies by actors not recognized as significant (lower-right cell in Table 8.1) is assumed to legitimize the GGI. As in the case of specific protest by actors who are recognized as significant, this fourth scenario includes expressions of positive legitimacy beliefs, as the protesters recognize (or at least do not directly challenge) its authority. Politicization of specific practices or policies is likely to be ignored (or at least not taken very seriously) by the GGI, because the GGI does not recognize the protesters as significant for its legitimacy.

This scenario includes GGIs that do not recognize non-state actors as significant audiences for their legitimacy claims. Many state-centered IGOs tend to ignore or try to co-opt oppositional civil society groups. A clear example is ASEAN. Although this regional IGO has recently adopted a "people-oriented" rhetoric and tentatively opened up for some limited engagement with selected CSOs, ASEAN considers neither civil society actors nor ordinary citizens as recognized legitimacy audiences (Uhlin 2016: ch. 7). As a result, more oppositional CSOs turn to outside protest activities. Demonstrations have occurred outside the ASEAN secretariat in Jakarta and at certain summit venues. Such protests have typically focused on specific issues, such as the establishment of a regional human rights mechanism, poor treatment of migrant workers, and alleged harms of trade liberalization. These protests did not challenge the overall authority of ASEAN and instead concentrated on specific issue areas and demanded specific policy responses. In this way the protesters implicitly recognized the overall authority of ASEAN as rightful, while criticizing certain policies. However, unlike in the case of protest against the ADB referred to above, the groups protesting against ASEAN were not recognized by the IGO as representing significant legitimacy audiences. Therefore, the ASEAN leadership could afford to ignore the protesters' demands. Some protests nevertheless resulted in modest policy reform, which was possible precisely because the protesters focused on specific issues rather than attempting to delegitimize the GGI as a whole.

These empirical illustrations indicate the potential of the analytical model introduced in the chapter for the study of protest and (de)legitimation in global governance. The model combines conceptual distinctions that have so far received limited attention in research on (de)legitimation processes related to GGIs and provides theoretical expectations of the likely relationships between different forms of protests and the legitimacy of GGIs. While the preceding empirical examples have focused on IGOs and a TGN, the model could also be applicable to hybrid and wholly private GGIs.

Concluding Remarks

This chapter has reviewed the literature on civil society protest against GGIs and found that, while this work offers conceptualizations of protest and identifies important empirical trends, it has engaged little with legitimacy theory. Similarly, a review of literature on legitimacy in global governance showed that this research has generally neglected civil society protest. The chapter has argued that these research fields can fruitfully be interlinked, but also that this rapprochement should be coupled to advances in our understanding of when and how civil society protest matters for the legitimacy of a GGI. To make such advances, the chapter has built on existing theory of legitimacy and (de)legitimation to propose a novel analytical model. The model points to two likely explanatory factors which have received limited attention in previous research. The first factor highlights whether protest is directed more generally against the overall authority of the GGI or more specifically at particular policies or practices of the GGI. The second factor highlights whether the GGI recognizes the protesting actors as being significant for its legitimacy. Based on this analysis we have identified four scenarios which sought to identify when and how protest matters for the legitimacy of GGIs. Protests are likely to also matter for GGI legitimacy by provoking changes in the legitimacy beliefs of other audiences, but the nature of such changes cannot be derived from our model as they depend on the reactions and beliefs of a number of different legitimacy-granting audiences, which must be studied empirically in each specific case.

A main argument emerging from this analysis is that protesters are more likely to matter for the legitimacy of a GGI when that GGI recognizes them as relevant legitimacy-granting actors. Protests of the diffuse type typically delegitimize the GGI, whereas specific protests tend to enhance the GGI's overall legitimacy while politicizing specific policies or practices. Hence, the analysis developed in this chapter suggests that the relationship between civil society protests and GGI legitimacy is far more complex than previous research has acknowledged.

This conclusion has implications for protest strategy. First, protesters who are not recognized by a GGI as significant could be advised to claim status as a recognized constituency. This can be done by mobilizing a mass following that the GGI cannot ignore, by influencing public opinion, or by seeking influential allies. Yet, paradoxically, the act of claiming recognition by the GGI as a significant actor in itself can seem to entail recognition of the GGI's rightful authority.

A second implication of this chapter for protest strategy is that, if protesters seek radical change (transformation), then they should clearly challenge the GGI's authority, contest the overall power of the GGI, and avoid focusing too much on its specific practices and policies. In contrast, if protesters seek moderate change (reform), then they should target specific practices and policies, but not the overall authority of the GGI. This reflects the distinction between different types of opposition against GGIs made by Kalm and Uhlin (2015: 61), where structural opposition aims to abolish or fundamentally transform the GGI, and non-structural opposition aims to change specific policies or projects, but not overall power structures.

Future research could apply this analytical model in more in-depth comparative case studies, which will require more attention to the operationalization of "diffuse" and "specific" protest, as well as the processes that generate recognition of civil society as (in)significant for the legitimacy of GGIs. More particularly, future studies could assess how far the diffuse-versus-specific distinction holds in concrete protest actions and what consequences for GGI legitimacy may follow when protests exhibit both diffuse and specific characteristics.

Likewise, future research needs to consider how protesting actors come to be recognized as significant legitimacy-granting actors, and how processes of recognition may differ across different types of GGIs and different issue areas. Also ripe for future study are the consequences of civil society protest for the legitimacy of hybrid GGIs that combine public and private elements, as well as wholly private GGIs. Finally, future work may reflect on how to incorporate other potentially significant factors into the analysis: for example, the legitimacy effects of discursive and behavioral delegitimation practices within protest; and the impact of outside protest as opposed to protest from within.

This chapter has offered an innovative take on how civil society protests relate to legitimation, delegitimation, and relegitimation of GGIs. Together, the three chapters of Part III have developed new analytical tools for studying processes of legitimation and delegitimation in global governance. Next, the volume turns to theories for analyzing the consequences of GGI legitimacy (and its absence).

Part IV
Consequences of Legitimacy

9

Consequences of Legitimacy in Global Governance

Thomas Sommerer and Hans Agné

What are the consequences of global governance institutions (GGIs) gaining, sustaining, and losing legitimacy? Do higher or lower levels of legitimacy among member governments, stakeholder groups, and the general public change the ways in which GGIs operate and affect their surroundings? It is a long-established wisdom in domestic politics that legitimacy—and related qualities such as trust, public support, and social capital—makes political institutions more effective (e.g. Weber 1922/1978; Dahl and Lindblom 1992; Putnam 1993; Fukuyama 1995; Rothstein 2003). However, so far, relatively little theoretical and empirical research has considered whether legitimacy has similar (or perhaps also different) consequences in global governance.

While Part II of this volume has surveyed the institutional and individual sources of sociological legitimacy, and Part III has explored practices of (de)legitimation of GGIs by various audiences, the logical next step taken in Part IV is to address the effects of legitimacy. In the present chapter, we explore multiple consequences of GGI legitimacy related to problem-solving effectiveness, while the following Chapter 10 zooms in on the effects of legitimacy crises on institutional complexity in global governance.

More specifically, the purpose of this chapter is to outline an agenda for comparative and large-scale research on the consequences of legitimacy in global governance. In the first section, we discuss how legitimacy is best conceptualized to avoid problems of tautology in the study of its effects. In the second section, we present a novel framework for studying legitimacy's consequences. We develop expectations about legitimacy's effects on the resources of GGIs, on the policy output of GGIs, on compliance with GGI policy, and, ultimately, on the problem-solving effectiveness of GGIs.

Our approach implies that we include multiple, but not all, relevant consequences of legitimacy in global governance. (For instance, one aspect that we bracket is strategic responses of GGIs to challenges of their legitimacy—see Gregoratti and Uhlin, this volume.) We argue that a multi-step approach to analyzing effects of GGI legitimacy has methodological advantages by allowing us to employ large-scale empirical research strategies to test the expected effects. In the third and final section of the chapter we discuss challenges involved in empirically studying legitimacy's effects and point towards potential solutions.

Advancing research on the consequences of legitimacy in global governance is important for three reasons. First, while the effects of legitimacy have attracted scholarly attention in comparative politics (CP), they have so far been a marginal concern in international relations (IR). Constructivists have for some time argued that the legitimacy of GGIs influences state behavior (Franck 1990; Hurd 1999), but they have not yet engaged in more systematic research of effects on problem solving. Theorists from other IR traditions have been skeptical of legitimacy's effects, to the point where they have neglected the concept altogether. Realists traditionally assume that states act on the basis of self-interest and relative power rather than legitimacy (Waltz 1979; Mearsheimer 1994/1995), while rational institutionalists argue that state compliance with international rules is contingent on GGIs possessing not legitimacy, but monitoring capacity and sanctioning power (Downs et al. 1996).

Second, extending the study of legitimacy's effects from CP to IR brings new opportunities to test the conditions under which legitimacy produces consequences in any political context. In comparison with domestic politics, global governance has a less centralized authority structure, provides greater opportunities for venue shopping, has higher institutional birth and death rates, and has weaker institutionalized procedures for coordinating policy across different issue areas. These and other differences between domestic and global politics expand the opportunities for scholars to theorize and examine when, how, and why legitimacy results in specific outcomes.

Third, to help solve problems that transcend individual countries, such as financial crises, epidemics, and climate change, we need to analyze the consequences of legitimacy in relation to those institutions which are specifically empowered to address these transboundary problems: GGIs like the International Monetary Fund (IMF), the World Health Organization (WHO), and the Forest Stewardship Council (FSC). While, for sure, domestic political institutions are central for mitigating such problems as well, limiting the study of legitimacy to the national level would reduce the practical usefulness of legitimacy research.

Conceptualizing Legitimacy for the Study of Its Effects

In Chapter 1, Tallberg et al. define legitimacy as the belief within a given audience that an institution's authority is appropriately exercised. In this section, we explain why emphasis in this definition on legitimacy as *audience beliefs* is crucial for studying legitimacy's effects on the operations and impacts of GGIs. Only if we separate beliefs and actions, and reserve legitimacy for the former, does it become meaningful and rewarding to study legitimacy's effects on the behavior of state and non-state actors.

This difference between our conceptualization of legitimacy and that of some other scholars is important to note. Gilley (2006: 500), for instance, compares legitimacy across states based on the definition that "a state is more legitimate the more that it is treated by its citizens as rightfully holding and exercising political power." Similarly, other researchers suggest that "voluntary compliance [by political subjects with rules] is the fundamental observable indicator of legitimacy" (McEwen and Maiman 1983: 258).

For the study of legitimacy's consequences, such a conceptualization either leads to tautological explanations or requires that many potential effects of legitimacy are excluded. The problem of tautology arises if the actions of audiences feature both as an indicator of legitimacy and as an indicator of its effects: that is, if legitimacy is measured in terms of the behavior that it is expected to produce (on the risk of tautology in explanations based on legitimacy, see Keohane 1997: 493). The problem of narrowing legitimacy's possible effects arises if scholars, owing to the risk of tautology, refrain from examining how legitimacy may affect the actions of state and non-state actors, since these actions are part of the very definition of legitimacy.

Conceptualizing legitimacy in terms of audience beliefs avoids these problems. It then becomes possible to theorize and examine if and when institutions that possess more legitimacy are better or worse at generating certain actions, such as rule-observing behavior. Moreover, this conceptualization of legitimacy is consistent with how the majority of social theorists use legitimacy to explain a very broad range of consequences (Weber 1922/1978; Beetham 2013). Hence, understanding legitimacy in terms of audience beliefs facilitates the construction of an ambitious research agenda on legitimacy's effects in global governance.

This choice of definition suggests an important knock-on question: whose legitimacy beliefs or perceptions is it relevant to observe? Expressed in other terms, who is the audience for the GGI? As Bexell and Jönsson indicate in their contribution to this volume, there are multiple ways of conceptualizing audiences. Here, we likewise observe legitimacy in relation to various audiences. The reason for not privileging one particular group of actors is not that we consider the question impossible to answer in principle (Agné 2010), but that we aim to stimulate a broad research agenda.

For instance, there is at present a lively and unsettled debate in international political theory on whether the audience (or subjects) of legitimate institutions must include affected stakeholders (Macdonald 2008), state governments (Keohane and Victor 2011), peoples united by their respective national identities (Smith 1984), the whole of humanity (Held 1995), or a rather amorphous multitude of actors (Hardt and Negri 2001). Likewise, in positive IR research, it is an important question whether consequences of legitimacy vary depending on whether the GGI's audience is conceptualized as member governments (Hurd 2007), civil society representatives (Steffek 2007), the general public (Dellmuth and Tallberg 2015), or all of the above. We remain agnostic on the issue of the relevant audience and suggest an inclusive approach that permits assessing the consequences of GGI legitimacy across multiple potential audiences.

Legitimacy's Effects: Resources, Outputs, Compliance, and Problem Solving

Having specified an understanding of legitimacy, this next section develops a theoretical framework for studying its effects on the problem-solving capacity of GGIs. This process requires theorization and the examination of a range of intermediary steps between legitimacy and problem-solving effectiveness.

Figure 9.1 gives a schematic overview of the consequences of legitimacy. First, legitimacy may affect the *resources* of an institution, which include its mandate, the willingness of political actors to participate, and the physical and financial assets of the institution (A). Second, legitimacy may affect the *policy outputs* of an institution, including binding as well as non-binding decisions (B). Third, legitimacy may impact *rule compliance*, including state implementation of international agreements as well as adherence among non-state actors to GGI-supported norms (C). Fourth, and finally, A to C taken together may also have consequences for the *problem-solving effectiveness* of a GGI in terms of, for instance, reducing ozone emissions, financial volatility, or military conflicts (D).[1]

As indicated by the arrows in Figure 9.1, we expect the legitimacy of a GGI to have direct effects on outcomes A to C, and an indirect effect on outcome D. Resources, policies, compliance, and problem-solving effectiveness are thus causally linked in a step-wise fashion. Some level of resources (A) is a

---

[1] Consequences B–D are elements of institutional performance (Gutner and Thompson 2010; Tallberg et al. 2016b), while consequence A is constitutive of the institution itself.

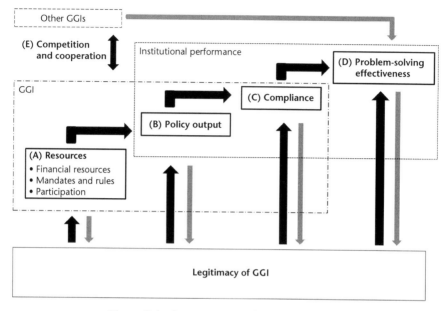

Figure 9.1. Consequences of GGI legitimacy

precondition for an institution to produce policy outputs (B). In turn, some level of policy outputs (B) is a precondition for there to be decisions that actors may comply with (C). In turn again, some level of compliance (C) is a precondition for problem-solving effectiveness (D). The multistep conditionality of A for B for C for D is a stylized depiction of the often more complicated real world of global governance. For instance, the case of the Group of Twenty (G20) demonstrates that even a GGI with a few own resources and little formally delegated authority can be an effective problem solver by orchestrating states and other actors (Viola 2015). Conversely, international organizations possessing resources, developing policy, and ensuring compliance may worsen existing problems or create new ones, if their basic analysis is wrong.

In addition, the upper-left corner of Figure 9.1 underlines that individual GGIs do not operate in isolation from each other, but often interact in ways that have consequences for the outcomes A–D. For example, when two GGIs such as the North Atlantic Treaty Organization (NATO) and the European Union (EU) occupy the same policy space (Hofmann 2009), changes in the legitimacy of one institution could affect the resource allocation, policy response, compliance rate, and problem-solving effectiveness of both institutions. We conceptualize patterns of cooperation and competition between GGIs as an additional outcome (E), potentially affected by legitimacy and with potential effects for outcomes A–D. In Chapter 10 of this volume, Fariborz Zelli further expands on the implications of legitimacy for regime complexes in global governance.

Existing IR, CP, and related literatures have studied all five potential consequences (A–E) to some extent. However, these earlier investigations have not been comprehensive or systematic, as the following overview will demonstrate. Moreover, drawing together various consequences in a single framework, and studying them jointly across the same empirical cases, offers unexploited methodological advantages.

Previous research on the problem-solving effectiveness of GGIs has confronted two challenges (Mitchell 2008). First, the causal chain from the independent variable of interest (in our case legitimacy) to problem-solving effectiveness is long, with many potential intervening and confounding variables. GGIs operate in complex environments, and changes in outcomes may not be directly related to measures taken by these institutions. Second, evidence on the effectiveness of GGIs is in short supply, since data for effectiveness indicators is typically collected by domestic institutions, which often does not lead to comparable data.

These difficulties are mitigated by taking our proposed multistep approach to legitimacy's effects. The problem of the long chain between cause (legitimacy) and effect (problem solving), and the abundance of confounding variables, is reduced by dividing this process into several shorter steps analyzed both independently and jointly. Moreover, the multistep approach increases the number of empirical observations available for assessing consequences of legitimacy.

In the remainder of this section, we theorize how and why each outcome (A–E) may be affected by legitimacy, and discuss how GGI resources, policy outputs, compliance rates, and interactions may condition problem-solving effectiveness. For these purposes, we draw on, synthesize, and venture beyond existing literature in both CP and IR. We also explain how the hypothesized effects may be consistent with causal mechanisms privileged in both rationalist and constructivist theory, emphasizing instrumental concerns and norm conformance, respectively.

(A) Resources

The first dimension of the framework involves resources. As we have argued above, resources may be considered a necessary condition for a GGI to sustain decision-making capacity, ensure rule compliance, and achieve problem-solving effectiveness. We apply a broad understanding of resources, since a strong GGI is not only defined by material aspects like the size of its budget and staff. Some authors have highlighted the role of other, less tangible resources of GGIs (Barnett and Finnemore 1999, 2004; Haas 2008). GGI resources also include institutional assets, such as recognized authority and organizational rules. For example, the power of the Appellate Body of the World Trade Organization (WTO) to adjudicate trade disputes among member states or the issuance of arrest warrants by the International Criminal Court (ICC) issuance are constituted by the act of delegation in the organizations' founding agreements. Strong institutional resources do not always come with strong material resources, as the combination of comprehensive mandates and limited staff in some GGIs illustrates.

So far, organizational resources have received limited attention in existing literature on legitimacy in global governance. Yet there are good reasons for redressing this neglect. Without resources of staff, policy mandate, functional decision rules, and participation, an institution will struggle to survive. Expressed less dramatically, the stability and operation of an institution is sensitive to increases and decreases of these resources. This expectation is well rooted in general institutionalist research (Meyer and Rowan 1977: 353), and likely extends to GGIs.

Constructivist scholarship in IR suggests several examples of how legitimacy may affect the resources of GGIs. Some argue that legitimacy considerations affect the institutional design of GGIs (Wendt 2001), for instance, in terms of weighting votes for states and granting access for non-state actors (Stephen 2016; O'Brien et al. 2000; Steffek and Nanz 2008). Others suggest that legitimacy affects the delegation of power to an institution in the first place, as when the ICC was created in response to the decreasing legitimacy of United Nations (UN) tribunals (Fehl 2004), or when the Asian Infrastructure Investment Bank (AIIB) was created in response to the decreasing legitimacy of the World Bank in the eyes of audiences in Asia. Consequences of legitimacy for GGI funding have received less attention so far, but a case in point may be the dramatically reduced contributions to the budget of the United Nations Educational, Scientific and Cultural Organization (UNESCO) following the accession of Palestine as a member state in 2011 (Hüfner 2015; for earlier examples, see Imber 1989).

Existing CP scholarship has explored the effect of legitimacy on state capacity, state failure, and the reform of institutional structures. A common question is whether states become weaker as a consequence of a legitimacy crisis (Gilley 2006, 2009; Migdal 2001: 52; Tilly 2005; Schubert 2008). So far, however, empirical studies have not been able to demonstrate a convincing link between legitimacy deficits and state breakdown (Booth and Seligson 2005). In organizational studies, institutional survival rates of non-profit organizations are linked to legitimacy, as measured by endorsements and interorganizational relationships (Baum and Oliver 1991; Singh et al. 1986).

In sum, the main expectation is that legitimacy will have positive effects on the resources vested in a GGI, as state and non-state actors will be more ready to commit competencies, funding, and involvement to GGIs. This effect may come about through causal mechanisms emphasized in either rationalist or constructivist theories, since both instrumental concerns and norm conformance may lead actors to confer additional resources on legitimate GGIs.

Proposition 1: An increase in the legitimacy of a GGI will increase its ability to attract resources.

(B) Policy Output

Our second dimension of the consequences of GGI legitimacy relates to policy output. Generating some level of policy measures is likely to be a necessary, but insufficient, condition for GGIs to attain problem-solving effectiveness (Tallberg et al. 2016b). While it is obvious that a deadlocked decision-making body cannot contribute to problem solving, a high volume of policy output is no guarantee either, since it says little about the quality of the policy. When studying the link between policy output and effectiveness, it is therefore essential to consider both the quantity and the quality of binding and non-binding decisions.

So far, policy output has not been a prominent topic in IR research, with the exception of certain studies on the UN (Holloway and Tomlinson 1995; Vreeland and Dreher 2014), the EU (Schulz and König 2000; Naurin and Wallace 2008), and the WTO (Elsig 2010). Given the limited scope of this literature, it is not surprising that legitimacy does not figure prominently among the potential explanations of decision-taking capacity in GGIs. Only a few IR scholars have explicitly studied these effects, while some have argued theoretically that increasing support for decisions should facilitate decision making (Fearon 1998; Zürn 2000). Gulbrandsen (2004) has argued that the legitimacy of the FSC among producer groups increases the recognition of this private global certification scheme.

Studying the effects of legitimacy on policy output is somewhat more common in CP. For instance, scholars have looked into the effects of state and local government legitimacy on the enactment of legislation, public spending, foreign aid, and climate change planning (e.g. Gilley 2009: 198, 2006; Cashmore and Wejs 2014).

The relationship between legitimacy and policy output is not straightforward. While it could be expected that a legitimacy crisis would bring gridlock to a decision-making body, the opposite outcome is plausible, too. An illustration of declining policy-making activity is the WTO General Council in the aftermath of civil society protests at the end of the 1990s (WTO 2017a). An illustration of increased decision taking is the ICC's greater activism following criticism from African countries (e.g. Clarke et al. 2016).

Thus, we formulate two competing expectations regarding the consequences of legitimacy on GGI decision making. These effects may be produced by causal mechanisms privileged by different theories. While rationalists would emphasize how legitimacy affects decision making through preferences and decision rules, constructivists would highlight socialization and informal norms of interaction.

Proposition 2a: An increase in the legitimacy of a GGI will lead to more policy outputs of this institution.

Proposition 2b: A decrease in the legitimacy of a GGI will lead to more policy outputs of this institution.

(C) Compliance

The third dimension in our framework refers to compliance with rules set by GGIs. Similar to resources and policy outputs, we understand rule compliance as a necessary condition for GGIs to contribute to problem solving. However, it is also far from a sufficient condition. Even if all members are in full compliance with the rules and policies of a GGI, its overall performance can be low due to, for instance, weak policy solutions, a lack of resources, or intervening external factors.

International organizations, transgovernmental networks, and transnational hybrid institutions often have the authority to make policy, but they rarely have any authority to implement their decisions by force. For instance, the Kimberley Process, a tripartite arrangement established in 2003 for the purpose of registering rough diamonds, has few sanctions for noncompliance and no body to monitor and enforce implementation (Wright 2004). Therefore, it is commonly argued that legitimacy is of particular importance for compliance in global governance, and ultimately for problem-solving effectiveness (Hurd 2007; Checkel 2001; Steffek 2003). As Ian Hurd (2007: 34) puts it, "[i]t is common in IR to assume that the main behavioural implication of legitimacy in IOs [international organizations] is higher rates of compliance by states with international rules" (see also Chayes and Chayes 1995; Simmons 1998; Mayntz 2010). Similarly, in international law, Franck (1990) argues that the legitimacy of rules exerts a "compliance pull" on governments. While IR scholars mostly understand compliance as a problem of governments following joint agreements, it is important to mention that supranational regulation directly addresses—and thus involves compliance by—private actors and individuals as well (Steffek 2007).

Similarly, CP literature dedicates much attention to the question of whether and how a legitimacy crisis leads to a decrease in compliance with rules and norms. That states depend heavily on legitimacy beliefs when it comes to law enforcement or tax collection is uncontroversial (Gilley 2009: 149; Tyler 1990; Sunshine and Tyler 2003). The phenomenon has been observed in different contexts and for a wide range of issues. For example, Levi (1997) found in a study of several American states that legitimacy was an important predictor of compliance with military conscription orders. Hauck and Kroese (2006) studied the effect of the legitimacy of marine and coastal management on fisheries compliance in South Africa. Other research has shown that this pattern of voluntary obedience can be observed not only for individuals, but also for groups and associations (Knoke and Wood 1981).

We therefore expect that legitimacy has a positive effect on compliance with GGI rules. While constructivism's emphasis on legitimacy's compliance pull is most featured in existing scholarship, it is conceivable that legitimacy could generate instrumentally motivated compliance as well, as actors strategically seek to avoid negative reputational repercussions from violating the rules of a GGI broadly perceived as legitimate.

Proposition 3: An increase in the legitimacy of a GGI will lead to higher compliance from the actors addressed by those rules.

(D) Problem-Solving Effectiveness

An extensive body of research in IR examines the effectiveness of international regimes, focusing primarily on environmental pollution (e.g. Young 1999; Miles et al. 2002), but also covering human rights violations (Simmons 2009; Hafner-Burton 2013), peacekeeping (Fortna 2004), and trade (Mansfield and Reinhardt 2008; Gray and Slapin 2012). These studies have given little attention to legitimacy as a potential explanation of problem-solving effectiveness. However, some scholars have argued theoretically that legitimacy is key to effective global governance (Heupel and Binder 2015; Hurd 1999), while others have emphasized the need to specify the conditions under which legitimacy has an impact on the problem-solving capacity of international organizations and regimes (Young 2011). In a case study on Somalia and Cambodia, Mersiades (2005) examines how local perceptions of the legitimacy of UN and African Union (AU) peacekeepers affected the success of the peacekeeping operations of these institutions. Lake and Fariss (2014) find that a lack of legitimacy was a core reason behind failed international efforts at state building in Iraq and Afghanistan.

Similar to IR, CP has paid relatively little attention to the consequences of legitimacy for the problem-solving effectiveness of political institutions. Some studies assess the relationship between legitimacy and performance measures, such as welfare gains (Gilley 2006) and regime effectiveness (Karklins 1994). More specific investigations focus on, for instance, the outbreak of violence as a consequence of a national government losing or trying to regain legitimacy (Byman et al. 1998). Schlyter et al. (2009) have assessed how legitimacy perceptions of forest owners in Sweden vis-à-vis international forest certification schemes has impacted their ecological effectiveness. Students of management have developed and tested hypotheses regarding the consequences of legitimacy for organizational success (Deephouse and Suchman 2008).

In large parts of the above-mentioned literature, the mechanisms that lead to legitimacy-driven changes in effectiveness remain rather vague or simply absent. This is where our suggested multistep approach with the chain from legitimacy to problem-solving effectiveness as a causal sequence in itself becomes useful. Yet the common denominator in existing research is the expectation that legitimacy has positive consequences on the effectiveness of political institutions:

Proposition 4: An increase in the legitimacy of a GGI will yield higher problem-solving effectiveness of this institution.

(E) Competition and Cooperation between GGIs

So far, we have discussed consequences of legitimacy in the context of an individual GGI. However, there are hundreds of global and regional governance arrangements, and GGIs seldom exist and operate in isolation from each other. Every global problem is targeted by more than one institution. An important implication of these functional overlaps is cooperation and/or competition between GGIs. Scholarly attention to such interinstitutional interaction has grown substantially during the last decade (e.g. Helfer 2004; Raustiala and Victor 2004; Oberthür and Gehring 2006; Frey 2008; Alter and Meunier 2009; Keohane and Victor 2011; Zelli and van Asselt 2013b; Eberlein et al. 2014; Risse 2016). GGIs compete for crucial resources like public attention, membership, financial support, and delegation of authority. Such contention can lead to the birth and death of institutions, as choices by states and non-state actors to join, fund, and participate are essential for GGIs to be created and survive. There is also competition among GGIs to secure compliance with their (sometimes contradictory) rules and to present the most attractive policy solutions to global problems. But cooperation occurs as well, and IR scholarship has pointed to multiple forms, from loose and informal arrangements to comprehensive and formalized collaboration.

Interestingly, one can observe instances of institutional cooperation on all four previously mentioned dimensions of legitimacy's effects. In terms of resources, for example, the World Bank has co-financed many projects with regional development banks (A). In terms of decision taking, the IMF and the

EU have coordinated their policy solutions to the financial crisis in Europe (B). In terms of compliance, NATO and the Organization for Security and Co-operation in Europe (OSCE) have cooperated in monitoring observance of conflict-resolution measures (C), while also working together to resolve the problem of violent conflicts as such (D).

As Zelli describes in Chapter 10, relatively little research has explored the effect of legitimacy on interactions among GGIs. The main exceptions are studies of organizational ecology, which have found that legitimacy increases survival rates across organizational populations (Hannan and Carroll 1992). In addition, some research in sociology has suggested that legitimacy affects interorganizational competition for resources (Salancik and Pfeffer 1978: 201).

Our expectation is that changes in legitimacy will affect interactions among GGIs. Those institutions which enjoy substantial legitimacy are more likely to be successful competitors, since they will be able to attract more resources and gain focal positions in their respective policy domains. Indeed, a GGI with high levels of legitimacy may have less need to collaborate with others (although other GGIs may seek to collaborate with it on account of its high levels of legitimacy). Conversely, GGIs low in legitimacy are more likely to lose standing relative to their competitors, and therefore can have stronger incentives to initiate cooperation with other institutions.

Proposition 5: Legitimacy will make a GGI stronger in relation to GGIs with less legitimacy and therefore also less likely to initiate cooperation with other GGIs.

Towards Empirical Research

Earlier efforts to research the effects of legitimacy in domestic and international politics have been partly stranded due to methodological difficulties in isolating such consequences empirically. The multistep approach proposed above reduces some of the typical methodological concerns by dividing the causal chain from legitimacy to effects into shorter steps, and by expanding the number of observable implications of the expectation that legitimacy has effects. Still, other methodological issues remain, and this section discusses three particular challenges as this agenda moves from theory to empirical testing.

Causality

A first major challenge is to establish the direction of causality between legitimacy and its expected effects. Not only may legitimacy contribute to the effectiveness of an institution, but successful problem solving may itself also be the reason why an institution is legitimate in the first place. This possibility is reflected, for instance, in the notion of *output legitimacy* (Scharpf 1999), which refers to legitimacy generated by effective resolution of societal problems. The standard way of addressing this problem of endogeneity is to analyze whether it is legitimacy or problem-solving effectiveness that tends to come first. The more specific methodological challenge, therefore, is to find data on the legitimacy of GGIs over time. (In a qualitative study, this observation would favor the selection of cases where GGIs have undergone a legitimacy crisis.)

A common way to operationalize and measure the legitimacy of political institutions is through public opinion surveys of people's confidence or trust in these institutions. However, whereas public opinion research on domestic political institutions offers long-time series for a large number of countries, the situation is less favorable with regard to GGIs, as discussed by Lisa Dellmuth in Chapter 3. Sources like the World Values Survey (WVS) and the Eurobarometer only cover a limited set of GGIs and short observation periods. The WVS covers eighteen mostly regional governance organizations, but offers relatively little continuity in institutional selection and country samples across its six waves to date since the early 1980s. Given this data situation, it is no surprise that only a few studies have so far exploited these resources for the study of legitimacy (Torgler 2008; Dellmuth and Tallberg 2015).

This leaves us with a few alternatives. One is to wait patiently for the future when better over-time survey data on GGIs may become available. This alternative is unsatisfying, given the time it may take and the urgent need to explore the consequences of GGI legitimacy. Another option would be to construct surveys that include retrospective questions. While this approach may be worthwhile, it involves problems like selective memory, time displacement, and the reinterpretation of the past in the light of the present (de Vaus 2013: 33; Smith 1984; Dex 1995).

A further option would be to base legitimacy assessments on media data for elite critique of or mass protests against GGIs (Della Porta and Tarrow 2005; Lindvall 2013; Tallberg et al. 2014). We find this to be the most promising approach. Figure 9.2 exemplifies how such measures may be used to paint a picture of the perceived legitimacy of the Association of South East Asian Nations (ASEAN) based on data from global newswires.

While this empirical approach has been criticized for a number of reasons, its key familiar weaknesses can be sufficiently overcome. Some argue that a focus on protests may overestimate critical minorities and underestimate silent support for political institutions (Herkenrath and Knoll 2011). However, negative indicators of critique and protest in newswires can be complemented by indicators of support and trust in public opinion surveys, in order to test whether a decrease in protest actually conforms to growing support. Where data on public opinion are not available, qualitative assessments of protest

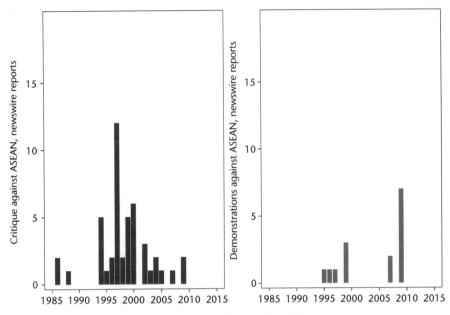

Figure 9.2. Challenges of ASEAN, media coverage

patterns can provide the required information. Whether protest data overestimate critical minorities can also be tested by considering elites and grassroots separately: if the trend in legitimacy is unaffected by a change in the specification of the audience (see conceptual discussion above), there should be less risk that the position of a particular group is overrepresented in the data. To illustrate this possibility, Figure 9.2 distinguishes between mass protests and elite critique. An even more fine-grained categorization of different elite groups may further reduce this problem. Finally, it has also been argued that media-based assessments of legitimacy are unreliable, because political opposition may not be forthcoming owing to a lack of resources or a fear of punishment under autocratic states (Heupel and Binder 2015; Scott 1985). However, this problem may be alleviated by controlling statistically for variation in political and civil liberties across states.

Operationalization of Legitimacy

A second major challenge to empirical analysis of legitimacy's effects concerns the need to distinguish legitimacy from such support of institutions that is fostered by self-interest alone. As already discussed in several other contributions to this volume, legitimacy refers to a reservoir of confidence in an institution that goes beyond short-term satisfaction with the GGI's distributional outcomes (e.g. Agné, this volume; Tallberg et al., this volume). However, separating out legitimacy beliefs from support driven by self-interest alone is easier said than done in empirical research. Some contributions to this volume suggest ways forward. For instance, Gregoratti and Uhlin propose a distinction between critiques that target the GGI as such and critiques that target only specific aspects of the institution, like individual policies. Only in the former case, Gregoratti and Uhlin suggest, does critique count against the legitimacy of the GGI. As we read their distinction, critique limited to particular policies is more likely to reflect the distributional self-interest of the critic than a principled objection to policymaking by this GGI as such.

Availability of Data on Legitimacy's Effects

A third major challenge for empirical research is the lack of availability of data for measuring the different consequences of legitimacy in a comparative design. Since this problem is more serious for quantitative than for qualitative research, we focus on the former and discuss how the construction of new data sets may help to rectify the situation.

With regard to the financial and administrative aspect of *GGI resources*, data on staff and budgets can be gathered from the *Yearbook of International Organizations* (UIA 2015) as well as GGI annual reports and growing digital archives (e.g. WHO 2017; WTO 2017b). Recent years have also brought new advances in coding large-N data on the mandate and design of GGIs (e.g. Hooghe and Marks 2015; Blake and Payton 2015; Tallberg et al. 2014).

Data on *policy output of GGIs* is more readily available today than for earlier generations of researchers, as archiving and digitalization strategies of GGIs have progressed. A result of this development is a new data set on thirty GGIs that contains all policy measures adopted by the main decision-making bodies of these organizations from 1980 to 2015 (Sommerer et al. 2016; Lundgren et al. 2017). Other recent data-collection efforts have focused on different types of GGI outputs, for instance, public communication by GGI secretariats (Ecker-Ehrhardt 2016).

Comparative quantitative data on *compliance with GGI decisions* are not available today, but it may with some effort be possible to construct them. The majority of existing data sets are limited to the EU (Mastenbroek 2005; Hartlapp and Falkner 2009) or individual international treaties and courts (e.g. Stiles and Thayne 2006; Hillebrecht 2014). An important constraint lies in the difficulty to establish comparable compliance measurements across GGIs working in different policy fields, using different types of policy outputs, and with varying levels of access to information on compliance. However, if comparative research on compliance limits its scope to the policies of GGIs in identical policy fields, then such problems of comparability may be reduced (see e.g. Simmons 2009).

The lack of comparable data on *problem-solving effectiveness* across GGIs may be addressed in a similar way, that is, by narrowing the policy scope to focus on specific outcomes. The UN, the World Bank, OSCE, the WHO, and other GGIs systematically collect data on outcome indicators pertaining to economic performance, health, environmental quality, victims of violent conflicts, etc. To the extent that the methodological challenge of controlling for confounding factors can be handled, data for assessing GGIs' effects on problem solving in specific domains exist.

Conclusion

Researching legitimacy's effects in global governance poses considerable challenges. The exercise involves conceptualizing legitimacy in a non-tautological way, disentangling complex causal relationships, and constructing new empirical measurements and data resources. However, as we have argued in this chapter, these challenges are not insurmountable, and rather present concrete research tasks. The motivation for pursuing this possibility with actual research is threefold.

First, although it is frequently assumed that legitimacy matters for problem-solving effectiveness in global governance, little systematic research has been done. In this chapter, we have shown how a multistep approach to this issue helps to answer some of the methodological problems that have prevented progress in the past.

Second, extending research on legitimacy's effects to GGIs opens up new opportunities to assess the scope conditions of theories of legitimacy that were developed in the context of domestic politics. Given the institutional and societal differences between global and domestic spheres, analyzing and comparing legitimacy in the two domains is likely to be particularly rewarding.

Third, if legitimacy indeed affects the problem-solving effectiveness of GGIs, then it is urgent to unveil those relationships, given their implications for transnational threats such as violent conflicts, poverty, climate change, epidemics, and financial crises. Anything short of systematic research on legitimacy's consequences would be a lost opportunity to help solve such global problems.

10

Effects of Legitimacy Crises in Complex Global Governance

Fariborz Zelli

Global governance institutions (GGIs) increasingly operate in a world of institutional complexity, polycentricity, and fragmentation. Processes of regulation and legalization in world politics have brought material and functional overlaps between GGIs—intergovernmental and transnational, global and regional. Few, if any, institutions can nowadays claim exclusive authority over a given issue of global governance.

Relations between GGIs can vary from synergy and coherence to tension and conflict, with considerable consequences for the governance activities of these institutions. In this competition over authority, the legitimacy of the respective GGIs may serve as a crucial resource. However, research has yet to explore this connection between legitimacy and complexity.

This chapter follows up on the previous contribution by Sommerer and Agné to focus specifically on the consequences of legitimacy for complexity and competition among GGIs. The ambition is to offer a novel analytical framework for systematically studying this connection. Treating legitimacy as an independent variable, the framework develops hypotheses about the consequences of legitimacy crises on three dimensions of complex governance: (1) *architecture*, i.e. the degree of complexity of the system in which the GGI is embedded; (2) *effectiveness* of the GGI within its increasingly complex environment; and (3) *modes of governance* employed by the GGI to navigate this complexity. In developing these expectations, the chapter primarily invokes examples from the domain of global climate governance, with its core institution the United Nations Framework Convention on Climate Change (UNFCCC), though the discussion also refers to illustrations from other issue areas.

The chapter's main message is that the legitimacy crisis of a central GGI may increase the complexity of its institutional environment, since dissatisfied actors will be motivated to build alternative institutions. In addition, institutional complexity may aggravate other effects of a legitimacy crisis, by reinforcing effectiveness losses and strengthening reliance on soft and indirect governance.

The chapter proceeds as follows. After a brief review of the state of the art and an introduction to the two key concepts (i.e. legitimacy and complexity), the ensuing three sections develop hypotheses that capture consequences of legitimacy crises for the three dimensions (i.e. architecture, effectiveness, and modes of governance). The concluding section summarizes the main arguments and outlines an agenda for further theory development and empirical testing.

State of the Art

As institutionalist and organizational ecology scholars have argued for some time, we cannot fully grasp key aspects of a GGI today—its establishment, growth, legitimacy, fairness, or effectiveness—without considering its institutional environment (e.g. Abbott et al. 2016; Young 2002). Greater complexity of this environment may significantly shape a GGI's operations and impacts. Complexity may foster inclusiveness and political experimentation, enhance or impede accountability, change bargaining settings, and bring interagency cooperation or conflict, to name but a few possible implications (Biermann et al. 2009).

As the next section will elaborate, there is much proliferation of concepts in this literature. However, the work has provided little in the way of explanatory approaches that help us to understand the underlying dynamics of a complex governance architecture. Such analysis would relate institutional complexity to constellations of power, interests, knowledge, norms, and discourses (Zelli and van Asselt 2013b).

One of the prominent gaps in explanatory theory concerns the relationship between legitimacy and institutional complexity. There are good reasons to believe that the legitimacy of GGIs affects institutional complexity, and vice versa. Recently, several scholars have noted this gap, calling for more systematic insights into the causal connections between the two factors (Abbott et al. 2016; Keohane and Victor 2011). We still know too little about how (lack of) legitimacy affects institutional environments, how we can assess the normative or sociological legitimacy of overall complex governance architectures, how the polycentric character of a governance area is used for legitimation or delegitimation, and how legitimacy audiences are constituted and shift in complex governance architectures (see Bexell and Jönsson, this volume).

These lacunae open up an extensive research program which can help us gain greater understanding of a GGI's legitimacy and the consequences thereof. Such knowledge may also yield targeted recommendations for enhancing legitimacy in complex environments. The remainder of this chapter makes a case for such an agenda.

Key Concepts

Legitimacy

This chapter follows the volume's sociological understanding of legitimacy: namely, as beliefs or perceptions within a given audience that an institution's exercise of authority is appropriate (Tallberg et al., this volume; cf. Tallberg and Zürn 2017). These beliefs may have a variety of institutional and contextual sources. Following Scholte and Tallberg (this volume), one can roughly differentiate between procedural sources of legitimacy that relate to input and throughput processes of an institution and performance-based sources of legitimacy that comprise all sorts of institutional output (cf. Scharpf 1999; Hurd 2007; Dellmuth, this volume).

When studying the consequences of legitimacy, this perception-based definition of legitimacy presents a risk of tautology. As Sommerer and Agné caution in Chapter 9, it is crucial to disentangle: (a) procedures and performances which generate legitimacy beliefs; (b) the legitimacy beliefs as such; and (c) consequences of these legitimacy beliefs for the procedures and performances of GGIs. To avoid circular reasoning, one needs to distinguish, for instance, the sources of the UNFCCC's legitimacy, the critical perceptions of the UNFCCC by the US and other member states in recent years, and the potential consequences of these legitimacy perceptions in terms of reaching a new climate agreement.

Legitimacy Crisis

The analytical framework developed in this chapter focuses specifically on the effects of *legitimacy crises*. Thus, the framework theorizes the effects of legitimacy in a particular setting. This is a choice motivated by pragmatic and methodological concerns. Legitimacy crises offer a good starting point for theorizing the effects of legitimacy on institutional complexity. Moments of crisis mark profound changes in the legitimacy of an institution and make it possible to identify clear cut-off points, which is useful when studying the consequences of legitimacy. An easy identification of potential consequences, in turn, makes it easier to assess whether these outcomes are in line with theory-based expectations.

Reus-Smit defines the legitimacy crisis of a GGI in two steps. First, it implies that the GGI in question "may suffer a decline in legitimacy, or may have trouble establishing robust legitimacy in the first place" (2007: 166). Such a crisis could be the result of targeted delegitimation practices (Bäckstrand and Söderbaum, this volume; Gregoratti and Uhlin, this volume). The challenge may happen acutely (critical point), but it may also be more chronic (critical phase), in the sense of a slowly evolving "legitimacy drift" (Stephen 2016: 8). Second, a criterion to grasp intensity is added in order to distinguish slight declines of legitimacy from critical points or phases "in which the imperative to adapt is heightened by the immanent possibility of death, collapse, demise, disempowerment, or decline into irrelevance" (Reus-Smit 2007: 166).

To provide further precision and operationalization, Reus-Smit's notion of an "imperative to adapt" ties legitimacy crisis to a potential reaction by the affected institution. This adaptation can take two major forms. First, a GGI may draw on material sources of power to compensate for the loss of legitimacy. Second, the GGI may recalibrate, "which necessarily involves the communicative reconciliation of the ... institution's social identity, interests or practices" (Clark and Reus-Smit 2007b: 154). This recalibration may imply that the GGI realigns "its realm of political action" to reorient itself towards its audience (Reus-Smit 2007: 167).

In light of Sommerer and Agné's previously noted caution, Reus-Smit's understanding of legitimacy crisis is challenging, since it incorporates possible adaptation by the affected institution, i.e. legitimation before or after crisis (see also Bäckstrand and Söderbaum, this volume). This chapter therefore uses an alternative version of Reus-Smit's definition, where adaptation by the GGI is not part of the legitimacy crisis as such, but a consequence thereof.

This chapter also adopts a constructivist reading of the crisis itself: not only legitimacy is perceived, but also the crisis. This is in line with Habermas' understanding that we can only speak of a crisis if members of a society "experience structural alterations as critical for continued existence and feel their social identity threatened" (1973/1976: 3). In other words, legitimacy crises result from how an institution is perceived by its audience (see also Bexell and Jönsson, this volume). As Reus-Smit notes, "What matters, it seems, is that consciousness, in the form of broad social perception of power without right, is essential to crises of legitimacy" (2007: 169).

In sum, a GGI is undergoing a legitimacy crisis *if a given audience perceives its legitimacy to be at a point or phase of critical vulnerability*. This situation requires the GGI to adapt in order to (re)gain audience beliefs that it exercises its authority appropriately.

Institutional Complexity

For a working definition of institutional complexity, this chapter follows the broad understanding of fragmentation presented by Biermann et al.

(2009). They state that many policy domains are marked by a "patchwork of international institutions that are different in their character (organizations, regimes, and implicit norms), their constituencies (public and private), their spatial scope (from bilateral to global), and their [predominant] subject matter" (2009: 16).

The concept of institutional fragmentation originated in the international law community (e.g. Hafner 2004; ILC 2006; Koskenniemi and Leino 2002), before being adapted by international relations (IR) scholars and extended to transnational arrangements and public-private partnerships. Still, the term fragmentation remains contested, because it suggests to some a preference for order or centrality. While this chapter treats the notion of fragmentation without prejudice, it will mostly use the more neutral word "complexity."

Other terms common in the literature to capture the same phenomenon, broadly speaking, are "governance experiment" (Hoffmann 2011), "polyarchic" or "polycentric" governance (Ostrom 2010), and "regime complex" (Orsini et al. 2013; Raustiala and Victor 2004), to name but a few. Regime complexes are defined in a rather additive manner as "loosely coupled sets of specific regimes" (Keohane and Victor 2011: 7; cf. Alter and Meunier 2009).

Notwithstanding such terminological divisions, all of these scholars would agree that institutional complexity is a structural characteristic of contemporary global governance (Zelli 2015). No policy domain today has all relevant provisions under a single institutional umbrella with universal membership (Biermann et al. 2009; Orsini et al. 2013). Hence, the central issue is not whether institutional complexity prevails, but the degree of complexity and its variation across issue areas. This chapter argues that, among a variety of possible factors, the degree of complexity may be determined by considering two dimensions: (1) core institutional centrality; and (2) legal and functional coherence (Biermann et al. 2009; Keohane and Victor 2011).

The degree of centrality is assessed through an examination of architectures, understood as the overarching systems of public, private, and hybrid institutions "that are valid or active in a given issue area of world politics" (Biermann et al. 2009: 15). One can differentiate between architectures with one core institution, architectures with two or more cores, and architectures with no clear hierarchy. The first type of architecture, for example, corresponds to a situation with one "core GGI," which is often intergovernmental in nature. Core GGIs are typically entrusted with a broad mandate covering main themes and key governance functions of a particular issue area. Examples include the UNFCCC in climate governance, the World Trade Organization (WTO) in commerce, and the World Health Organization (WHO) in disease control. Such situations still leave spaces for other institutions, but usually in the periphery of the issue area and its governance.

Legal coherence refers to the extent that major norms, principles, and rules overlap between GGIs. Sometimes formal mechanisms are put in place to manage such overlaps, such as conflict clauses within the affected treaties, conflict resolution rules in a third treaty, or cooperation agreements among institutions (van Asselt 2014). Functional coherence addresses whether other institutions complement, duplicate, or compete with the governance functions of the GGI, such as agenda setting, policy formulation, decision making, financing, implementation, and evaluation (Zelli et al. 2017).

Combining the two dimensions of centrality and coherence, Biermann and colleagues speak of a synergistic or low degree of complexity in a global governance domain when almost all countries participate in the core GGI, and when this institution "provides for effective and detailed general principles that regulate the policies in distinct yet substantially integrated institutional arrangements" (2009: 20). An example is the global governance architecture for ozone layer depletion. At the core of this regime is the Ozone Secretariat, which administers the 1985 Vienna Convention, the 1987 Montreal Protocol, and a series of amendments that add new substances to the regulatory system. There are only a few arrangements that are external to the Ozone Secretariat, and they are largely supportive of the core regime. For instance, a bilateral agreement between China and the US eventually spurred the adoption of the most recent amendment to the ozone regime in October 2016.

At the other end of the continuum, a high or conflictive degree of complexity characterizes a global governance area when GGIs are hardly connected, have different decision-making and voting procedures, and produce conflicting policy outcomes. One prominent example is the regulation of genetic resources. Here, two GGIs attempt to regulate the same issue: the Secretariat of the Convention on Biological Diversity (CBD) and the WTO through its agreement on Trade-Related Aspects of Intellectual Property Rights (TRIPS). The CBD reaffirms the sovereign rights of states over their biological resources, while TRIPS seeks to strengthen and harmonize national systems of private intellectual property rights. As Rosendal suggests, a virtual "arms race" has taken place through additional agreements that take sides with one or the other of the two conflicting GGIs (2006: 94; also Oberthür and Pożarowska 2013).

Having established this chapter's conceptualization of legitimacy crisis and institutional complexity, the following sections in turn explore three possible causal connections between legitimacy and complexity. In these discussions, legitimacy crisis is treated as the independent variable, while institutional complexity is considered either as a dependent variable (in the next section on consequences for the institutional architecture) or as a conditioning variable (when qualifying the consequences of a legitimacy crisis for a GGI's effectiveness and governance mode).

Impacts of Legitimacy Crises on the Global Governance Architecture

This section develops an argument that a legitimacy crisis of a core GGI may impact the shape of the broader governance architecture. *When a leading GGI undergoes a legitimacy crisis, the governed that have sufficient means to do so may establish alternative institutions to fill the legitimacy gaps, thus adding to the complexity of the existing governance architecture.*

This expectation may materialize along different causal pathways, depending on the more fundamental conditions in which both legitimacy crises and institutional complexity are embedded. In the following, I briefly elaborate two structural types of such pathways: a set of power-based ones that refer to the behavior of hegemonic states; and an interest-based one that relies on constellations of preferences among states or other key actors. The two types of pathways share the rationalist assumption that actors seek to maximize their interests, and the effects of the pathways may in practice be complementary.

First, a set of power-based causal mechanisms draws on instrumental multilateralism and the works of Ikenberry (2003) and Kindleberger (1973, 1981). From this viewpoint, the above hypothesis would reflect the behavior of a hegemon or a coalition of powerful states. Power here refers to states' economic, military, and more issue-specific resources. Once a critical degree of dissatisfaction with a core GGI is reached, such a coalition may use its resources to initiate or develop rival arenas that better suit its interests. The ultimate goal of these steps is to reach relative gains over rival states (Morse and Keohane 2014). The resulting alternative institutions increase the institutional complexity—not necessarily in terms of centrality, but definitely by adding legal or functional incoherence.

Such behavior would be in line with two types of causal mechanisms that different strands of neorealist theory in IR ascribe to powerful states. On the one hand, dissatisfied powerful states try to maximize their autonomy from the ailing GGI by seeking to leave, veto, or otherwise delegitimize it (see also Bäckstrand and Söderbaum, this volume). On the other hand, powerful states try to keep or enhance their influence, i.e. "the measure of control a state has over its international environment" (Baumann et al. 2001: 40). Establishing a rival institution is one strategy that would satisfy both needs. Moreover, powerful members may force or incentivize other actors to join in their strategies, adding to the effects of a legitimacy crisis.

These alternative GGIs are likely to have a decision structure that reflects the interests of the powerful states that pushed for their creation, for instance, taking the form of clubs where these states hold the majority of the votes (Karlsson-Vinkhuyzen and McGee 2013). Apart from decision making, the establishment of arrangements that favor the powerful may also extend to other governance functions like financing, implementation, and enforcement.

One empirical example that illustrates most of these theory-guided expectations is the creation of a series of new climate and energy institutions in the early 2000s. Intriguingly, these forums were established right after the US withdrawal from the Kyoto Protocol (cf. Eckersley 2007; Karlsson-Vinkhuyzen and van Asselt 2009). In June 2001, US president George W. Bush formally rejected the protocol, which he considered "fatally flawed" (White House 2001). With this assessment, Bush questioned the legitimacy of the protocol and United Nations (UN) climate negotiations in terms of poor performance (failing to avoid dangerous climate change), but also in terms of unfair and inefficient procedures (differentiating responsibilities among country groups and relying on top-down emissions targets) (Bodansky 2002: 1). Australia, a key member of the US-led coalition in climate negotiations, withdrew from Kyoto for the same reasons, and did not change its course until December 2007 under a new government (Lawrence 2009).

This double withdrawal marked a phase of severe legitimacy crisis for the UNFCCC. Harsh skepticism towards the GGI's procedural and performance-based legitimacy was paired with widespread perceptions that the UNFCCC had reached a critical point where it had to change fundamentally or be replaced. In July 2005, the Australian minister for environment and heritage, Ian Campbell, stated: "It's quite clear the Kyoto Protocol won't get the world to where it wants to go...We've got to find something that works better; Australia is working on that with partners from around the world" (International Herald Tribune, July 28, 2005). The withdrawal of two major emitters from the Kyoto Protocol, in turn, intensified the sense of a critical phase. Most remaining parties also reduced their support for the treaty (Eckersley 2015). The UNFCCC leadership responded with perseverance, but also denial. The president of the sixth Conference of the Parties to the UNFCCC, Jan Pronk, asserted after the withdrawal of the US and Australia that Kyoto was "the only game in town" (IISD 2001: 13).

Yet this was no longer the case. Several new climate governance institutions were created in the early 2000s that brought together member states and corporate actors, such as the Carbon Sequestration Leadership Forum (June 2003), the International Partnership for Hydrogen and Fuel Cells in the Economy (November 2003), and the Global Methane Initiative (November 2004). Further initiatives emerged after the Kyoto Protocol's entry into force, such as the (now defunct) Asia-Pacific Partnership on Clean Development and Climate (APP) in January 2006 and the Major Economies Process on Energy Security and Climate Change in September 2007 (McGee and Taplin 2009; Skodvin and Andresen 2009; Zelli 2011).

All of these forums fit the definition of transgovernmental networks (TGNs) used in this volume (Tallberg et al., this volume). They all have their head-quarters in Washington, DC and were also launched there, with the exception of the APP, which started in Sydney. None of these TGNs had more than twenty-five members at their founding stage, and until now they are mostly limited to industrialized countries and large emerging economies. Poorer countries like small island states or least-developed countries are excluded. The US, Australian, and Japanese governments bear a major part of the costs of these partnerships (van Asselt 2007; Brewer 2008).

Apart from adding more institutions to the global climate governance architecture, some of these minilateral initiatives were created as alternative models and rival forums to the UNFCCC, thus increasing institutional inco-herence in this domain. This goes in particular for the APP (van Asselt 2007). The above statement by Minister Campbell was made in conjunction with his informal announcement of the partnership, which was explicitly character-ized as a "Kyoto substitute" (International Herald Tribune, July 28, 2005). Likewise, Australian prime minister John Howard stated on several occasions that the APP is "significantly better than the Kyoto Protocol on reducing greenhouse gas emissions" (ABC News, May 20, 2007). Hence, the building of these new institutions involved a delegitimation of the UNFCCC, pointing at the mutual relationship between institutional complexity and legitimacy. Similarly, German environment minister Gabriel wondered at the time whether another club-like forum, the Major Economies Process, was intended to "halt the whole United Nations process in climate protection and go a special way" (EU Digest 2007).

A second type of causal pathway shows that it is not necessarily the most powerful states that push for the establishment of complementary or rival institutions. Following neoliberal institutionalist theory, and in particular a situation-structuralist approach (Zürn 1993), one can expect that highly asymmetric constellations of interest eventually generate a variety of institu-tional solutions (cf. Keohane and Victor 2011). They may especially do so if the incumbent core institution is perceived as weak or not legitimate.

Thus, non-hegemonic states and non-state actors might also be incentivized to establish alternative institutions. In such cases the main motivation is that these players cannot reach any considerable gains through an incumbent GGI. Decisions or reforms that would provide such benefits are blocked due to strong differences of preference among major groups of member states.

This interest-based causal pathway follows a rationalist logic of action as well. This notwithstanding, the main differences compared to the power-based causal pathway are: the broader realm of actors (not only states) and the motivations of the actors who care for absolute gains (how much do I get?) rather than relative gains (how much more or less than the others do I get?). Moreover, the chances of success may vary more, as they depend on the coalition-building efforts and available resources of these less powerful initiators. The resulting new institutions might become outright rivals of the leading GGI, but they may also just turn into insignificant side arenas.

One illustrative policy field is global energy governance. As Van de Graaf (2013) observes, the creation in 2009 of the International Renewable Energy Agency (IRENA) goes back to an asymmetry of preferences over the handling of renewable energy within the core GGI, the International Energy Agency (IEA). Countries with major renewables industries like Germany, Denmark, and Spain did not at the time perceive the IEA as a reliable forum to support research, development, and diffusion of these technologies. The perception of biased or unfair procedures and performances heightened over the years, leading to heated debates and mounting requests for programmatic reform of the core GGI. When this reform was held off, the three countries exploited the legitimacy crisis and, together with other IEA parties, established IRENA as an ambitious rival forum at the heart of an already complex institutional environment.

As previously noted, power-based and interest-based pathways to the creation of rival GGIs may also be complementary. A case in point is international trade governance, where the WTO is the core GGI. WTO regulations cover a wide range of issues beyond trade in goods, such as services, intellectual property rights, and sanitary measures. Moreover, these regulations are enforced by an unprecedented dispute settlement system (cf. van Asselt 2014).

Yet lack of progress in the WTO's Doha Round, initially scheduled for conclusion in 2005 but still ongoing, has led many to question the WTO's relevance as a global forum for trade negotiations. Meanwhile, bilateral and regional arrangements have grown dramatically as an alternative mode of trade governance. As of March 2017, 270 regional trade agreements were in force (WTO 2017c). These alternative arrangements vary considerably in their approaches to economic, social, and environmental issues. Moreover, many of them create further legal incoherence in the global trade architecture by failing to eliminate tariffs and regulations as requested by the WTO (WTO and UNEP 2016). The rise of bilateralism and regionalism raises questions about potential delegitimizing motivations and about consequences for the coherence of the global trade architecture.

These alternative agreements were formed by a large variety of states. As one of their main incentives, they referred to what they perceived to be an uncertain and insufficient performance of the WTO, making it necessary to ensure international rule making by other means, even if that meant going beyond WTO rules (Jinnah and Morgera 2013; Kellner 2016). Most of the bilateral trade agreements do not include trade hegemons, which suggests interest-based rather than power-based motivations behind them. Still, major trading powers like the US, the European Union (EU), and China were the main initiators of several prominent bilateral and so-called mega-regional trade agreements.

Such mega-regionals include, for instance, the Comprehensive Economic and Trade Agreement (CETA) between Canada and the EU, the Transatlantic Trade and Investment Partnership (TTIP), and the Trans-Pacific Partnership (TPP). It is an unresolved question whether the envisaged dispute-settlement mechanisms of these mega-regionals threaten the authority of the WTO and its Dispute Settlement Body (Schill 2017). However, TTIP and TPP face an uncertain future after the new US administration withdrew from negotiations in January 2017, showing that hegemonic behavior may change and not necessarily lead to further institution building.

Impacts of Legitimacy Crises on GGI Effectiveness

While the previous section discussed consequences of a core GGI's legitimacy crisis for its institutional environment, this section and the next concentrate on consequences of a legitimacy crisis for the GGI itself. The major pathways that lead from a GGI's legitimacy to its effectiveness are discussed in detail in Chapter 9. There, Sommerer and Agné distinguish between consequences for resources, policy output, compliance, and problem-solving effectiveness. The first repercussion, effects on resources, includes the willingness of political actors to participate as well as the physical and financial assets that are made available to an institution. The other three consequences relate to what the literature often characterizes as three stages of effective performance: namely, the norms produced by the core GGI (*output*); the GGI's behavioral effects on relevant actors (*outcome*); and the ultimate effectiveness of the GGI with regard to its subject matter (*impact*) (cf. Easton 1965; Tallberg et al. 2016b; Underdal 2004; Wolf 1991).

Sommerer and Agné (this volume) expect that a decline in legitimacy will reduce an institution's effectiveness in all of these areas, as reduced legitimacy discourages relevant actors from adopting, expanding, and following key rules and norms. In addition, these consequences are strongly linked to the institutional environment in which the GGI is embedded: "Those institutions which enjoy substantial legitimacy are more likely to be successful competitors, since they will be able to attract more resources and gain focal positions in their respective policy domains" (Sommerer and Agné, this volume).

Building on these insights, this section advances the hypothesis that *institutional complexity intensifies the detrimental consequences of a legitimacy crisis on a core GGI's output, outcome, and impact effectiveness.* Thus institutional complexity is a context variable, that is, a "phenomenon whose presence activates or magnifies the action of a causal law or hypothesis" (Van Evera 1997: 9–10).

How exactly can institutional complexity intensify effectiveness losses through a legitimacy crisis? The literature on regime complexes and polycentricity offers a few suggestions, including notions of forum shopping and forum shifting. Both imply consequences for all three types of effectiveness, but particularly an institution's output. Forum shopping involves playing one institution off against another as states and other actors seek to maximize their interests (Benvenisti and Downs 2007; Raustiala and Victor 2004). This strategy implies a certain acceptance of the core GGI, since actors change back and forth between institutions depending on what venue best suits their interests in a given case. With forum shifting, on the other hand, actors fully move to an alternative institution. For a core GGI, this is "a highly disintegrative strategy because it aims to disconnect negotiation forums" (Orsini 2013: 42; see also Helfer 2004, 2009).

Forum shopping and shifting reinforce the negative effects of a legitimacy crisis for institutional effectiveness. Neoliberal institutionalists suggest that major GGIs are normally attractive for key actors because they lower the transaction costs of cooperation (Keohane 1984, 1988). However, with the growth of alternative venues, other rationalist mechanisms like forum shopping and shifting come to the fore. The more alternatives, the easier it is for member states and other actors to change forums. Also, the diversity of choice hampers sustained interaction which creates a sense of common destiny among a given constellation of actors. This, in turn, diminishes some of the assumed effects of iterated games, like diffuse reciprocity (Scharpf 1997).

Global climate governance in the early 2000s well illustrates such dynamics. The various TGNs founded in this period, in particular the APP and the Major Economies Process, provided forum-shopping opportunities for states that were not satisfied with the Kyoto Protocol (Van Asselt 2007). By not differentiating between states in the burden sharing of emission reductions, and by favoring a bottom-up approach, these new fora constituted alternatives for the future of international climate politics.

The TGNs injected an element of competition into the governance architecture, and they reinforced the difficulties of the crisis-ridden UNFCCC process to reach significant output effectiveness, namely, a successor treaty to the Kyoto Protocol. By offering attractive alternatives, the TGNs further undermined the willingness of parties to join a new climate treaty that would continue to differentiate responsibilities between developing and developed countries. As a result, the 2009 Copenhagen climate summit failed to produce such a treaty, reinforcing the sense of a legitimacy crisis (Bodansky 2016; Falkner 2016).

Impacts of Legitimacy Crises on GGI Governance Mode

Finally, institutional complexity may reinforce the effects of a legitimacy crisis on the governance mode of a GGI. The notion of governance mode bundles different procedural dimensions of a GGI, i.e. overarching ways in which a GGI relates to its members when deciding, implementing, evaluating, or enforcing certain policies. The hypothesis that will be developed in this section states: *a core GGI undergoing a legitimacy crisis may increasingly rely on soft and indirect approaches, with institutional complexity further intensifying this trend.* This expectation is inspired by Abbott and colleagues (2015: 21), who predict such a tendency for those GGIs that lack "a high degree of taken-for-granted legitimacy vis-à-vis the targets of regulation or public goods production." In short, legitimacy (or its absence) is likely to affect a GGI's choice of governance mode.

Abbott and colleagues distinguish four types of governance modes based on two dimensions. The hard-soft dimension separates mandatory and enforceable rules from non-binding and self-regulating approaches. The direct-indirect dimension asks whether or not rules apply directly to target actors. "Indirect" suggests that the governing institution addresses target actors via a third party. Combining the two dimensions yields four ideal types of governance modes: hierarchy (direct and hard), collaboration (direct and soft), delegation (indirect and hard), and orchestration (indirect and soft) (Abbott et al. 2015: 9).

Across its various objectives and functions, an institution may use all four types of governance modes at the same time, albeit in particular mixes. But, as Abbott and colleagues observe, GGIs have far less capacity than states to adopt hard and direct rules: "States are reluctant to grant authority to [GGIs] to govern states hierarchically through binding international law with strong enforcement mechanisms" (2015: 11).

Add a legitimacy crisis to this default situation, and the perceived appropriateness of direct and hard governance dwindles further. A GGI whose authority is questioned by key audiences, such as major member states, can hardly expect acceptance of this intrusive type of governance. A crisis may thus further constrain a GGI's options.

This constraining effect may be stronger if the GGI operates in a complex institutional environment. In such an architecture, orchestration as a form of voluntary coordination may present an attractive alternative, in two ways. First, a complex environment means more competition. Dynamics of forum shopping and forum shifting will make it even less likely that hard and direct modes will be accepted from a GGI whose legitimacy is questioned. Skeptical governments and non-state actors will be tempted to turn to a readily available alternative that they consider more appropriate and less intrusive. In such a severe situation, orchestration—rather than the more intrusive options of collaboration and delegation—may offer a last resort for a GGI to keep governments and other actors from forum shopping. Second, a complex environment puts extra cross-institutional coordination demands on an already challenged GGI. Not surprisingly, a comparison of complex environmental governance architectures by Stokke and Oberthür finds that top-down cross-venue "coordination by overarching institutions appears difficult to realize" (2011: 316). Compared to the three other governance modes, orchestration offers the easiest alternative here, as it relies on less demanding coordination tasks such as serving as a clearing house or establishing overarching funding criteria for other initiatives.

Again, global climate governance offers examples of this dynamic. Following the failure of the 2009 Copenhagen summit, many state and non-state actors perceived the UNFCCC as incapable of reaching a new agreement, unless it would undergo a drastic change of direction (Victor 2016). This choice between change or disempowerment corresponds to Reus-Smit's "imperative to adapt" at the heart of a legitimacy crisis. What happened in the aftermath of Copenhagen can indeed be interpreted as a recalibration or reinvention. Instead of further promoting the hierarchical, top-down approach of binding targets for industrialized countries only, the UNFCCC secretariat and chairpersons at climate summits gave in to the demands of leading members and pragmatically embraced the polycentric nature of climate governance (van Asselt and Bößner 2016).

The legitimacy crisis, materializing in the growing resistance of a critical mass of member states against a continuation of the command-and-control approach, eventually forced the UNFCCC into an orchestrator role. Indeed, when the Paris Agreement was finally reached, it established a retreat solution in terms of governance mode. In several regards, it resembled the non-binding, non-discriminatory, and bottom-up elements of the APP and other institutional competitors (Falkner 2016). The agreement includes all state parties in its mitigation effort, but allows each member to set its own "nationally determined contributions," thus putting the design and output of obligatory greenhouse gas reduction measures mostly back into the hands of country governments.

The shift towards orchestration was observable already one year before Paris as two brief final examples illustrate. First, the Non-State Actor Zone for Climate Action (NAZCA) platform established a registry that gives the UNFCCC secretariat a system to keep track of commitments by a wide variety of non-state actors, including municipal and regional networks, private-led initiatives, investor networks, and public-private climate governance partnerships (Zelli and van Asselt 2015). Second, the Lima-Paris-Action Agenda, launched in 2014, encouraged new governance initiatives and became a major pillar in the Paris negotiations (van Asselt and Bößner 2016: 58–60).

Strikingly, this shift coincides with a new wave of minilateral initiatives that further add to cross-institutional collaboration rather than to incoherence. Unlike several of the climate clubs from the early 2000s, these recent initiatives are explicitly supportive of the UNFCCC. Some were even launched at UNFCCC conferences like the 2015 Paris summit, among them, the Carbon Pricing Leadership Coalition, convened by the World Bank, and the Mission Innovation, which pledged to double governmental investment in clean energy research and development by 2020. Recent years have also seen more coalition building by developing countries, mainly to cooperate with rather than to challenge the UN climate regime. One example is the International Solar Alliance, initiated by India, that seeks to enhance collaboration among state and non-state actors on the deployment of solar energy technologies (van Asselt and Bößner 2016).

If this trend continues, the shift of the UN climate regime towards a mode of orchestration may turn out to be effective crisis management. It may spur a new institutional division of labor which turns the previously delegitimating effect of institutional complexity (at least partly) into a legitimating one.

Conclusions

What are the consequences of having more or less legitimacy for GGIs competing in an increasingly complex institutional environment? To address this question, this chapter has explored the relationship between legitimacy crises and institutional complexity. The discussion has focused on possible implications of legitimacy crises on three dimensions of complex governance: the shape of the institutional architecture; the effectiveness of GGIs; and the governance mode of GGIs. The first hypothesis held that a legitimacy crisis may intensify the complexity of the surrounding architecture, by increasing incentives for dissatisfied audiences to build additional and rival institutions. The second and third hypotheses treated institutional complexity as a context variable that reinforces the impacts of a legitimacy crisis. Complexity further catalyzes effectiveness losses through forum shopping and selective compliance by states and other actors. Complexity may also reinforce shifts of weakened GGIs towards soft and indirect governance modes, as a strategy to stay relevant when lacking the authority and legitimacy necessary for hierarchical coordination.

These expectations have primarily been illustrated through developments in the area of global climate governance, where a legitimacy crisis caused the US to withdraw from the Kyoto Protocol and spurred the creation of competing minilateral GGIs in the form of TGNs. These rival institutions, in turn, may have reduced the output effectiveness of the UNFCCC, which eventually failed to reach a successor agreement to the Kyoto Protocol. As a consequence, the UNFCCC was forced to adapt both to mounting resistance against hierarchical solutions and to its growing institutional environment. The UNFCCC secretariat facilitated negotiations towards the state-driven Paris Agreement and moved increasingly towards orchestration as its principal governance mode. This chain of events also underlines the importance of analytically distinguishing between a legitimacy crisis and its consequences. The US withdrawal from Kyoto and the Copenhagen summit failure were each consequences of a prior legitimacy crisis, but once perceived as being critical turning points, they constituted crises that generated consequences in their own right.

Figure 10.1 summarizes the analytical framework with its three hypotheses. This visualization does not capture the overarching structural conditions in which these connections are embedded or the considerable reinforcement potential between legitimacy crisis and complexity. As Sommerer and Agné (this volume) argue, we have to picture a feedback loop leading from effectiveness loss back to the legitimacy crisis of a GGI. The complexity of this relationship indicates that more theoretical and empirical research is needed to identify the various mechanisms at work. I therefore conclude by suggesting three directions for future research inspired by the framework in this chapter.

First, these expectations need to be further detailed and subjected to empirical testing, including systematic comparison across cases. In the same vein, a research program on legitimacy-complexity dynamics could incorporate major scope conditions more thoroughly, such as constellations of power and interests, as well as cognitive, ideational, and discursive structures. With the help of associated theories, these conditions could be elaborated into further hypotheses and causal mechanisms. They would allow for richer multivariate analyses and for more informed insights on which factors are most influential for specific GGIs and their surrounding institutional complexes.

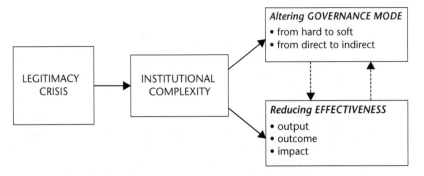

Figure 10.1. Summary of analytical framework

Second, as discussed in the introduction, this chapter pursued a relatively easy explorative path by focusing on the phenomenon of legitimacy crisis with its reasonably clear consequences. However, further research could enquire, conversely, whether a significant increase in a core GGI's legitimacy would lead to a decrease in institutional complexity. Or does the low mortality rate of GGIs render such an effect unlikely?

Third, researching legitimacy and institutional complexity may also provoke normative considerations. Is legitimacy a generally desirable property of a complex architecture, or does institutional complexity make trade-offs between legitimacy and effectiveness even harder to avoid? How can we craft sensible strategies to improve legitimacy in light of the many unintended consequences that a complex system entails?

These questions once more suggest that individual GGIs, their legitimacy, and their problem-solving effectiveness do not exist in a vacuum, but are part of and shaped by a broader institutional environment. Taking this embeddedness into account will make our analyses of the consequences of legitimacy more challenging, but also more accurate and policy-relevant.

Part V
Commentaries

11

Challenges in the Empirical Study of Global Governance Legitimacy

Steven Bernstein

This volume's sociological and comparative approach marks a major step forward in the empirical study of legitimacy in global governance. For at least twenty years, scholars have debated what intergovernmental and non-state institutions must do to gain or maintain legitimacy in response to crises, perceived legitimacy (especially democratic) deficits, or gridlock in global governance (e.g. Coicaud and Heiskanen 2001; Buchanan and Keohane 2006; Reus-Smit 2007; Hale et al. 2013). Yet, the diagnoses of legitimacy challenges and normative prescriptions to address them have not been matched by empirical analyses of "whether, why, how and with what consequences" global governance institutions (GGIs) gain or lose legitimacy in the first place (Tallberg et al., this volume). The contributions to this volume should be commended for their engagement with multiple strands of this debate, and concrete steps to generate answers to these questions. The volume thus marks a significant step forward in the sociological study of legitimacy in global governance.

Such an ambitious research program naturally comes with significant challenges. Here I focus on three: (1) differentiating political communities of legitimation, which may have varying mixes of audiences that constitute them, and the implications of those mixes for who matters, what gets legitimated, and with what consequences; (2) overcoming the trade-off of gains in empirical tractability achieved through a focus on actor strategies at the expense of attention to evolving norms and cultural factors that may underpin actors' expectations about what legitimacy requires; (3) theory building that can link legitimacy sources, (de)legitimation practices, audiences, and consequences of legitimacy across different types of institutions. After some conceptual ground clearing, I discuss each challenge, the strengths and limitations of the volumes' admirable efforts to address them, and implications for the broader research agenda I expect it to spark.

Conceptual Context: Sociological *and* Political

Whereas the approach to legitimacy in this volume is sociological, the type of legitimacy studied is *political*. Political legitimacy concerns governance and authority relationships. This focus deserves explicit attention since much of the extant sociological literature concerns legitimacy in non-political realms—e.g. organizations or firms that compete for legitimacy in the marketplace or society but are not public or political in the sense of the GGIs studied here. Even ostensibly "private" or hybrid institutions that the volume addresses—such as the Marine Stewardship Council (MSC) or the Internet Corporation for Assigned Names and Numbers (ICANN)—have a public or political aspect. They claim authority—and thereby require political legitimacy—to govern some type of public good or concern as opposed to provide a rule, good, or service for the private benefit or ends of its members (Bernstein 2014). Thus while much can be learned from the sociological literature on legitimation, the distinction between its traditional focus on appropriateness and political legitimacy's focus on rule brings with it important stakes. Political legitimization always involves some giving up (or over) of autonomy. Thus, despite contributors' assiduous avoidance of "making theoretical-normative judgments about legitimacy and the right to rule," normative implications cannot be far removed from the study of GGIs, even if research is focused on legitimacy as it is as opposed to how it ought to be (Bäckstrand and Söderbaum, this volume).

A second implication of a sociological approach to political legitimacy is the importance of power. In that regard, the premise of the volume, that legitimacy is functional for the smooth operation of global governance, contains a duality. Inis Claude, the scholar most associated with introducing the study of legitimacy to international relations, put it well: Legitimacy can make rulers "more secure in the possession of power and more successful in its exercise" (Claude 1966: 368). Like Max Weber (1922/1978), Claude emphasized that legitimacy, by linking power and authority, can be looked at from two perspectives. Not only can it support authority necessary for order, but by making it acceptable and appropriate in the eyes of the community granting legitimacy, it may reinforce underlying power relationships. The volume's focus on legitimation and delegitimation and sensitivity to who matters—audiences or constituencies who can grant, withhold, or undermine legitimacy—opens up questions of power, voice, and the substance of what gets legitimated. The next stage of research might explore even further these issues using the frameworks introduced here.

Problem of Political Community and Diversity of Audiences

Perhaps the most difficult research challenge for sociological approaches to legitimacy in global governance is the problem of political community, that is, who "matters" in legitimating the authority of GGIs. I self-consciously use the term political community because it is the language generally used by political theorists when discussing who is subject to authority and who must generate the legitimacy required for that authority. The reason community matters is simple; political legitimacy at its most basic is a condition under which *"people who are subject to and affected by a governing framework* perceive its exercise of authority to be appropriate" (Tallberg et al., this volume; italics added). Who the "people" are, what counts as "affected," and how they are constituted by legitimating audiences—the empirical focus for the chapters in this volume— pose significant research challenges because they vary widely in composition, power, and relevance across institutions and geographies. Their composition has important implications not only for questions of voice, influence, and accountability, but also for what gets legitimated and with what consequences, as illustrated in the chapter by Bexell and Jönsson. The volume not only tackles these questions, but by design opens up the question of the relationship between abstract notions of political community and the mixes of audiences that might comprise them by focusing on the full range of GGIs— intergovernmental *and* non-state and hybrid institutions—across issue areas of security, economic, and sustainable development governance.

When Claude in the 1960s famously wrote about the "collective legitimization" function of the United Nations, or Henry Kissinger highlighted legitimacy's importance for international stability, the answer to the community question seemed obvious. Sovereign states—mainly the great powers at that— constituted the audience that mattered; legitimation of shared rule occurred essentially through a consensus among them (Kissinger 1957; Claude 1966). The world has clearly changed, even as scholarship on international legitimacy has taken some time to catch up (e.g. compare Franck 1990 and Hurd 2007 with Held and Koenig-Archibugi 2005, Seabrooke 2007, and Bernstein 2011). As the volume's editors put it, "In today's more globalized world politics, legitimacy for GGIs comes not only from governments, but also from civil society organizations, business associations, political parties, media channels, and ordinary citizens" (Tallberg et al., this volume).

When particular groups matter, though, or under what conditions and with what effects on the authority or resilience of that institution, or their "affected" audiences, is a complicated issue.

The chapter by Bexell and Jönsson tackles the question head on. Their primary goal is to understand how what Seabrooke (2007) calls the "social constituency of legitimation" is constituted. Their first cut at an answer is to draw a distinction between constituencies ("audiences with institutionalized political bonds to a governing authority") and observers (who lack such connections) and between GGI-targeted and self-appointed audiences. These neat divisions, in place of the array of overlapping categories that characterizes the existing literature on political communities, provide useful analytical leverage to investigate "who matters" in granting legitimacy and where to focus attention when looking at how legitimacy is buttressed or undermined.

Determining who "matters" within and between these categories is trickier, since as institutions become more visible or their effects are felt by different communities, audiences' engagement in practices of legitimation and delegitimation clearly influences whether they matter or not for granting or contesting legitimacy. Similarly, who feels affected is not only directly related to what the institution does (its policies and everyday practices), but also who perceives a stake, the reach of the institution, and the chains of accountability. For example, principals who may be the immediate constituency of legitimation (e.g. governments in the case of international organizations) may accept the institution's authority but face pressure from their own legitimating constituencies (citizens) if the institution appears to them to violate its mandate, scope, procedures (including accountability), or functions. Such disjunctures can be expected to put pressure on the formal boundaries of constitutive and observer audiences, but boundary shifts that result through modified voting procedures or new accountability arrangements may or may not coincide with abstract notions of the political community, if defined by notions such as "affected" people.

Legitimacy challenges to the International Monetary Fund (IMF) and the World Bank in the late 1990s and early 2000s illustrate such tensions (Tussie, this volume). Legitimacy challenges not only from their "constituency" (especially developing countries) but also challenges to accountability from observer audiences within states forced these institutions to reconsider their voting structure. These changes came about not only because of the increased reach of IMF and World Bank programs into what had been considered domestic policy domains, but also because civil society groups, including in funding states, put pressure on their own governments to press for changes in these institutions' policies and practices. Seabrooke (2007) has highlighted that the response of GGIs to shift boundaries of these audiences, at least in the case of the IMF, are fraught with complications. He argues that the attempt to expand what he calls the "social constituency of legitimation" by creating new initiatives to directly address domestic audiences affected by IMF discipline created a mismatch with the IMF's core legitimating principle of sovereign non-interference on which rightful membership is based. Seabrooke recommended instead that the IMF focus more on improving deliberation with member states, including through regional or like-minded groups of officials, experts, and stakeholders such as non-governmental organizations (NGOs), private interests, and trade unions. Whether or not one agrees with Seabrooke's diagnosis or recommendation, this example highlights the challenge of working with these categories and the importance in analyzing the consequences of shifts in the boundaries between constituencies and observers: the lack of fit between legitimating principles, an expanding realm of GGI action, and the misfired attempt to change institutional arrangements to redefine (or recognize changes in) constituencies who grant legitimacy can as easily exacerbate as ameliorate legitimacy challenges.

Bexell and Jönsson articulate a twofold strategy for empirical research to address the dilemma of shifting boundaries: recognize that "constituency" and "observer" audiences are not given a priori, and focus on practices. The first insight is helpful, but over and understates the research challenge. It overstates the problem (which is good news for empirical research) because expectations about who should be recognized as constituents is closely related to what GGIs actually do compared to the overall audience's normative expectations or perceptions of what GGIs ought to be doing based on existing institutional bonds. Disjunctures can often be "read" empirically off of media accounts, official statements, and debates in political forums that identify new expectations around who should be included as a relevant audience of legitimation, be it state or non-state actors or citizens and elites. While such work requires interpretation, it may not be especially controversial empirically since such pressures to address mismatches between political action by GGIs and legitimating audiences often results in explicit attempts at institutional reform to recognize new constituents or changing arrangements (voting weights, decision-making structures, accountability mechanisms) among current constituents. Returning to the example of international financial institutions, the composition and scope of those included in shifting constituencies of legitimation did not arise overnight. Rather, they evolved both because of a new set of programs that extended hard rules or conditions into new areas of domestic policy and because these changes occurred at a time when global pressures and support to democratize global governance was on the rise (e.g. Held 1995; Zürn 2000; Payne and Samhat 2004). The precise reasons for these pressures are varied and debated—including the Cold War's end, globalization, civil society campaigns, and growing sense of a democratic deficit in GGIs and Europe in particular. However, reference to these trends is easily identifiable empirically in official documents and debates.

The bad news for empirical research is that Bexell and Jönsson understate how much these audiences may differ depending on the GGI in question. This is not simply a matter of functional scope or governmental versus non-governmental, but also of expectations around the type of legitimacy that is relevant as well as which audiences the GGI views as relevant or believes can materially hurt or empower it. With intergovernmental organizations, some audiences easily map onto the "constituency/observer" categories. For example, states (governments) are important constituents because they fund, vote, and oversee GGIs formally accountable to them. While traditional hierarchical lines of accountability are fundamental to legitimacy, other chapters in the volume highlight that delegitimation may come from discontent outside or further up these chains. Focusing too much on the division between constituencies and observers risks missing how *who matters*, and why, may change even if formal lines of accountability do not, or why pressures may mount to change those lines of accountability.

Meanwhile, non-state institutions generally require tighter links to their audiences because their legitimacy is less given. Their core constituency is often corporate actors in the sectors they aim to regulate and sometimes civil society groups with an interest in the pursuit of the GGI's mandate, especially in the social and environmental areas (e.g. sustaining forests or fisheries or promoting labor or human rights). Those GGIs that directly aim to regulate the market may also require legitimation from less organized "observers"— such as consumers or wider publics—who may be largely passive but can influence an organization through public opinion or market behavior (boycotts, consumer behavior). It's no surprise that the International Organization for Standardization (ISO) sees its core constituency as national standard-setting associations made up largely of industry players affected by the standards and governments who are responsible for the regulatory environment in the countries where these industries operate. However, when demands increase to take into account additional values—as they did in the cases of the ISO 14000 series of environmental standards or the newer ISO 26000 "guideline" standard on corporate social responsibility (CSR)—the ISO had to institutionally adapt its decision-making structures (to accept greater input from civil society groups and public consultations). In effect, these changes simply recognized the shifting boundary between constituents and observers (Hahn and Weidtmann 2016).

More complicated still is when outside groups or changing circumstances act to shift audiences. For example, Gregoratti and Uhlin in their excellent chapter point out that, "In certain circumstances, protests may in fact unsettle prevalent understandings of who grants legitimacy, potentially constituting new significant audiences." One line of research suggested by their analysis could involve identifying conditions under which GGIs react to or ignore such efforts. One might hypothesize, for example, that GGIs marginalize or criminalize such protests at their peril when they are linked to changing norms of participation or to shifting practices or policies of GGIs that reach or directly affect new audiences. Examples of GGIs' responses to such pressures include an ongoing series of World Trade Organization (WTO) transparency initiatives over the last fifteen years, the World Bank's introduction of new accountability mechanisms, including the Inspection Panel in 1993 (where communities and individuals adversely affected by projects can launch complaints) and the more recent introduction of a Grievance Redress Service (where complaints can be brought directly to World Bank management). Gregoratti and Uhlin's example of the Asian Development Bank's (ADB) expansion of consultation processes reflects similar dynamics. Whatever their efficacy, these reforms recognize wider social audiences of legitimacy to stave off delegitimation.

On audience constitution, Bexell and Jönsson argue that audiences are "constructed" through "practices," both their own and the GGIs' who target particular audiences for legitimation. Their extensive discussion of power dynamics in such practices is instructive, and modest, self-consciously raising more questions than they can answer. Perhaps the most uncomfortable question of all—which cannot be directly addressed within a strictly sociological approach—is "who matters" compared to "who should matter." A number of contributors observe that resources to participate or GGI targeting of particular elites to represent constituencies of legitimation has implications for what gets legitimated or perceptions of legitimacy. These observations inevitably raise questions of whether the processes, chains of accountability, or recognition of audiences in theory matches actual practices, and with what consequences for governance outcomes. It also points to the need for sensitivity to how such power dynamics may bias research findings, if, for example, research strategies inadvertently reinforce such biases by surveying groups of "elites" or "citizens" based on predefined categories that ignore differences in engagement, expert knowledge, or cultural, gender, or class backgrounds. Failure to take these factors into account in evaluating their responses might skew understandings of how or why individuals view GGIs as legitimate or not, as discussed in Dellmuth's chapter in this volume.

Interaction of Strategies and Norms

The volume's focus on practices of legitimation and delegitimation—and the discursive, institutional, and behavioral strategies in pursuit of them—is one of its signal contributions (Bäckstrand and Söderbaum, this volume). The advantages for empirical research to such an approach are many, not least the observability of such strategies. Nonetheless, the volume's almost exclusive focus on actors, with the exception of Scholte's chapter (5) on social structure, has trade-offs, including much less attention to the institutional and normative environment in which they act (cf. Bernstein 2011).

The impulse to focus on process over structure is understandable. It "brings attention to the role of actors, practices and strategies in the acquisition, maintenance, contestation, and transformation of legitimacy" (Bäckstrand and Söderbaum, this volume). It also resonates with recent work on international practices (Adler and Pouliot 2011b); taking more seriously that literature's understanding of practices as "competent performances" offers one fruitful way to correct the imbalance toward agency because it can bring into play expectations around which types of practices are "competent" in legitimating or delegitimating an institution. Competency is often tied to norms or expectations of the communities who grant or withhold legitimacy or to "background knowledge" (Adler and Pouliot 2011b). Thus, practices link both to the dispositions of actors in terms of their perceptions of legitimacy (which can inform their motivations to support or withdraw support from an institution) and also define the types of strategies and reasons or arguments at their disposal. As Bäckstrand and Söderbaum put it, favorably citing Adler and Pouliot (2011a: 4–5), studying (de)legimation as a social practice, while including strategic acts of political performance, transcends a strict focus on intention because they involve "dynamic material and ideational processes that enable structures to be stable or to evolve, and agents to reproduce or transform structures" (Bäckstrand and Söderbaum, this volume).

This formulation also points to the social embeddedness of practices (i.e. the link to "background knowledge"), attention to which is largely missing from the volume's research strategy, even as a number of chapters recognize its importance in theory. As Chapter 1 points out, recognition of social embeddedness "opens up spaces for actors to draw on prevailing norms to shape legitimacy perceptions" (Tallberg et al., this volume). I thus encourage future research to fully exploit this opening to explore the links between (de)legitimation practices and the broader normative and institutional environment that gives them meaning.

Such an approach is also consistent with recent scholarship on international institutions, norms, and practices, which, in different ways, view GGIs as embedded in normative environments in which they compete for legitimacy and in which audiences generate expectations of what they should be doing (Dingwerth and Pattberg 2009, Bernstein 2011, 2014; Raymond and DeNardis 2015; Abbott et al. 2016). Thus, actors that challenge the legitimacy of an institution are likely to draw on these norms or expectations, which in turn are often linked to sources of legitimacy.

For example, the legitimacy crisis that hit the WTO in 1999 did not necessarily challenge its mission. Rather, civil society campaigns targeted practices that did not fit with the WTO's own legitimacy claims or with broader evolving normative expectations around GGIs in the 1990s. These demands stemmed from mismatches between the WTO's self-perception as a largely legal and technical organization on one hand, and normative expectations around sovereignty, democracy, accountability, and legal process in regard to affected publics on the other. Thus, civil society groups especially took issue with its dispute-settlement system, which had more authority than the pre-1994 system under the General Agreement on Tariffs and Trade (GATT) and increasingly ruled on allegedly "behind the border" trade barriers that could include areas such as environmental regulation. Specific demands included greater access to information, avenues for civil society interaction, and legal reforms such as the ability to submit amicus briefs when disputes could have wider societal implications.

Perhaps with some irony, the WTO currently faces delegitimation from an unlikely source, the United States, previously a staunch defender of legalization of the trade regime. The Trump Administration is drawing on the reascendance of sovereignty norms to justify holding up the appointment of new members of the Appellate Body, effectively putting the legalized dispute-resolution system in jeopardy (Elsig et al. 2017).

Both examples illustrate my broader point, that drawing connections between shifts in expectations around appropriate sources of legitimacy to strategies of actors may be one of the most important and interesting set of findings from this project. This means realigning/connecting research on practices of legitimation, the sources of legitimacy, and the normative and institutional environment of GGIs. Bäckstrand and Söderbaum anticipate this move when they write about discursive practices, stating that, "[i]n many cases, legitimating agents make explicit associations between themselves and commonly perceived sources of legitimacy, such as the purported democratic credentials, technocratic standards, and fairness of a governing institution" (Bäckstrand and Söderbaum, this volume).

Putting the Pieces Together

Taken on their own, each section of the volume contributes a strong conceptual toolkit for the sociological study of legitimacy in global governance. For example, in Part II, Scholte and Tallberg's Table 4.1 on institutional sources of legitimacy smartly synthesizes and extends extant scholarship, which opens the door for empirical investigations of what different audiences may actually demand of GGIs to grant them legitimacy. The six institutional features they derive (democratic procedure, democratic performance, technocratic procedure, technocratic performance, fair procedure, and fair performance) nicely capture most key categories in more unwieldy sociological and normative typologies. Importantly, they also create operationalizable categories appropriate for comparative empirical work. While one might quibble that such typologies can overplay the divisibility of these features in practice, it is compelling that different GGIs vary across these features in how they make authority claims.

Similarly, treating sources of legitimacy (Part II), processes of legitimation and delegitimation (Part III), and consequences of legitimacy (Part IV) separately makes good initial sense from a research design perspective. Part II addresses the empirical question—often taken for granted—of what actors look for in assessing whether to accept an institution as appropriate, while Part III takes the acceptance or contestation of the institution as a starting point to ask how actors engage in (de)legitimation to reinforce or undermine perceptions of legitimacy. Part IV similarly separates evaluations of legitimacy (dealt with in Parts II and III) from its consequences.

Still, the introduction of separate typologies of sources and (de)legitimation practices, the latter in Chapter 6, raises the question of whether the two could be productively linked in future research. On its face, researching (de)legitimation practices can be agnostic as to the sources of legitimacy targeted. Yet, intuitively, identifying the sources of legitimacy should tell us something about how institutions gain and lose legitimacy, especially if both sources of legitimacy and practices of (de)legitimation are socially embedded. That is, what practices are likely to work and what and who they target may depend very much on the sources of legitimacy relevant for a particular GGI. Similarly, the likelihood of successful legitimation or delegitimation likely depends in part on the audiences targeted (or that engage) in legitimation or delegitimation practices who may view particular sources as more or less important. Thus, the very sets of institutional features identified by Scholte and Tallberg (this volume) that may explain variation in sources of legitimacy (e.g. degree of authority, institution type or function, legitimating audience characteristics, shifts in legitimating norms over time) may be central to developing hypotheses on which strategies are likely to work or when we are likely to see legitimacy challenges. As they rightly point out, "[identifying] characteristics of the GGIs themselves that can underpin or undermine audience perceptions of GGIs' legitimacy . . . is important not least because it identifies circumstances that members and staff of GGIs can address with strategies to enhance the legitimacy of their organization in the eyes of its audiences" (Scholte and Tallberg, this volume). The inverse is equally plausible—this focus can identify circumstances that delegitimating agents may exploit in their strategies if they perceive legitimacy deficits linked to alternative sources of legitimacy salient for relevant audiences of legitimation.

The payoff in such synthesis could be hypotheses that cut across the volume's themes. Indeed, many of the volume's rich empirical examples already hint at such linkages. For example, one simple hypothesis is that *discursive legitimacy challenges are more likely to succeed when they successfully highlight disjunctures between sources of legitimacy on which a GGI bases its authority and practices of the GGI.* Or, in the language of practices, discursive delegitimation strategies are advantageous when GGIs perform legitimacy "incompetently."

African governments' criticism of the International Criminal Court (ICC) "for allegedly failing to resolve conflicts, for imposing 'double standards,' and for being inconsistent with domestic laws" is of this type (Bäckstrand and Söderbaum, this volume).

A related hypothesis is that *strategies of (de)legitimation generally will be more likely to succeed when they adapt to or exploit disjunctures that arise between legitimacy sources and changed circumstances or shocks that shift the boundaries between constituents and observers.* Something like this process arguably occurred in the case of climate change, where the 2015 Paris Agreement now explicitly recognizes the role of non-state and sub-state actors in achieving its goals. This institutional legitimation practice reflected changed material circumstances where cities, partnerships, foundations, etc. had been acting on climate change while multilateral institutional arrangements focused on formal national commitments floundered, thus pressure mounted to recognize their role and status (Bäckstrand et al. 2017). This, and other features of the Paris agreement also support two of Zelli's propositions (this volume) on consequences of legitimacy challenges. One likely consequence, he argues, is increased institutional complexity; another is that core GGIs, such as the United Nations Framework Convention on Climate Change (UNFCCC), may increasingly rely on soft and indirect modes of governance such as orchestration.

At the same time, attention to broader norms would highlight that shifting practices of law encouraged greater participation of non-state actors, especially when they are relevant for implementation. One sees a similar pattern with the new Sustainable Development Goals (SDGs) (Bexell and Jönsson, this volume; Bernstein 2017). These trends are even more amplified in non-state governance arenas, such as environmental and social standard setting, where "thicker" consensus among stakeholders and practices of "publicness" are increasingly expected (Pauwelyn et al. 2014; Raymond and DeNardis 2015; Bernstein 2014). The above hypothesis similarly provides insight into the case of the Southern African Development Community (SADC) (Bäckstrand and Söderbaum, this volume), where withdrawal of support occurred when those expectations of stakeholder participation were not met.

The corollary is that GGIs well matched to broader norms may be resilient in response to pressures for change because they "fit" with that broader normative environment (Bernstein 2011). To be clear, returning to normative and power arguments raised earlier, durable does not necessarily mean good—resilience may reflect resources to strategically adapt and the norms and discourses that legitimate them may reflect or reinforce unequal power relationships. For example, while some transnational and regional civil society groups, especially those who adhere to a justice discourse, challenge "neoliberalism," many GGIs associated with neoliberal policies and practices have successfully maintained legitimacy, even as they respond to delegitimation practices by shifting their procedures or mode of authority. For example, Jacqueline Best has documented how the IMF and World Bank have shifted over the last decade to a governing strategy centered on "best practices" and flexible standards in global development policy as opposed to law-like rules that seemed to dictate neoliberal policies. The new strategy, she argues, provides a way for these GGIs to relegitimate their missions and promote the "universal value of their institutions' efforts" (Best 2014: 116; Broome and Seabrooke, 2012).

The IMF example, like the example of the US challenge to the WTO appellate body mentioned earlier, highlight that the links between legitimacy and its consequences for GGIs and their problem-solving effectiveness may not be linear. Sommerer and Agné's chapter (this volume) take an important first step by analytically separating audience beliefs from four possible consequences of legitimacy (resources, policy outputs, compliance, and problem-solving effectiveness). They also provide some propositions on how those four consequences might interact (e.g. attracting more resources may increase problem-solving effectiveness). However, returning to the IMF and WTO examples suggests further insights and propositions can be developed from the work on sources of legitimacy and practices as developed in the other sections of the volume. As Best (2014) shows, the IMF has been very successful in developing new legitimating strategies following what was arguably a legitimacy crisis in the 1990s and early 2000s (when it even looked for a while like its services were less needed). Its ability to weather those delegitimation challenges (continuing to attract resources, finding new ways to generate compliance, etc.) is arguably linked to relegitimation strategies sensitive to its root sources of legitimacy but reformulated: e.g. sovereign non-interference reformulated as country ownership and from technical expertise to a focus on standards, benchmarks, and best practice. Whether the WTO can similarly adapt in the face of changing beliefs from a powerful member of its core constituency is an open question.

The comparative nature of legitimacy and legitimation so excellently explored in this volume provides a way forward to generate even more theoretical linkages and refinements across sources, practices, the normative and institutional environments in which GGIs operate, and consequences, as discussed in different sections of the volume. As empirical work gets underway and forces further conversations among those themes and insights, the promise is enormous for both the contributors and others inspired by this volume for major advances in research on legitimacy and legitimation in global governance.

12

Bringing Power and Markets In

Diana Tussie

The concepts of legitimacy and legitimation have been central to political theory since the writings of Max Weber. Legitimacy gives meaning to authority and is instrumental to the effectiveness of political systems. In modern liberal societies, legitimacy constitutes the foundation of democratic life. In global governance institutions (GGIs), legitimacy is primarily the result of the relationship between actors, processes, and institutions, as perceived by the audiences, be it states, non-state actors, or individuals. As is clear when reading the chapters in this book, there are plenty of reasons to debate how legitimacy and legitimation sustain contemporary global governance. Chapter 1 (Tallberg et al.) states upfront that while legitimacy bolsters GGIs, it is not static and can decline and needs to be maintained and regained. And there is every reason to think that change will be accelerating.

An institution is legitimate when its authority is accepted as appropriate, and worthy of support by relevant audiences. In a sociological sense, legitimacy will vary across audiences and issue areas and over time. But who are the relevant audiences in global governance? As Dellmuth fleshes out in her chapter on individual sources of legitimacy beliefs, preferences and context matter. We have long struggled with the problem of cultural diversity or time-bound beliefs, such as in the debates about child and labor rights, human rights, or gender issues. The social embeddedness of legitimacy beliefs means that the universal does not actually have a transcendental voice for us. Each of us enters debates on legitimacy with a sense for the different challenges we face. How then can we grapple with the question of legitimacy when the liberal order is itself under challenge from within *and* without? As academics we are aware of popular discontent and have sought to quell public skepticism and even fears of GGIs. We need to do more to capture the simmering conflict. It is at this point that I want to start my reflections.

The commentary will advance in two sections. The first will address the influence of geopolitical change on legitimacy beliefs vis-à-vis GGIs. My argument for this section is that in times of transition the sources of legitimacy, which are examined in Part II of this volume, are themselves sites of contestation. Contestation is a point this book makes loud and clear. With the exception of Scholte's chapter on societal sources of legitimacy, the book is generally agnostic on deeper structural interpretations on what shapes legitimacy and legitimation of global governance. The line of my own argument is that global power transitions expose limits to the liberal order and intimate a return of contestation of geopolitics.

The second section will argue that we need to bring markets into the picture. The emergence of legitimacy concerns is reflective of the changing nature of global governance structures that go beyond the nation-state. The legitimacy of global governance is fragile partly because it is believed to be stacked in favor of markets. Private and market actors' preferences have dominated the representation of interests in multilateral negotiation and decision making. Legitimacy of GGIs in this conjuncture requires that domestic governance is not totally set off track by international markets. It requires the space for countries to achieve a social bargain in which people are protected and markets are "embedded" (Ruggie 1982) or, at the very least, restrained in such a way that international market actors do not gain disproportionate influence at the expense of the public. I will focus my commentary on intergovernmental GGIs, but the argument is equally applicable to non-state and hybrid GGIs. For example, the Bill and Melinda Gates Foundation illustrates how the influence of monopolistic market giants-turned-philanthropists able to arbitrate the political environment in such organizations as the World Health Organization (WHO) raises increasingly visible dilemmas in global governance. More broadly, the discussion brings to light the legitimacy problem associated with wealth distribution. As Harman (2016) shows, the legitimacy problem here is twofold: first, with regard to the criteria used to assess the presence or absence of legitimacy in global governance; and, second, how analysis of legitimacy does not fully account for how we understand the legitimate basis of rule drawn from private wealth.

Geopolitics

Chapter 2 by Agné argues that in global politics reflections on legitimacy have grown among scholars previously concerned with global democracy. Legitimacy has in recent years often supplemented, and sometimes replaced, the concept of democracy in accounts of global governance. In my view, this shift must be understood against the backdrop of an ideological shift in global governance. The ideational underpinnings of the GGIs are imbued with the Western ideal of legitimacy, particularly after the fall of the Berlin Wall which appeared to demonstrate the historical possibility of peaceful change and substantive agreement on societal ends sought.

To take a step back in the argument, during the Cold War, for example, global governance had provided a venue for legitimating power by member states. The paradigm of security, for one, was closely tied up with the concept of *national* security. It faded rapidly in the early 1990s as the risk of nuclear war between the two superpowers disappeared. There was a turn to more liberal practices freed from the ropes of ideological conflict and Cold War rivalry. Many saw the emergence of human rights and the responsibility to protect as a constitutional moment (Kennedy 2008). Liberal economic and political ideas gained ground around the world as country after country from Eastern Europe to the developing world were also following the path of liberal economic reform. Bill Clinton, the charismatic "globalist," was in the White House leading the world twinning free markets and democracy.

The primacy of the Western worldview gave GGIs substantive legitimacy and power. Liberalism gained force in the prominence given to markets, trade, democratic governance, human rights, the rule of law, and good governance. There was a rise in pluralism and new audiences of GGIs as civil society activists gained ground in achieving changes in the global governance, such as debt relief, access to essential medicines, the curtailing of a multilateral agreement on investment and the banning of landmines.

In parallel to the shifting geopolitics of the post-Cold War a new framework of appropriate global governance developed and took hold. The concept of security, for instance, was reworked. Security should aim to protect and empower populations. It materialized in the United Nations Development Programme (UNDP) benchmark report *New Dimensions of Human Security*. Likewise, the new geopolitics enabled widespread contestation and delegitimation of Bretton Woods institutions which came under fire because of stabilization and adjustment claimed to have served the interests of American banks and to have resulted in the "lost decade" in developing countries. Here again, there was a window of opportunity for the UNDP to challenge the legitimacy of the austerity policies.

The *Human Development Report* produced under the inspiration of Amartya Sen and the leadership of Mahbub ul Haq installed the value of freedom over that of austerity. Human development was meant to expand freedom. The conception of development became less centered on state policies and more on people. With the de-escalation of conflict, the United Nations also became an advocate for democracy, a subject that had remained out of bounds and out of sight throughout the Cold War. Each of these revisions was an effort to retrofit global governance to the moment and sustain the legitimacy of GGIs (Thérien 2015). Liberalism reigned supreme.

At the beginning of the twenty-first century the structural dynamic has grown combative again. In this milieu the vision of an overarching common good has faded. While previous research had emphasized the contestation and delegitimation performed by non-state actors, this book shows that today GGI staff and member states also engage in delegitimation practices, for instance, by withdrawing from membership, articulating public criticism, or creating rival institutions (Bäckstrand and Söderbaum, this volume; Gregoratti and Uhlin, this volume; Zelli, this volume). The declining economic power of the West and the rising clout of China and other emerging countries have in fact eroded the public legitimacy of many GGIs constructed in the postwar and Cold War era. Dissatisfaction with the limitations of the liberal cosmopolitan vision is increasingly heard in policy circles accompanied by nationalistic and populist overtones. As Dellmuth elaborates in this volume, perceptions of GGI legitimacy relate to circumstances of the audience, their ideological leanings, and their degrees of political awareness. Instead of the end of history, what we see is that the revenge of revisionist powers was galvanized to delegitimize financial GGIs.

The 2008 global financial crisis became a wake-up call for revisionist powers—new and old—that are economically, politically, and culturally different to established powers. What came to the fore were financial excesses and bursting financial bubbles. Rules were no longer seen to be right and just in the view of developing countries in the Global South. These rules by economic GGIs propagated disequilibria rather than order and hence rulers had no right to paternalism in the eyes of developing countries. It became unacceptable to be at the receiving end of such rules and having to prove one's worth in such institutions.

The legitimacy crisis for economic GGIs turned out to be a transformative event. It offered political momentum to the group of countries coming together as BRIC (Brazil, Russia, India and China), until then a mere asset class of the four biggest emerging economies put together in 2001 by Jim O' Neill, chairman of Goldman Sachs. O'Neill's category morphed into a formal association with the blowout, eight years later. It shook the mode of BRIC from external (marginal) role adscription to assume ownership and a shared aspiration to change the outsized role of the United States in GGIs. Running high on that wave, BRIC held their founding summit in 2009 in Yekaterinburg in Russia. In a short communiqué they made clear that they would move together "to advance the reform of financial GGIs, so as to reflect changes in the world economy . . . We also believe that there is a strong need for a stable, predictable and more diversified international monetary system" (BRIC 2009).

Taken one by one some of these countries have not lived up to expectations. Russia and Brazil have both fallen into recession, while China, the principal engine of world growth, has seen a sharp contraction in overall economic activity. Brazil's economic woes were compounded by corruption and the impeachment of Dilma Rousseff (Hopewell 2017). But there is no doubt that strategic cooperation continues with China in the lead, intent on rebalancing the voice in GGIs with its relative economic weight and significant political power.

The vigorous revival of geopolitics falls into this context of countries fighting for redefinition and assertion. This occurred long before Brexit and long before Trump announced a wall to keep off migrants, threatened to invade Venezuela, and to withdraw from migration, trade, and climate agreements. In fact, the turn of the ruling elite in many countries to unconstrained economic and political nationalism is not unrelated to the arrival of new actors. Deinstitutionalization, new divides, and a more ideology-prone world reappears, requiring states to reassess how they conduct themselves in the storm. An important theme within the foreign policy imaginary of, for instance, Russia, turns on the idea of a country that "other countries do not respect as fully they should, a country that is not given its due" (Guzzini 2013: 229).

Nationalism is not only the preserve of would-be great powers (Hurrell 2006), but also for Trump-like geopolitics wanting to show off raw power. The successes and failures of contention are not always measured, for instance, by whether the wall is finally built or the invasions thwarted but by the new tone in GGIs and the very real possibility of enforcing "take it or leave it" procedures to settle conflict. The essential point is that there are real conflicts that unsettle popular and elite beliefs in the legitimacy of GGIs. Conflicts have amplified the pull of geopolitical rivalry to redress "universal" norms that have multiplied from current power holders who fear disruption of their control and authority and from respondents with newly gained awareness and drive. The mismatch is threatening because both sides frame their demands in terms of legitimacy even if they can be transparently self-serving. The argument is that in times when a significant number of countries are rethinking their strategic positioning in the world, the sources of legitimacy are themselves a site of contestation which then makes legitimacy very often indeterminate and not obvious.

As the volume shows there is a wide spectrum of legitimation and delegitimation practices, which is classified as discursive, institutional, and behavioral. In this vein, as liberal optimism fades, contested conceptions may become a central feature of GGIs. The chapter by Bäckstrand and Söderbaum shows legitimation and delegitimation as processes of justification and contestation. Research on protest, like much of social movement theory, has not deployed the vocabulary of "legitimacy" as illustrated in the chapter by Gregoratti and Uhlin. For those interested in the politics and agency of such processes, this uneasy relationship provides both a focal point for the politics of GGIs and an impetus to new forms of political engagement by new audiences such as civil society and business.

The return to geopolitical competition does not mean that its lure is able to provide a stable "fix." In such a fragile imbalance, the debate on the legitimacy of GGIs tends to oscillate like a pendulum without coming to a halt. My argument is that large processes of political and social change are marked by a period of competition as actors measure their forces. Global rule setting by GGIs has been pushed this way and that by political and ideological trends, subject to contradictory forces. Hence the current challenge may not materialize fully, but there is prone to be adaptation to make some room for new demands. We need to rethink research on legitimacy as a program for a world in transition, as a dynamic process in which political and economic arrangements demand change in the understandings of legitimacy (Kennedy 2008). As the rules of engagement are recreated and reconfigured, a shared vision of the world is more likely to take hold. Thus legitimacy might be conceptualized as an ongoing process of legitimation and delegitimation as illustrated by the chapters in Part III of the book. GGIs will always serve some audiences' interests and agendas better than others. This point needs to be made since there is nothing natural or neutral about governing. This leads me to the second part of my commentary focusing on the role of markets.

Markets

Given contestation of contemporary global governance, we need to pay close attention to the relationship of markets to the question of GGI legitimacy. As markets expand globally, governments find that the tools and the tradeoffs that once worked to keep social stability no longer work. "Even the most powerful of formally democratic states, the United States, has seen a weakening of democracy" (Murphy 2016: 36), which many authors link to the ascendance and dominance of global markets. My concern here is that the study of legitimacy might become divorced from the force of global markets and unwittingly condone or leave unquestioned *whose* needs are being met by governance arrangements. Such a contention opens up an expansive subject matter which is beyond the scope of these commentaries. But the point that I want to raise is that global politics and global markets must come together to enhance our understanding of legitimacy dynamics.

We need to ask boldly how important economic forces are in relation to the legitimacy of GGI. This is a less immanent perspective than the book has chosen. In their chapter, Scholte and Tallberg suggest that legitimacy beliefs are shaped by institutional features of GGIs related to procedure and performance. Among such features, the chapter suggests that three—democratic, technocratic, and fairness qualities—are most central in generating audience beliefs in GGI legitimacy. I will argue here that the interaction with the power dynamics in economic structure also matters. In Polanyian fashion, brushing aside connotations of economic determinism, we know that market forces condition and spill over to GGI. The legitimacy of GGIs requires a social bargain in which people are protected and markets are "embedded" or restrained in such a way that private actors do not gain extraordinarily at the expense of the public, enabling a reconciliation of markets and societies in Ruggie's (1982) classical terms.

As the chapters in this volume show so interestingly, there are variations of legitimacy perceptions across GGIs. Those which possess the highest authority—such as the International Monetary Fund (IMF) or the World Bank—are typically among the GGIs which the public most often criticize for having democratic deficits. In contrast, general purpose GGIs, such as the European Union (EU) and the Association of South East Asian Nations (ASEAN), are umbrella organizations—similar to national governments—covering a full spectrum of problems and actors. Even if governments can be considered as the prime actors as members of interstate GGIs, the private sector is often in the driver's seat because of its importance for growth and funding. Performance matters as the legitimacy of a GGI derives partly from its impacts, irrespective of how the institution made the relevant policy (Scholte and Tallberg, this volume).

Even though the concept of legitimacy cannot be equated to the concept of justice, distributional outcomes will ultimately matter. The fairness of distributional consequences lies at the heart of contestation. Distributional outcomes are intimately tied to legitimacy, in terms of the typology developed by Scholte and Tallberg in Chapter 4. Fair procedure and performance capture perceptions that process and outcome are just, equitable, and impartial vis-à-vis implicated actors. This suggests that the substance of policies also demands analysis. Substantive outcomes take place within a power structure. Many issues in global economic governance, such as intellectual property and finance, exhibit a huge discrepancy between narrow representation (unfair procedure) and the huge societal footprint of these policy areas. These are issues of substantive legitimacy (performance)—why is it that one policy is more desirable than another? (Sell 2016: 32) This brings us to Susan Strange's concerns with winners and losers in governance contests—*cui bono*?

What substantive benefits do we want to achieve and for whom? Corporate scandals and business behavior in general are very much in the spotlight, as well as the deep imbrication of governments and GGIs in patterns of governance that fail to control the more destructive tendencies of markets. Some of these patterns are considered deeply illegitimate by significant segments of the public. For one, the offshore industry that allows tax avoidance and evasion has come under the spotlight because there is a widespread perception that offshore centers shift the burden of taxation to ordinary taxpayers and give multinational companies an edge over smaller competitors. Many now hold that such asymmetry can no longer be deemed as collateral damage. The struggle between markets and democracy sits uneasily with such a settlement—a tug requiring adjustment both at the level of the state and GGIs.

State and market relations are co-constitutive as they are themselves a form of power struggle. International political economy opens the window to economic incentives that offer political opportunities and pose threats. Taking the market as central (rather than as an additional or incidental component of a political analysis) provides further insight into the contestation over GGIs by specifying the interactive elements of markets as both drivers of and respondents to opportunities and threats. Here, the aim is to explicitly link international political economy to the dynamics of contestation, legitimacy, and legitimation. Economically sensitive analyses of legitimacy will find that corporations have been able to place initiatives under the aegis of global governance in a way that risks disconnecting international institutions from the democratic legitimacy on which their creation was premised. They may be writing rules or have found ways to either capture or avoid state control. Firms themselves push for the very "gaps" in public governance that are necessary for their business models to thrive globally.

To take the case of trade as an example, the General Agreement on Tariffs and Trade (GATT) model was one of shallow integration and limited cooperation—mutual adjustment of policy—rather than aiming to change domestic governance arrangements to best practices. When agreement could not be reached, the default option was respect for national regulation. Until the Uruguay Round and the creation of the World Trade Organization (WTO) in 1994, GATT rules by and large did not intrude within the domestic political economy of states. They pertained to external barriers to trade, not to national regulation. Furthermore, it was not essential to be a GATT member nor when being a member to follow all the rules of trade liberalization. Such centrally planned economies as Cuba, Poland, Romania, Czechoslovakia, Hungary, and Yugoslavia were members. In contrast, Venezuela, Ecuador, and Mexico, for instance, were not.

Trade negotiations in the last three decades have incorporated into its sphere more and more diverse issues and agendas from financial services, investment protection, and intellectual property. Trade agreements result in package-dealing negotiations whereby countries exchange concessions across several issue areas with negligible economic or political sense. Trade diplomacy seen previously as largely inconsequential now looms large on all fronts. Trade itself is an inherently distributive policy. It has a direct impact on consumption, production, fiscal revenues, and employment. The distribution of gains both among and within countries is a matter of serious contention. The requirement to grant reciprocity in negotiations whereby the gains of one external sector call for one or more internal sectors to adjust to heightened import competition have increased domestic sensitivity to the adjustment process.

Trade has thus acquired an unprecedented salience for domestic politics. Moreover, a foreign offer of market access for a particular good or sector acts as bait by creating an in-country vested interest that will lobby the government. That lobby pushes to get its interest as exporters to the forefront against all other interests, even as many of these groups are seldom aware they will also be paying a cost by virtue of the principle of reciprocity in trade negotiations. The market for palm oil, for example, is liberalized to facilitate country A's exports but A will reciprocate by offering a government contract or stricter intellectual property protection for a specific drug that businesses in country X seek. The fact that trade negotiations have expanded their sway over so many aspects compounds the seriousness of this problem. Reciprocity across such broad issues has important distributional effects and political implications for domestic governance. Exporting coalitions become strong constituencies at the expense of the constituency that is thrown in as a "concession." Trade becomes a framework for gaming conflicts among interests internal to other states.

The new trade agreements suffer from additional legitimacy challenges with the advent of the Trump Administration and its attack on the liberal trade order. As first conceptualized most notably by Cox (1987), the state is "internationalized"—there is a reworking of domestic institutions and national agencies to serve "global" purposes. Trade agreements today suction whole areas of regulation from the realm of ordinary legislation, replacing it with what is known as "legislation by treaty" (Lind 2017). States are disciplined to favor the preference of global markets. As put by Streeck (2014), such treaties provide institutional protection of the global market economy from democratic interference and oversight. Favorable laws and regulations that business is unable to persuade national legislatures to enact can be repackaged, masked, and enshrined in complex trade treaties. These treaties tend to be drafted by committees in tandem with corporate lobbyists, then sent for ratification to legislatures. The issue in relation to the substance of legitimacy is that these trade agreements transmute domestic governance. In many policy domains, institutions, laws, and processes cater to global market demands, enshrining the primacy of economic growth over social equality. While states are rebalanced to enact global market needs, domestic interests are marginalized and disparaged as "vested" (Hameiri and Jones 2015).

Most of these agreements include "investor-state dispute settlement" pro-visions that allow corporations to sue national governments in international tribunals, with no appeal mechanisms and influenced by corporate lawyers. Companies have mostly won their cases and states have had to pay huge costs and astronomical fines. A shadow of arbitrator bias in favor of investors and failure to take into account situations of massive economic downturns, as was the case of the Argentine crisis in 2001, have triggered severe questioning of the balance between the interests of foreign investors and national citizens. Unsurprisingly, domestic audiences are sometimes frustrated with this trade-off. Bolivia, Venezuela, Ecuador, Indonesia, South Africa, Italy, and Russia have withdrawn from such investment treaties while Argentina refused to comply. All told, we are now compelled to range much more widely over the balance of interests associated with particular forms and arenas of governance. When rules are encapsulated in treaties as substitutes for rules made democrat-ically by states, questions of legitimacy "of broad social perception of power without right" (Zelli, this volume) insistently arise. "As a result citizens increas-ingly perceive their governments, not as their agents, but as those of other states or of international organizations such as the IMF or the EU immeasurably more insulated from electoral pressure than was the nation state" (Streeck 2011: 26). No wonder so many voters have revolted. The force of contestation continues and indeed is perhaps even stronger.

These considerations aside, it is the case that one of the most vibrant avenues of political economy research in recent years has taken the dysfunc-tion of markets and substantive distributive questions as a central preoccupa-tion. Increasingly we have come to question who captures free trade and to whose benefit. How do trade agreements affect distributional choices? Are these agreements driving global wage competition? Who captures the rent? Where is the money parked? The reaction against the disembeddedness of markets is a type of countermovement, society re-embedding itself and push-ing back against the primacy of markets leading to outcomes that are far from socially accepted. Examining these implications of the distributional effects of markets should be high on the future agenda of research on legitimacy in global governance.

Conclusion

This volume goes a long way to help us think afresh about how the study of legitimacy and legitimation of GGIs needs to evolve in order to accommodate the associated conceptual, theoretical, and empirical challenges that are now laid before us. The set of questions raised by this volume are central in global governance research and will leave a mark for future research. The chapters also reflect on the new challenges that have been presented to us by contemporary events such as the Eurozone crises, Brexit, and the Trump presidency, which prompt a re-examination of some of our assumptions. Common to both sociological and normative understandings of legitimacy is the value of legitimacy as a means to justify and practice power. The more overarching research question posed here relates to the nature of the relationship between normative and sociological legitimacy. Are they mutually dependent or complementary? Can we hold a stark dichotomy when the established order is so severely challenged?

This commentary has argued for a more engaged political economy perspective on the question of legitimacy in global governance. Patterns of governance are themselves unstable, continuously in flux, in some cases merely embryonic, in others longstanding but fragile, and so on—even if some become entrenched over a more extended period of time. The revival of contested geopolitics is actually or potentially disrupting and delegitimatizing GGIs, challenging the normalization of Western and neoliberal global governance (Brassett and Tsingou 2011), and possibly sowing the seeds of new patterns of governance. Naturally, state-level responses are not sufficient. In the process we might "need to scale down our ambitions with respect to global economic integration ... [and] ... do a better job of writing the rules for a thinner version of globalization" (Rodrik 2002: 3). As a new normative legitimacy less infused with the hyper-liberal *Zeitgeist* takes shape, it will be prone to affect real sociological legitimacy.

Zelli (this volume) brings these questions to the fore by arguing that individual GGIs, their legitimacy, and their problem-solving effectiveness do not exist in a vacuum, but are part of and shaped by a broader institutional environment. Taking this embeddedness into account will make our analyses of the consequences of legitimacy more challenging, but also more accurate and policy-relevant. The scholarship focusing on what a legitimate form of global governance might look like may need to grapple much more with the fact that many new actors in global governance will be distancing themselves from the continued dominance of the neoliberal agenda both within and across states. Social science can do little, if anything, to help resolve the polarized politics, the rise of nationalism, the structural tensions, and the contradictions underlying the economic and social disorders. What we need to continue to do is examine the new forms of governance that are emerging, and in whose interests they are operating. As scholars we must attend to this process, not assume it away. Of course, there is nothing inevitable about change. It is definitely not linear, and if structure matters, a lot of agency, as this volume shows, makes a difference.

Bibliography

Abbott, Kenneth W., and Steven Bernstein. 2015. The High-Level Political Forum on Sustainable Development: Orchestration by Default or Design. *Global Policy* 6(3): 222–33.

Abbott, Kenneth W., Philipp Genschel, Duncan Snidal, and Bernhard Zangl. 2015. Orchestration: Global Governance through Intermediaries. In *International Organizations as Orchestrators*, edited by Kenneth W. Abbott, Philipp Genschel, Duncan Snidal, and Bernhard Zangl, pp. 3–36. Cambridge: Cambridge University Press.

Abbott, Kenneth W., Jessica F. Green, and Robert O. Keohane. 2016. Organizational Ecology and Institutional Change in Global Governance. *International Organization* 70(2): 247–77.

Acosta, Alberto. 2013. Extractivism and Neoextractivism: Two Sides of the Same Curse. In *Beyond Development: Alternative Visions from Latin America*, edited by Miriam Lang and Dunia Mokrani, pp. 61–86. Amsterdam: Transnational Institute.

Adler, Emanuel, and Vincent Pouliot. 2011a. International Practices. *International Theory* 3(1): 1–36.

Adler, Emanuel, and Vincent Pouliot, eds. 2011b. *International Practices*. Cambridge: Cambridge University Press.

African Union. 2017. The Imperative to Strengthen Our Union. Report on the Proposed Recommendations for the Institutional Reform of the African Union. The Kagame Report. Decision on the Institutional Reform of the African Union, Assembly/AU/Dec. 606 (XXVII).

Agné, Hans. 2010. Why Democracy Must Be Global: Self-Founding and Democratic Intervention. *International Theory* 2(3): 381–409.

Agné, Hans. 2016. Accountability's Effect: Reaction Speed and Legitimacy in Global Governance. *Global Governance* 22(4): 575–94.

Agné, Hans. 2018. Democratism: Towards an Explanatory Approach to International Politics. *Review of International Studies*. http://dx.doi.org/10.1017/S0260210518000025.

Agné, Hans, Lisa Maria Dellmuth, and Jonas Tallberg. 2015. Does Stakeholder Involvement Foster Democratic Legitimacy in International Organizations? An Empirical Assessment of a Normative Theory. *Review of International Organizations* 10(4): 465–88.

Agnew, John. 2005. *Hegemony: The New Shape of Global Power*. Philadelphia, PA: Temple University Press.

Agnew, John, and Stuart Corbridge. 1995. *Mastering Space: Hegemony, Territory and International Political Economy*. London: Routledge.

Albrow, Martin. 1996. *The Global Age: State and Society beyond Modernity*. Cambridge: Polity.

Alter, Karen J. 2008. Agents or Trustees? International Courts in Their Political Context. *European Journal of International Relations* 14(1): 33–63.

Alter, Karen J. 2014. *The New Terrain of International Law: Courts, Politics, Rights*. Princeton, NJ: Princeton University Press.

Alter, Karen J., and Sophie Meunier. 2009. The Politics of International Regime Complexity. *Perspectives on Politics* 7(1): 13–24.

Ameli, Saied Reza. 2011. The Organization of Islamic Conference, Accountability and Civil Society. In *Building Global Democracy: Civil Society and Accountable Global Governance*, edited by Jan Aart Scholte, pp. 146–62. Cambridge: Cambridge University Press.

Amin, Samir. 1973. *Unequal Development*. New York, NY: Monthly Review Press.

Anderson, Christopher J. 1998. When in Doubt, Use Proxies: Attitudes toward Domestic Politics and Support for European Integration. *Comparative Political Studies* 31(5): 569–601.

Anderson, Christopher J., and Michael S. Reichert. 1995. Economic Benefits and Support for Membership in the EU: A Cross-National Analysis. *Journal of Public Policy* 15(3): 231–49.

Anievas, Alexander, Nivi Manchanda, and Robbie Shilliam, eds. 2015. *Race and Racism in International Relations: Confronting the Global Colour Line*. Abingdon: Routledge.

Archibugi, Daniele. 2008. *The Global Commonwealth of Citizens: Toward Cosmopolitan Democracy*. Princeton, NJ: Princeton University Press.

Archibugi, Daniele, Mathias Koenig-Archibugi, and Raffaele Marchetti, eds. 2012. *Global Democracy: Normative and Empirical Perspectives*. Cambridge: Cambridge University Press.

Arendt, Hannah. 1956. Authority in the Twentieth Century. *Review of Politics* 18(4): 403–17.

Armingeon, Klaus, and Besir Ceka. 2014. The Loss of Trust in the European Union during the Great Recession since 2007: The Role of Heuristics from the National Political System. *European Union Politics* 15(1): 82–107.

Ba, Alice D. 2013. The Association of Southeast Asian Nations: Between Internal and External Legitimacy. In *Legitimating International Organizations*, edited by Dominik Zaum, pp. 133–61. Oxford: Oxford University Press.

Bäckstrand, Karin. 2011. The Democratic Legitimacy of Global Governance after Copenhagen. In *Oxford Handbook of Climate Change and Society*, edited by John Dryzek, Richard Norgard, and David Schlosberg, pp. 669–84. Oxford: Oxford University Press.

Bäckstrand, Karin, and Eva Lövbrand. 2016. The Road to Paris: Contending Climate Governance Discourses in the Post-Copenhagen Era. *Journal of Environmental Policy and Planning*. DOI: 10.1080/1523908X.2016.1150777.

Bäckstrand, Karin, Jonathan Kuyper, Björn-Ola Linnér, and Eva Lövbrand, eds. 2017. Non-State Actors in Global Climate Governance from Copenhagen to Paris and Beyond. Special issue, *Environmental Politics* 24(4): 561–79.

Bandy, Joe, and Jackie Smith, eds. 2005. *Coalitions across Borders: Transnational Protest and the Neoliberal Order*. Lanham, MD: Rowman and Littlefield.

Barber, Benjamin R. 1984. *Strong Democracy: Participatory Politics for a New Age*. Berkeley, CA: University of California Press.

Barker, Rodney. 1990. *Political Legitimacy and the State*. Oxford: Oxford University Press.

Barker, Rodney. 2001. *Legitimating Identities: The Self-Presentation of Rulers and Subjects*. Cambridge: Cambridge University Press.

Barker, Rodney. 2007. Democratic Legitimation: What Is It, Who Wants It, and Why? In *Legitimacy in an Age of Globalization*, edited by Achim Hurrelmann, Steffen Schneider, and Jens Steffek, pp. 19–34. Basingstoke: Palgrave Macmillan.

Barnett, Michael. 2011. *Empire of Humanity: A History of Humanitarianism*. Ithaca, NY: Cornell University Press.

Barnett, Michael. 2013. Humanitarian Governance. *Annual Review of Political Science* 16: 379–98.

Barnett, Michael, and Martha Finnemore. 1999. The Politics, Power, and Pathologies of International Organizations. *International Organization* 53(4): 699–732.

Barnett, Michael, and Martha Finnemore. 2004. *Rules for the World: International Organizations in Global Politics*. Ithaca, NY: Cornell University Press.

Bauer, Michael W., and Jörn Ege. 2016. Bureaucratic Autonomy of International Organizations' Secretariats. *Journal of European Public Policy* 23(7): 1019–37.

Baum, Joel, and Christine Oliver. 1991. Institutional Linkages and Organizational Mortality. *Administrative Science Quarterly* 36(2): 187–218.

Baumann, Rainer, Volker Rittberger, and Wolfgang Wagner. 2001. Neorealist Foreign Policy Theory. In *German Foreign Policy since Unification: Theories and Case Studies*, edited by Volker Rittberger, pp. 37–67. Manchester: Manchester University Press.

Bechtel, Michael M., Jens Hainmueller, Dominik Hangartner, and Marc Helbling. 2015. Reality Bites: The Limits of Framing Effects for Salient and Contested Policy Issues. *Political Science Research and Methods* 3(3): 683–95.

Beetham, David. 1991. *The Legitimation of Power*. Atlantic Highlands, NJ: Humanities Press International.

Beetham, David. 2012. Political Legitimacy. In *The Wiley-Blackwell Companion to Political Sociology*, edited by Edwin Amenta, Kate Nash, and Alan Scott, pp. 120–9. Chichester: Wiley-Blackwell.

Beetham, David. 2013. *The Legitimation of Power*. 2nd ed. Basingstoke: Palgrave Macmillan.

Beetham, David, and Christopher Lord. 1998. *Legitimacy and the EU*. London: Addison Wesley Longman.

Bell, Duncan S.A. 2002. Language, Legitimacy, and the Project of Critique. *Alternatives* 27(3): 327–50.

Benvenisti, Eyal, and George W. Downs. 2007. The Empire's New Clothes: Political Economy and the Fragmentation of International Law. *Stanford Law Review* 60(2): 595–632.

Bernauer, Thomas, and Robert Gampfer. 2013. Effects of Civil Society Involvement on Popular Legitimacy of Global Environmental Governance. *Global Environmental Change* 23(2): 439–49.

Bernstein, Steven. 2001. *The Compromise of Liberal Environmentalism*. New York, NY: Columbia University Press.

Bernstein, Steven. 2005. Legitimacy in Global Environmental Governance. *International Journal of Comparative Labour Law and Industrial Relations* 1(1): 139–66.

Bernstein, Steven. 2011. Legitimacy in Intergovernmental and Non-State Global Governance. *Review of International Political Economy* 18(1): 17–51.

Bernstein, Steven. 2014. The Publicness of Private Global Environmental and Social Governance. In *The Return of the Public in Global Governance*, edited by Jacqueline Best and Alexandra Gheciu, pp. 120–48. Cambridge: Cambridge University Press.

Bernstein, Steven. 2017. The United Nations and the Governance of Sustainable Development Goals. In *Governance through Goals: New Strategies for Global Sustainability*, edited by Norichika Kanie and Frank Biermann, pp. 213–39. Cambridge, MA: MIT Press.

Bernstein, Steven, and Benjamin Cashore. 2007. Can Non-State Global Governance Be Legitimate? An Analytical Framework. *Regulation and Governance* 1(4): 347–71.

Best, Jacqueline. 2014. *Governing Failure: Provisional Expertise and the Transformation of Global Finance*. Cambridge: Cambridge University Press.

Best, Jacqueline, and Matthew Paterson, eds. 2010. *Cultural Political Economy*. Abingdon: Routledge.

Bevir, Mark. 2013. *Governance: A Very Short Introduction*. Oxford: Oxford University Press.

Bexell, Magdalena. 2014. Global Governance, Legitimacy and (De)legitimation. *Globalizations* 11(3): 289–99.

Bexell, Magdalena, ed. 2015a. *Global Governance, Legitimacy and Legitimation*. Abingdon: Routledge.

Bexell, Magdalena. 2015b. The Post-2015 Consultations: Fig Leaf Policy or Test Bed for Innovation? In *Global Trends 2015. Prospects for World Society*, edited by Michèle Roth, Cornelia Ulbert, and Tobias Debiel, pp. 129–46. Bonn: SEF, INEF and Käte Hamburger Kolleg/Centre for Global Cooperation Research.

Bieler, Andreas, Werner Bonefeld, Peter Burnham, and Adam David Morton. 2006. *Global Restructuring, State, Capital and Labour: Contesting Neo-Gramscian Perspectives*. Basingstoke: Palgrave Macmillan.

Biermann, Frank, Philipp Pattberg, Harro van Asselt, and Fariborz Zelli. 2009. The Fragmentation of Global Governance Architectures: A Framework for Analysis. *Global Environmental Politics* 9(4): 14–40.

Binder, Martin, and Monica Heupel. 2015. The Legitimacy of the UN Security Council: Evidence from Recent General Assembly Debates. *International Studies Quarterly* 59(2): 238–50.

Black, Julia. 2008. Constructing and Contesting Legitimacy and Accountability in Polycentric Regulatory Regimes. *Regulation and Governance* 2(2): 137–64.

Blake, Daniel J., and Autumn Lockwood Payton. 2015. Balancing Design Objectives: Analyzing New Data on Voting Rules in Intergovernmental Organizations. *Review of International Organizations* 10(3): 377–402.

Bodansky, Daniel. 1999. The Legitimacy of International Governance: A Coming Challenge for International Environmental Law? *American Journal of International Law* 93(3): 596–624.

Bodansky, Daniel. 2002. *U.S. Climate Policy after Kyoto: Elements for Success*. Washington, DC: Carnegie Endowment for International Peace.

Bodansky, Daniel. 2016. The Paris Climate Change Agreement: A New Hope? *American Journal of International Law* 110(2): 288–319.

Boddice, Rob, ed. 2012. *Anthropocentrism: Humans, Animals, Environments*. Leiden: Brill.

Bohman, James. 2007. *Democracy across Borders: From Dêmos to Dêmoi*. Cambridge, MA: MIT Press.

Bond, Patrick. 2012. *Politics of Climate Justice: Paralysis Above, Movement Below*. Durban: University of KwaZulu-Natal Press.

Bonditti, Philippe, Didier Bigo, and Frédéric Gros, eds. 2017. *Foucault and the Modern International: Silences and Legacies for the Study of World Politics*. New York, NY: Palgrave Macmillan.

Booth, John A., and Mitchell A. Seligson. 2005. Political Legitimacy and Participation in Costa Rica: Evidence of Arena Shopping. *Political Research Quarterly* 58(4): 537–50.

Bourdieu, Pierre. 1993. *The Field of Cultural Production*. Cambridge: Polity.

Bradbury, Jonathan. 2009. Constituency. In *The Concise Oxford Dictionary of Politics*. 3rd ed., edited by Iain McLean and Alistair McMillan. Oxford: Oxford University Press.

Brassett, James, and Eleni Tsingou. 2011. The Politics of Legitimate Global Governance. *Review of International Political Economy* 18(1): 1–16.

Braudel, Fernand. 1958. History and the Social Sciences: The *Longue Durée'*. In *On History*, pp. 25–54. Chicago, IL: University of Chicago Press.

Braun, Daniela, and Markus Tausendpfund. 2014. The Impact of the Euro Crisis on Citizens' Support for the European Union. *Journal of European Integration* 36(3): 231–45.

Brewer, Thomas L. 2008. Climate Change and Technology Transfer: A New Paradigm and Policy Agenda. *Climate Policy* 8(5): 516–26.

BRIC. 2009. Joint Statement of the BRIC Countries' Leaders. January 16. http://en.kremlin.ru/supplement/209. Accessed December 4, 2017.

Broome, André, and Leonard Seabrooke. 2012. Seeing Like an International Organisation. *New Political Economy* 17(1): 1–16.

Bruen, Carlos, Ruraí Brugha, Angela Kageni, and Francis Wafula. 2014. A Concept in Flux: Questioning Accountability in the Context of Global Health Cooperation. *Globalization and Health* 10(73): 3–15.

Brunnée, Jutta, and Stephen J. Toope. 2010. *Legitimacy and Legality in International Law: An Interaction Account*. Cambridge: Cambridge University Press.

Buchanan, Allen. 2002. Political Legitimacy and Democracy. *Ethics* 112(4): 689–719.

Buchanan, Allen, and Robert Keohane. 2006. The Legitimacy of Global Governance Institutions. *Ethics and International Affairs* 20(4): 405–37.

Bueger, Christian, and Frank Gadinger. 2015. The Play of International Practice. *International Studies Quarterly* 59(3): 449–60.

Buhari-Gulmez, Didem. 2010. Stanford School on Sociological Institutionalism: A Global Cultural Approach. *International Political Sociology* 4(3): 253–70.

Bühlmann, Marc, and Ruth Kunz. 2011. Confidence in the Judiciary: Comparing the Independence and Legitimacy of Judicial Systems. *West European Politics* 34(2): 317–45.

Burke, Sara. 2014. What an Era of Global Protest Says about the Effectiveness of the Human Rights Language to Achieve Social Change. *SUR: International Journal of Human Rights* 11(20): 27–33.

Büthe, Tim, and Walter Mattli. 2011. *The New Global Rulers: The Privatization of Regulation in the World Economy*. Princeton, NJ: Princeton University Press.

Buzan, Barry. 2004. *From International to World Society? English School Theory and the Social Structure of Globalization*. Cambridge: Cambridge University Press.

Byman, Daniel, Ever Byman, and Stephen Van Evera. 1998. Why They Fight: Hypotheses on the Causes of Contemporary Deadly Conflict. *Security Studies* 7(3): 1–50.

Caldeira, Gregory A., and James L. Gibson. 1992. The Etiology of Public Support for the Supreme Court. *American Journal of Political Science* 36(3): 635–64.

Caldeira, Gregory A., and James L. Gibson. 1995. The Legitimacy of the Court of Justice in the European Union: Models of Institutional Support. *American Political Science Review* 89(2): 356–76.

Caldwell, Mark. 2015. African Union Criticizes International Criminal Court at Member States' Meeting. *Deutsche Welle*, November 19. http://www.dw.com/en/african-union-criticizes-international-criminal-court-at-member-states-meeting/a-18862799. Accessed November 18, 2017.

Campbell, David E. 2006. What Is Education's Impact on Civil and Social Engagement? In *Measuring the Effects of Education on Health and Civic Engagement: Proceedings of the Copenhagen Symposium*. Paris: OECD.

Carey, Sean. 2002. Undivided Loyalties: Is National Identity an Obstacle to European Integration? *European Union Politics* 3(4): 387–413.

Carlile, Paul R., Davide Nicolini, Ann Langley, and Haridimos Tsoukas, eds. 2013. *How Matter Matters: Objects, Artifacts, and Materiality in Organization Studies*. Oxford: Oxford University Press.

Carr, Edward Hallett. 1946. *The Twenty Years' Crisis 1919–1939*. 2nd ed. London: Macmillan.

Cashmore, Matthew, and Anja Wejs. 2014. Constructing Legitimacy for Climate Change Planning: A Study of Local Government in Denmark. *Global Environmental Change* 24(2): 203–12.

Chalmers, Adam W., and Lisa M. Dellmuth. 2015. Fiscal Redistribution and Public Support for European Integration. *European Union Politics* 16(3): 386–407.

Chandler, David. 2014. *Resilience: The Governance of Complexity*. Abingdon: Routledge.

Chapman, Terrence L. 2009. Audience Beliefs and International Organization Legitimacy. *International Organization* 63(4): 733–64.

Chayes, Abram, and Antonia H. Chayes. 1995. *The New Sovereignty: Compliance with International Regulatory Agreements*. Cambridge, MA: Harvard University Press.

Checkel, Jeffrey T. 2001. Why Comply? Social Learning and European Identity Change. *International Organization* 55(3): 553–88.

Chong, Dennis, and James N. Druckman. 2007. Framing Theory. *Annual Review of Political Science* 10(1): 103–26.

Christiano, Thomas. 2010. Democratic Legitimacy and International Institutions. In *The Philosophy of International Law*, edited by Samantha Besson and John Tasioulas, pp. 119–37. Oxford: Oxford University Press.

Christin, Thomas. 2005. Economic and Political Basis of Attitudes towards the EU in Central and East European Countries in the 1990s. *European Union Politics* 6(1): 59–82.

Clark, Ian. 2003. Legitimacy in a Global Order. *Review of International Studies* 29(1): 75–95.

Clark, Ian. 2005. *Legitimacy in International Society*. Oxford: Oxford University Press.

Clark, Ian. 2007. *International Legitimacy and World Society*. Oxford: Oxford University Press.

Clark, Ian. 2011. *Hegemony in International Society*. Oxford: Oxford University Press.

Clark, Ian, and Christian Reus-Smit, eds. 2007a. Resolving International Crises of Legitimacy. Special issue, *International Politics* 44(2/3).

Clark, Ian, and Christian Reus-Smit. 2007b. Preface. *International Politics* 44(2/3): 153–6.

Clarke, Kamari, Abel S. Knottnerus, and Eefje de Volder. 2016. *Africa and the ICC*. Cambridge: Cambridge University Press.

Claude, Jr., Inis L. 1966. Collective Legitimization as a Political Function of the United Nations. *International Organization* 20(3): 367–79.

Cogan, Jacob Katz, Ian Hurd, and Ian Johnstone, eds. 2016. *The Oxford Handbook of International Organizations*. Oxford: Oxford University Press.

Cohen, Gerald Allan. 2008. *Rescuing Justice and Equality*. Cambridge, MA: Harvard University Press.

Coicaud, Jean-Marc, and Veijo Heiskanen, eds. 2001. *The Legitimacy of International Organizations*. Tokyo: United Nations University Press.

Coleman, Lara Montesinos, and Karen Tucker. 2011. Between Discipline and Dissent: Situated Resistance and Global Order. *Globalizations* 8(4): 397–410.

Commission on Global Governance. 1995. *Our Global Neighborhood: The Report of the Commission on Global Governance*. Oxford: Oxford University Press.

Converse, Philip E. 1964. The Nature of Belief Systems in the Mass Public. In *Ideology and Discontent*, edited by David E. Apter, pp. 206–61. New York, NY: Free Press.

Cooper, Andrew F. 2008. *Celebrity Diplomacy*. Boulder, CO: Paradigm.

Cox, Robert W. 1981. Social Forces, States and World Orders: Beyond International Relations Theory. *Millennium: Journal of International Relations* 10(2): 126–55.

Cox, Robert W. 1983. Gramsci, Hegemony and International Relations: An Essay in Method. *Millennium: Journal of International Relations* 12(2): 162–75.

Cox, Robert W. 1987. *Production, Power, and World Order: Social Forces in the Making of History*. New York, NY: Columbia University Press.

Crittendon, John. 1962. Ageing and Party Affiliation. *Public Opinion Quarterly* 26(4): 583–8.

Crouch, Colin, and Wolfgang Streeck, eds. 1997. *The Political Economy of Modern Capitalism: Mapping Convergence and Diversity*. London: Sage.

Cudworth, Erika, and Stephen Hobden. 2018. *The Emancipatory Project of Posthumanism*. Abingdon: Routledge.

Daase, Christopher, and Nicole Deitelhoff. 2014. Zur Rekonstruktion globaler Herrschaft aus dem Widerstand. Internationale Dissidenz, Working paper 1.

Dahl, Robert A. 1999. Can International Organizations be Democratic? A Skeptic's View. In *Democracy's Edges*, edited by Ian Shapiro and Casiano Hacker-Cordon, pp. 19–36. Cambridge: Cambridge University Press.

Dahl, Robert A., and Charles Lindblom. 1992. *Politics, Markets, and Welfare*. 2nd ed. New Brunswick, NJ: Transaction Press.

Dalton, Russell J., and Robert Duval. 1986. The Political Environment and Foreign Policy Opinions: British Attitudes toward European Integration, 1972–1979. *British Journal of Political Science* 16(1): 113–34.

Dauvergne, Peter, and Genevieve LeBaron. 2014. *Protest Inc*. Cambridge: Polity Press.

de Vaus, David. 2013. *Surveys in Social Research*. London: Routledge.

de Vreese, Claes H., and Hajo G. Boomgaarden. 2005. Projecting EU Referendums: Fear of Immigration and Support for European Integration. *European Union Politics* 6(1): 59–82.

de Wilde, Pieter, and Michael Zürn. 2012. Can the Politicization of European Integration Be Reversed? *Journal of Common Market Studies* 50(S1): 137–53.

Death, Carl. 2010. *Governing Sustainable Development: Partnerships, Protests and Power at the World Summit*. London: Routledge.

Death, Carl. 2011. Summit Theatre: Exemplary Governmentality and Environmental Diplomacy in Johannesburg and Copenhagen. *Environmental Politics* 20(1): 1–19.

Death, Carl. 2015. Disrupting Global Governance: Protest at Environmental Conferences from 1972 to 2012. *Global Governance* 21(4): 579–98.

Deephouse, David L., and Mark Suchman. 2008. Legitimacy in Organizational Institutionalism. In *The Sage Handbook of Organizational Institutionalism*, edited by Royston Greenwood, Christine Oliver, Roy Suddaby, and Kerstin Sahlin-Andersson, pp. 49–77. London: Sage.

Della Porta, Donatella, ed. 2016. *The Global Justice Movement: Cross-National and Transnational Perspectives*. New York, NY: Routledge.

Della Porta, Donatella, and Sidney J. Tarrow, eds. 2005. *Transnational Protest and Global Activism*. Lanham, MD: Rowman and Littlefield.

Della Porta, Donatella, Abby Peterson, and Herbert Reiter, eds. 2006. *The Policing of Transnational Protest*. Aldershot: Ashgate.

Delli Carpini, Michael X., and Scott Keeter. 1996. *What Americans Know about Politics and Why It Matters*. New Haven, CT: Yale University Press.

Dellmuth, Lisa M. 2016. The Knowledge Gap in World Politics: Assessing the Sources of Citizen Awareness of the United Nations Security Council. *Review of International Studies* 42(2): 673–700.

Dellmuth, Lisa M., and Adam W. Chalmers. 2017. All Spending Is Not Equal: European Union Public Spending, Policy Feedback and Citizens' Support for the EU. *European Journal of Political Research*. DOI: 10.1111/1475-6765.12215.

Dellmuth, Lisa M., and Jonas Tallberg. 2015. The Social Legitimacy of International Organisations: Interest Representation, Institutional Performance, and Confidence Extrapolation in the United Nations. *Review of International Studies* 41(3): 451–75.

Dellmuth, Lisa M., and Jonas Tallberg. 2016a. Elite Communication and Popular Legitimacy in Global Governance. Unpublished.

Dellmuth, Lisa M., and Jonas Tallberg. 2016b. What Drives the Association between Domestic and International Legitimacy? Paper presented at the ECPR Joint Sessions, Pisa, April 24–28.

Dellmuth, Lisa M., Jan Aart Scholte, and Jonas Tallberg. 2017. Institutional Sources of Popular Legitimacy in Global Governance. Paper presented at the Annual Convention of the International Studies Association, Baltimore, February 22–25.

Derman, Brandon B. 2014. Climate Governance, Justice, and Transnational Civil Society. *Climate Policy* 14(1): 23–41.

Desai, Radhika. 2013. *Geopolitical Economy: After US Hegemony, Globalization and Empire.* London: Pluto.

Dex, Shirely. 1995. The Reliability of Recall Data: A Literature Review. *Bulletin de methodologie sociologique* 49(1): 58–89.

DiMaggio, Paul, and Walter Powell. 1983. The Iron Cage Revisited: Institutional Isomorphism and Collective Rationality in Organizational Fields. *American Sociological Review* 48(2): 147–60.

Dingwerth, Klaus. 2007. *The New Transnationalism: Transnational Governance and Democratic Legitimacy.* Basingstoke: Palgrave Macmillan.

Dingwerth, Klaus. 2014. Global Democracy and the Democratic Minimum: Why a Procedural Account Alone Is Insufficient. *European Journal of International Relations* 20(4): 1124–47.

Dingwerth, Klaus. 2017. Field Recognition and the State Prerogative: Why Democratic Legitimation Recedes in Private Transnational Sustainability Regulation. *Politics and Governance* 5(1): 75–84.

Dingwerth, Klaus, and Philipp Pattberg. 2009. World Politics and Organizational Fields: The Case of Transnational Sustainability Governance. *European Journal of International Relations* 15(4): 707–43.

Dingwerth, Klaus, Henning Schmidtke, and Tobias Weise. 2016. Speaking Democracy: Why International Organizations Adopt a Democratic Rhetoric. Unpublished.

Djelic, Marie-Laure, and Kerstin Sahlin-Andersson, eds. 2006. *Transnational Governance.* Cambridge: Cambridge University Press.

Dolan, Kathleen. 2011. Do Women and Men Know Different Things? Measuring Gender Differences in Political Knowledge. *Journal of Politics* 73(1): 97–107.

Downs, George W., David M. Rocke, and Peter N. Barsoom. 1996. Is the Good News about Compliance Good News about Cooperation? *International Organization* 50(3): 379–406.

Druckman, James N., and Kjersten R. Nelson. 2003. Framing and Deliberation: How Citizen Conversation Limits Elite Influence. *American Journal of Political Science* 47(4): 729–45.

Dryzek, John S. 2006. *Deliberative Global Politics: Discourse and Democracy in a Divided World.* Cambridge: Polity.

Eagly, Alice H., and Chaiken Shelly. 1993. *The Psychology of Attitudes.* Fort Worth, TX: Harcourt Brace Jovanovich College.

Easton, David. 1965. *A Systems Analysis of Political Life.* New York, NY: John Wiley.

Easton, David. 1975. A Re-Assessment of the Concept of Political Support. *British Journal of Political Science* 5(4): 435–57.

Eberlein, Burkhard, Kenneth Abbott, Julia Black, Errol Meidinger, and Stepan Wood. 2014. Transnational Business Governance Interactions: Conceptualization and Framework for Analysis. *Regulation and Governance* 8(1): 1–21.

Ebrahim, Alnoor, and Edward Weisband, eds. 2007. *Global Accountabilities: Participation, Pluralism, and Public Ethics*. Cambridge: Cambridge University Press.

Ecker-Ehrhardt, Matthias. 2012. Cosmopolitan Politicization: How Perceptions of Interdependence Foster Citizens' Expectations in International Institutions. *European Journal of International Relations* 18(3): 481–508.

Ecker-Ehrhardt, Matthias. 2016. Why Do Citizens Want the UN to Decide? Cosmopolitan Ideas, Particularism and Global Authority. *International Political Science Review* 37(1): 99–114.

Ecker-Ehrhardt, Matthias, and Bernhard Wessels. 2013. Input-oder Output-Politisierung internationaler Organisationen? Der kritische Blick der Bürger auf Demokratie und Leistung. In *Die Politisierung der Weltpolitik*, edited by Michael Zürn and Matthias Ecker-Ehrhardt, pp. 36–60. Berlin: Suhrkamp Verlag.

Eckersley, Robyn. 2007. Ambushed: The Kyoto Protocol, the Bush Administration's Climate Policy and the Erosion of Legitimacy. *International Politics* 44(2–3): 306–24.

Eckersley, Robyn. 2015. Multilateralism in Crisis? In *Research Handbook on Climate Governance*, edited by Karin Bäckstrand and Eva Lövbrand, pp. 505–15. Cheltenham: Edward Elgar.

Edkins, Jenny. 2008. Biopolitics, Communication and Global Governance. *Review of International Studies* 34(1): 211–32.

Edkins, Jenny, and Nick Vaughan-Williams, eds. 2009. *Critical Theorists and International Relations*. Abingdon: Routledge.

Edwards, Martin S. 2009. Public Support for the International Economic Organizations: Evidence from Developing Countries. *Review of International Organizations* 4(2): 185–209.

Eichenberg, Richard, and Russel J. Dalton. 1993. Europeans and the European Community: The Dynamics of Public Support for European Integration. *International Organization* 47(4): 507–34.

Eisenstadt, Shmuel N. 2000. Multiple Modernities. *Daedalus* 129: 1–29.

Eisentraut, Sophie. 2013. Autokratien, Demokratien und die Legitimität internationaler Organisationen. Eine vergleichende Inhaltsanalyse staatlicher Legitimationsanforderungen an die UN-Generalversammlung. *Zeitschrift für Internationale Beziehungen* 20(3): 3–33.

El-Ghazali, Abdel Hamid Hasan. 2001. *The Way to the Revival of the Muslim Ummah*. Cairo: Al-Falah Foundation.

Elsig, Manfred. 2010. The World Trade Organization at Work: Performance in a Member-Driven Milieu. *Review of International Organizations* 5(3): 345–63.

Elsig, Manfred, Mark Pollack, and Gregory Shaffer. 2017. Trump Is Fighting an Open War on Trade: His Stealth War on Trade May Be Even More Important. *Washington Post*, September 27. https://www.washingtonpost.com/news/monkey-cage/wp/2017/09/27/trump-is-fighting-an-open-war-on-trade-his-stealth-war-on-trade-may-be-even-more-important/?utm_term=.82e3f28dc64c. Accessed December 1, 2017.

Elster, Jon. 1982. The Case for Methodological Individualism. *Theory and Society* 11(4): 453–82.

Erman, Eva. 2016. Global Political Legitimacy beyond Justice and Democracy? *International Theory* 8(1): 29–62.

Erman, Eva, and Sofia Näsström. 2013. *Political Equality in Transnational Democracy.* Basingstoke: Palgrave Macmillan.

EU Digest. 2007. Canada.com: Bush Climate Proposal Gets Mixed Reviews in Europe. http://eu-digest.blogspot.de/2007/06/canadacom-bush-climate-proposal-gets.html. Accessed April 28, 2017.

Falkner, Robert. 2016. The Paris Agreement and the New Logic of International Climate Politics. *International Affairs* 92(5): 1107–25.

Fearon, James D. 1998. Bargaining, Enforcement, and International Cooperation. *International Organization* 52(2): 269–305.

Featherstone, Mike, Scott Lash, and Roland Robertson, eds. 1995. *Global Modernities.* London: Sage.

Fehl, Caroline. 2004. Explaining the International Criminal Court: A "Practice Test" for Rationalist and Constructivist Approaches. *European Journal of International Relations* 10(3): 357–94.

Ferguson, Niall. 2002. *Empire: The Rise and Demise of the British World Order and the Lessons for Global Power.* London: Allen Lane.

Finnemore, Martha, and Kathryn Sikkink. 1998. International Norm Dynamics and Political Change. *International Organization* 52(4): 887–917.

Fischer, Frank. 1989. *Technocracy and the Politics of Expertise.* London: Sage.

Fisher, Dana. 2010. COP-15 in Copenhagen: How the Merging of Movements Left Civil Society out in the Cold. *Global Environmental Politics* 10(2): 1–11.

Fortna, Virginia P. 2004. Does Peacekeeping Keep Peace? International Intervention and the Duration of Peace after Civil War. *International Studies Quarterly* 48(2): 269–92.

Foucault, Michel. 1969/1989. *The Archaeology of Knowledge.* London: Routledge.

Fox, Oliver, and Peter Stoett. 2016. Citizen Participation in the UN Sustainable Development Goals Consultation Process: Toward Democratic Governance? *Global Governance* 22(4): 555–74.

Franck, Thomas M. 1990. *The Power of Legitimacy among Nations.* Oxford: Oxford University Press.

Frank, André Gunder. 1966. *The Development of Underdevelopment.* New York, NY: Monthly Review Press.

Frey, Bruno S. 2008. Outside and Inside Competition for International Organizations: From Analysis to Innovations. *Review of International Organizations* 3(4): 335–50.

Fukuyama, Francis. 1992. *The End of History and the Last Man.* New York, NY: Free Press.

Fukuyama, Francis. 1995. *Trust: The Social Virtues and the Creation of Prosperity.* New York, NY: Free Press.

Furia, Peter. 2005. Global Citizenship, Anyone? Cosmopolitanism, Privilege and Public Opinion. *Global Society* 19(4): 331–59.

Gabel, Matthew J. 1998a. Economic Integration and Mass Politics: Market Liberalization and Public Attitudes in the European Union. *American Journal of Political Science* 42(3): 936–53.

Gabel, Matthew J. 1998b. *Interests and Integration: Market Liberalization, Public Opinion, and European Union.* Ann Arbor, MI: University of Michigan Press.

Gabel, Matthew J. 1998c. Public Support for European Integration: An Empirical Test of Five Theories. *Journal of Politics* 60(2): 333–54.

Gabel, Matthew J., and Harvey D. Palmer. 1995. Understanding Variation in Public Support for European Integration. *European Journal of Political Research* 27(1): 3–19.

Gabel, Matthew, and Kenneth F. Scheve. 2007a. Estimating the Effect of Elite Communication on Public Opinion Using Instrumental Variables. *American Journal of Political Science* 51(4): 1013–28.

Gabel, Matthew, and Kenneth F. Scheve. 2007b. Mixed Messages: Party Dissent and Mass Opinion on European Integration. *European Union Politics* 8(1): 37–59.

Gelot, Linnéa. 2012. *Legitimacy, Peace Operations and Global-Regional Security: The African Union-United Nations Partnership in Darfur*. London: Routledge.

Gelot, Linnéa, and Tom Tieku. 2017. An African Perspective on Global Governance. In *Global Governance from Regional Perspectives: A Critical View*, edited by Anna Triandafyllidou, pp. 119–40. Cambridge: Cambridge University Press.

Gerard, Kelly. 2015. Explaining ASEAN's Engagement of Civil Society in Policy-Making: Smoke and Mirrors. *Globalizations* 12(3): 365–82.

Giddens, Anthony. 1984. *The Constitution of Society: Outline of the Theory of Structuration*. Cambridge: Polity.

Giddens, Anthony. 1985. *The Nation-State and Violence*. Cambridge: Polity.

Gill, Stephen. 1992. *American Hegemony and the Trilateral Commission*. Cambridge: Cambridge University Press.

Gill, Stephen. 2000. Toward a Postmodern Prince? The Battle in Seattle as a Moment in the New Politics of Globalization. *Millennium: Journal of International Studies* 29(1): 131–40.

Gill, Stephen. 2008. *Power and Resistance in the New World Order*. Basingstoke: Palgrave Macmillan.

Gill, Stephen, ed. 2015. *Critical Perspectives on the Crisis of Global Governance: Reimagining the Future*. Basingstoke: Palgrave Macmillan.

Gilley, Bruce. 2006. The Meaning and Measure of State Legitimacy: Results for 72 Countries. *European Journal of Political Research* 45(3): 499–525.

Gilley, Bruce. 2009. *The Right to Rule: How States Win and Lose Legitimacy*. New York, NY: Columbia University Press.

Gilpin, Robert. 1987. *The Political Economy of International Relations*. Princeton, NJ: Princeton University Press.

Gilpin, Robert. 1988. The Theory of Hegemonic War. *Journal of Interdisciplinary History* 18(4): 591–613.

Gleditsch, Kristian Skrede, and Michael D. Ward. 2008. Diffusion and the International Context of Democratization. *International Organization* 60(4): 911–33.

Goddard, Stacie E., and Ronald R. Krebs. 2015. Rhetoric, Legitimation, and Grand Strategy. *Security Studies* 24(1): 5–36.

Godsäter Andréas. 2016. *Civil Society Regionalization in Southern Africa. The Cases of Trade and HIV/AIDS*. London: Routledge.

Godsäter, Andréas, and Fredrik Söderbaum. 2017. Civil Society Participation in Regional Social Policy: The Case of HIV/AIDS in the Southern African Development Community (SADC). *Global Social Policy* 17(2): 119–36.

Goldsmith, Jack L., and Eric A. Posner. 2005. *The Limits of International Law*. Oxford: Oxford University Press.

Government of Sweden. 2017. Feminist Foreign Policy. Available at: http://www.gov ernment.se/government-policy/feminist-foreign-policy/. Accessed December 17, 2017.

Gray, Julia, and Jonathan B. Slapin. 2012. How Effective Are Preferential Trade Agreements? Ask the Experts. *Review of International Organizations* 7(3): 309–33.

Graz, Jean-Christophe, and Andreas Nölke, eds. 2008. *Transnational Private Governance and Its Limits*. London: Routledge.

Gregoratti, Catia. 2014. Global Days of Actions, Global Public Transcripts and Democracy. *Global Discourse* 4(2–3): 353–66.

Grigorescu, Alexandru. 2007. Transparency of Intergovernmental Organizations: The Roles of Member States, International Bureaucracies and Nongovernmental Organizations. *International Studies Quarterly* 51(3): 625–48.

Grigorescu, Alexandru. 2010. The Spread of Bureaucratic Oversight Mechanisms across Intergovernmental Organizations. *International Studies Quarterly* 54(3): 871–86.

Grigorescu, Alexandru. 2015. *Democratic Intergovernmental Organizations? Normative Pressures and Decision-Making Rules*. New York, NY: Cambridge University Press.

Grimm, Dieter. 1995. Does Europe Need a Constitution? *European Law Journal* 1(3): 282–302.

Gronau, Jennifer. 2016. Signaling Legitimacy: Self-Legitimation by the G8 and the G20 in Times of Competitive Multilateralism. *World Political Science* 12(1): 107–45.

Gronau, Jennifer, and Henning Schmidtke. 2016. The Quest for Legitimacy in World Politics: International Institutions' Legitimation Strategies. *Review of International Studies* 42(3): 535–57.

Grzanka, Patrick R., ed. 2014. *Intersectionality: A Foundations and Frontiers Reader*. Boulder, CO: Westview.

Guastaferro, Barbara, and Manuela Moschella. 2012. The EU, the IMF and the Representative Turn: Addressing the Challenge of Legitimacy. *Swiss Political Science Review* 18(2): 199–219.

Gulbrandsen, Lars H. 2004. Overlapping Public and Private Governance: Can Forest Certification Fill the Gaps in the Global Forest Regime? *Global Environmental Politics* 4(2): 75–99.

Gutner, Tamar, and Alexander Thompson. 2010. The Politics of IO Performance: A Framework. *Review of International Organizations* 5(3): 227–48.

Guzzini, Stefano. 2013. *The Return of Geopolitics in Europe? Social Mechanisms and Foreign Policy Identity Crises*. Cambridge: Cambridge University Press.

Haas, Ernst B. 2008. *Beyond the Nation State: Functionalism and International Organization*. Colchester: ECPR Press.

Habermas, Jürgen. 1973/1976. *Legitimation Crisis*. London: Heinemann.

Habermas, Jürgen. 1996. *Between Facts and Norms: Contributions to a Discourse Theory of Law and Democracy*. Cambridge, MA: MIT Press.

Hadden, Jennifer. 2015. *Networks in Contention: The Divisive Politics of Climate Change*. Cambridge: Cambridge University Press.

Hafner, Gerhard. 2004. Pros and Cons Ensuing from Fragmentation of International Law. *Michigan Journal of International Law* 25(4): 849–63.

Hafner-Burton, Emilie M. 2013. *Making Human Rights a Reality*. Princeton, NJ: Princeton University Press.

Hahn, Rüdiger, and Christian Weidtmann. 2016. Transnational Governance, Delibera-tive Democracy, and the Legitimacy of ISO 26000: Analyzing the Case of a Global Multistakeholder Process. *Business and Society* 55(1): 90–129.

Hale, Thomas. 2016. All Hands on the Deck: The Paris Agreement and Nonstate Climate Action. *Global Environmental Politics* 16(3): 12–22.

Hale, Thomas, and David Held, eds. 2011. *Handbook of Transnational Governance: Institutions and Innovations*. Cambridge: Polity.

Hale, Thomas, David Held, and Kevin Young. 2013. *Gridlock: Why Global Cooperation Is Failing When We Need It Most*. Cambridge: Polity Press.

Hall, Rodney Bruce, and Thomas J. Biersteker, eds. 2004. *The Emergence of Private Authority in Global Governance*. Cambridge: Cambridge University Press.

Halliday, Terence C., Susan Block-Lieb, and Bruce G. Carruthers. 2010. Rhetorical Legitimation: Global Scripts as Strategic Devices of International Organizations. *Socio-Economic Review* 8(1): 77–112.

Hameiri, Shahar, and Lee Jones. 2015. Global Governance as State Transformation. *Political Studies* 64(4): 793–810.

Hanna, Philippe, Frank Vanclay, Esther Jean Langdon, and Jos Arts. 2016. Conceptu-alizing Social Protest and the Significance of Protest Actions to Large Projects. *Extract-ive Industries and Society* 3(1): 217–39.

Hannan, Michael T., and Glenn Carroll. 1992. *Dynamics of Organizational Populations: Density, Legitimation, and Competition*. Oxford: Oxford University Press.

Hansson, Stina, and Sofie Hellberg, with Maria Stern, eds. 2015. *Studying the Agency of Being Governed*. London: Routledge.

Hardt, Michael, and Antonio Negri. 2001. *Empire*. Cambridge, MA: Harvard University Press.

Harman, Sophie. 2016. The Bill and Melinda Gates Foundation and Legitimacy in Global Health Governance. *Global Governance* 22(3): 349–68.

Harteveld, Eelco, Tom van der Meer, and Catherine E. de Vries. 2013. In Europe We Trust? Exploring Three Logics of Trust in the European Union. *European Union Politics* 14(4): 542–65.

Hartlapp, Miriam, and Gerda Falkner. 2009. Problems of Operationalization and Data in EU Compliance Research. *European Union Politics* 10(2): 281–304.

Harvey, David. 2005. *A Brief History of Neoliberalism*. Oxford: Oxford University Press.

Hauck, Maria, and Marcel Kroese. 2006. Fisheries Compliance in South Africa: A Decade of Challenges and Reform 1994–2004. *Marine Policy* 30(1): 74–83.

Haunss, Sebastian. 2007. Challenging Legitimacy: Repertoires of Contention, Political Claims Making, and Collective Action Frames. In *Legitimacy in an Age of Global Politics*, edited by Achim Hurrelmann, Steffen Schneider, and Jens Steffek, pp. 156–72. Basingstoke: Palgrave Macmillan.

Held, David. 1995. *Democracy and the Global Order: From the Modern State to Cosmopolitan Governance*. Cambridge: Polity Press.

Held, David, and Mathias Koenig-Archibugi, eds. 2005. *Global Governance and Public Accountability*. Oxford: Blackwell Publishing.

Held, David, and Kyle McNally, eds. 2014. *Lessons from Intervention in the 21st Century: Legality, Feasibility and Legitimacy*. Durham: Durham University/Wiley-Blackwell.

Helfer, Laurence R. 2004. Regime Shifting: The TRIPS Agreement and New Dynamics of International Intellectual Property Lawmaking. *Yale Journal of International Law* 29(1): 1–83.

Helfer, Laurence R. 2009. Regime Shifting in the International Intellectual Property System. *Perspectives on Politics* 7(1): 39–44.

Hempel, Lamont C. 1996. *Environmental Governance: The Global Challenge.* Washington, DC: Island Press.

Herkenrath, Mark, and Alex Knoll. 2011. Protest Events in International Press Coverage: An Empirical Critique of Cross-National Conflict Databases. *International Journal of Comparative Sociology* 52(3): 163–80.

Hermet, Guy, Ali Kazancigil, and Jean-François Prud'homme, eds. 2005. *La gouvernance. Un concept et ses applications.* Paris: Karthala.

Heupel, Monika, and Martin Binder. 2015. The Legitimacy of the UN Security Council: Evidence from Recent General Assembly Debates. *International Studies Quarterly* 59(2): 238–50.

Hewstone, Miles. 1986. *Understanding Attitudes to the European Community: A Social-Psychological Study in Four Member-States.* Cambridge: Cambridge University Press.

Hillebrecht, Courtney. 2014. *Domestic Politics and International Human Rights Tribunals: The Problem of Compliance.* Cambridge: Cambridge University Press.

Hobolt, Sara B. 2012. Citizen Satisfaction with Democracy in the European Union. *Journal of Common Market Studies* 50(1): 88–105.

Hoffmann, Matthew J. 2011. *Climate Governance at the Crossroads: Experimenting with a Global Response after Kyoto.* Oxford: Oxford University Press.

Hofmann, Stephanie. 2009. Overlapping Institutions in the Realm of International Security: The Case of NATO and ESDP. *Perspectives on Politics* 7(1): 45–52.

Hollander, Jocelyn A., and Rachel L. Einwohner. 2004. Conceptualizing Resistance. *Sociological Forum* 19(4): 533–54.

Holloway, Steven K., and Rodney Tomlinson. 1995. The New World Order and the General Assembly: Bloc Realignment at the UN in the Post-Cold War World. *Canadian Journal of Political Science* 28(2): 227–54.

Hooghe, Liesbet, and Gary Marks. 2005. Calculation, Community and Cues: Public Opinion on European Integration. *European Union Politics* 6(4): 419–43.

Hooghe, Liesbet, and Gary Marks. 2009. A Postfunctionalist Theory of European Integration: From Permissive Consensus to Constraining Dissensus. *British Journal of Political Science* 39(1): 1–23.

Hooghe, Liesbet, and Gary Marks. 2015. Delegation and Pooling in International Organizations. *Review of International Organizations* 10(3): 305–28.

Hopewell, Kristen. 2015. Multilateral Trade Governance as Social Field: Global Civil Society and the WTO. *Review of International Political Economy* 22(6): 1128–58.

Hopewell, Kristen. 2017. The BRICS—Merely a Fable? Emerging Power Alliances in Global Trade Governance. *International Affairs* 93(6): 1377–96.

Hüfner, Klaus. 2015. *What Can Save UNESCO?* Berlin: Frank and Timme GmbH.

Hurd, Ian. 1999. Legitimacy and Authority in International Politics. *International Organization* 53(2): 379–408.

Hurd, Ian. 2007. *After Anarchy: Legitimacy and Power in the United Nations Security Council*. Princeton, NJ: Princeton University Press.

Hurd, Ian. 2008. Myths of Membership: The Politics of Legitimation in UN Security Council Reform. *Global Governance* 14(2): 199–217.

Hurrell, Andrew. 2006. Hegemony, Liberalism and Global Order: What Space for Would-Be Great Powers? *International Affairs* 82(1): 1–19.

Hurrelmann, Achim. 2017. Empirical Legitimation Analysis in International Relations: How to Learn from the Insights—and Avoid the Mistakes—of Research in EU Studies. *Contemporary Politics* 23(1): 63–80.

Hurrelmann, Achim, and Steffen Schneider, eds. 2014. *The Legitimacy of Regional Integration in Europe and the Americas*. Basingstoke: Palgrave.

Hurrelmann, Achim, Steffen Schneider, and Jens Steffek, eds. 2007. *Legitimacy in an Age of Globalization*. Basingstoke: Palgrave Macmillan.

IISD. 2001. Summary of the Resumed Sixth Session of the Conference of the Parties to the UN Framework Convention on Climate Change: 16–27 July 2001. *Earth Negotiations Bulletin* 12: 176.

Ikenberry, G. John. 2001. *After Victory. Institutions, Strategic Restraint, and the Rebuilding of Order after Major Wars*. Princeton, NJ: Princeton University Press.

Ikenberry, G. John. 2003. Is American Multilateralism in Decline? *Perspectives on Politics* 1(3): 533–50.

Ikenberry, G. John. 2004. Liberalism and Empire: Logics of Order in the American Unipolar Age. *Review of International Studies* 30(4): 609–30.

ILC. 2006. Fragmentation of International Law: Difficulties Arising from the Diversification and Expansion of International Law. Report of the Study Group of the International Law Commission. A/CN.4/L.682. April 13. Geneva: ILC.

Imber, Mark. 1989. *The USA, ILO, UNESCO and IAEA: Politicization and Withdrawal in the Specialized Agencies*. Berlin: Springer.

Inglehart, Ronald. 1970. Cognitive Mobilization and European Identity. *Comparative Politics* 3(1): 45–70.

Inglehart, Ronald, and Jacques-René Rabier. 1978. Economic Uncertainty and European Solidarity: Public Opinion Trends. *Annals of the American Academy of Political and Social Science* 440(1): 66–97.

Inglehart, Ronald, and Christian Welzel. 2005. *Modernization, Cultural Change, and Democracy: The Human Development Sequence*. Cambridge: Cambridge University Press.

Inglehart, Ronald, Jacques-René Rabier, and Karlheinz Reif. 1991. The Evolution of Public Attitudes toward European Integration. In *Eurobarometer: The Dynamics of European Public Opinion*, edited by Karlheinz Reif and Ronald Inglehart, pp. 111–31. London: Macmillan.

Ishay, Micheline R. 2004. *The History of Human Rights: From Ancient Times to the Globalization Era*. Berkeley, CA: University of California Press.

Janssen, Joseph I.H. 1991. Postmaterialism, Cognitive Mobilization and Support for European Integration. *British Journal of Political Science* 21(4): 443–68.

Jerdén, Björn. 2016. *Waiting for the Rising Power: China's Rise in East Asia and the Evolution of Great Power Politics*. PhD dissertation, Department of Political Science, Stockholm University.

Jetschke, Anja. 2009. Institutionalizing ASEAN: Celebrating Europe through Network Governance. *Cambridge Review of International Affairs* 22(3): 407–26.

Jinnah, Sikina, and Elisa Morgera. 2013. Environmental Provisions in American and EU Free Trade Agreements: A Preliminary Comparison and Research Agenda. *Review of European, Comparative and International Environmental Law* 22(3): 324–39.

Johnson, Tana. 2011. Guilt by Association: The Link between States' Influence and the Legitimacy of Intergovernmental Organizations. *Review of International Organizations* 6(1): 57–84.

Jönsson, Kristina. 2014. Legitimation Challenges in Global Health Governance: The Case of Non-Communicable Diseases. *Globalizations* 11(3): 301–14.

Kalm, Sara, and Anders Uhlin. 2015. *Civil Society and the Governance of Development: Opposing Global Institutions.* Basingstoke: Palgrave Macmillan.

Kaltenthaler, Karl, and William J. Miller. 2013. Social Psychology and Public Support for Trade Liberalization. *International Studies Quarterly* 57(4): 784–90.

Karklins, Rasma. 1994. Explaining Regime Change in the Soviet Union. *Europe-Asia Studies* 46(1): 29–45.

Karlsson-Vinkhuyzen, Sylvia I., and Jeffrey McGee. 2013. Legitimacy in an Era of Fragmentation: The Case of Global Climate Governance. *Global Environmental Politics* 13(3): 56–78.

Karlsson-Vinkhuyzen, Sylvia I., and Harro van Asselt. 2009. Introduction: Exploring and Explaining the Asia-Pacific Partnership on Clean Development and Climate. *International Environmental Agreements* 9(3): 195–211.

Karns, Margaret P., Karen A. Mingst, and Kendall W. Stiles. 2015. *International Organizations: The Politics and Processes of Global Governance.* 3rd ed. Boulder, CO: Rienner.

Karp, Jeffrey A., Susan A. Banducci, and Shaun Bowler. 2003. To Know It Is to Love It? Satisfaction with Democracy in the European Union. *Comparative Political Studies* 36(3): 271–92.

Keck, Margaret E., and Kathryn Sikkink. 1998. *Activists beyond Borders: Advocacy Networks in International Politics.* Ithaca, NY: Cornell University Press.

Kellner, Tobias. 2016. *Going beyond Pure Economics: The EU's Strategic Motivation to Negotiate the Transatlantic Trade and Investment Partnership (TTIP).* Bruges: College of Europe.

Kennedy, David. 2008. The Mystery of Global Governance. *Ohio Northern University Law Review* 34(3): 827–60.

Keohane, Robert O. 1984. *After Hegemony. Cooperation and Discord in the World Political Economy.* Princeton, NJ: Princeton University Press.

Keohane, Robert O. 1988. International Institutions: Two Approaches. *International Studies Quarterly* 32(4): 379–96.

Keohane, Robert O. 1997. International Relations and International Law: Two Optics. *Harvard International Law Journal* 38(2): 487–502.

Keohane, Robert O. 2006. The Contingent Legitimacy of Multilateralism. In *Multilateralism under Challenge? Power, Institutional Order, and Structural Change,* edited by Edward Newman, Ramesh Thakur, and John Tirman, pp. 56–76. Tokyo: United Nations University Press.

Keohane, Robert O., and David G. Victor. 2011. The Regime Complex for Climate Change. *Perspectives on Politics* 9(1): 7–23.

Keohane, Robert O., Stephen Macedo, and Andrew Moravcsik. 2009. Democracy-Enhancing Multilateralism. *International Organization* 63(1): 1–31.

Khagram, Sanjeev, and Peggy Levitt, eds. 2008. *The Transnational Studies Reader: Intersections and Innovations*. New York, NY: Routledge.

Kindleberger, Charles P. 1973. *The World in Depression 1929–1939*. London: Penguin Press.

Kindleberger, Charles P. 1981. Dominance and Leadership in the International Economy: Exploitation, Public Goods, and Free Rides. *International Studies Quarterly* 25(1): 242–54.

Kirton, John J., Joseph P. Daniels, and Andreas Freytag, eds. 2001. *Guiding Global Order: G8 Governance in the Twenty-First Century*. Aldershot: Ashgate.

Kissinger, Henry. 1957. *A World Restored: Metternich, Castlereagh and the Problems of Peace 1812–22*. Boston, MA: Houghton Mifflin.

Kissinger, Henry. 1964. *A World Restored*. New York, NY: Gosset Dunlap.

Knoke, David, and James R. Wood. 1981. *Organized for Action: Commitment in Voluntary Associations*. New Brunswick, NJ: Rutgers University Press.

Koenig-Archibugi, Mathias. 2011. Is Global Democracy Possible? *European Journal of International Relations* 17(3): 519–42.

Koenig-Archibugi, Mathias. 2015. Could a World State Be Democratic? Unpublished.

Kooiman, Jan. 2003. *Governing as Governance*. London: Sage.

Koopmans, Ruud, and Paul Statham, eds. 2010. *The Making of a European Public Sphere: Media Discourse and Political Contention*. Cambridge: Cambridge University Press.

Koskenniemi, Martti, and Päivi Leino. 2002. Fragmentation of International Law? Postmodern Anxieties. *Leiden Journal of International Law* 15(3): 553–79.

Krasner, Stephen D. 1999. *Sovereignty: Organized Hypocrisy*. Princeton, NJ: Princeton University Press.

Krishna, Sankaran. 2009. *Globalization and Postcolonialism: Hegemony and Resistance in the Twenty-First Century*. Lanham, MD: Rowman and Littlefield.

Kritzinger, Sylvia. 2003. The Influence of the Nation-State on Individual Support for the European Union. *European Union Politics* 4(2): 219–41.

Krücken, Georg, and Gili S. Drori, eds. 2009. *World Society: The Writings of John W. Meyer*. Oxford: Oxford University Press.

Kuyper, Jonathan W. 2016. Systemic Representation: Democracy, Deliberation, and Nonelectoral Representatives. *American Political Science Review* 110(2): 308–24.

Kuyper, Jonathan W., and Karin Bäckstrand. 2016. Accountability and Representation: Non-State Actors in UN Climate Diplomacy. *Global Environmental Politics* 16(2): 61–81.

Lake, David A., and Christopher J. Fariss. 2014. Why International Trusteeship Fails: The Politics of External Authority in Areas of Limited Statehood. *Governance* 27(4): 569–87.

Lamb, Robert D. 2014. *Rethinking Legitimacy and Illegitimacy: A New Approach to Assessing Support and Opposition across Disciplines*. Lanham, MD: Rowman and Littlefield.

Larner, Wendy, and William Walters, eds. 2004. *Global Governmentality: Governing International Spaces*. Abingdon: Routledge.

Lawrence, Peter. 2009. Australian Climate Policy and the Asia Pacific Partnership on Clean Development and Climate (APP). From Howard to Rudd: Continuity or Change? *International Environmental Agreements* 9(3): 281–99.

Lechner, Frank J., and John Boli. 2005. *World Culture: Origins and Consequences*. Oxford: Blackwell.

Lenz, Tobias. 2012. Spurred Emulation: The EU and Regional Integration in Mercosur and SADC. *West European Politics* 35(1): 155–73.

Lenz, Tobias, and Alexandr Burilkov. 2017. Institutional Pioneers in World Politics: Regional Institution Building and the Influence of the European Union. *European Journal of International Relations* 23(3): 654–80.

Lenz, Tobias, and Lora A. Viola. 2017. Legitimacy and Institutional Change in International Organisations: A Cognitive Approach. *Review of International Studies* 43(5): 939–61.

Lenz, Tobias, Jeanine Bezuijen, Liesbet Hooghe, and Gary Marks. 2015. Patterns of International Authority: Task Specific vs. General Purpose. Special issue, *Politischen Vierteljahresschrift* 49: 131–56.

Levi, Margaret. 1997. *Consent, Dissent, and Patriotism*. Cambridge: Cambridge University Press.

Lind, Michael. 2017. The New Class War. *American Affairs* 1(2).

Lindberg, Leon N., and Stuart A. Scheingold. 1970. *Europe's Would-Be Polity: Patterns of Change in the European Community*. Englewood Cliffs, NJ: Prentice Hall.

Lindvall, Johannes. 2013. Union Density and Political Strikes. *World Politics* 65(3): 539–69.

Lipset, Seymour Martin. 1960. *Political Man: The Social Basis of Politics*. New York, NY: Doubleday and Company.

Livingstone, Sonia. 2015. Active Audiences? The Debate Progresses But Is Far from Resolved. *Communication Theory* 25(4): 439–46.

Lotze, Walter. 2013. Building the Legitimacy of the African Union: An Evolving Continent and Evolving Organization. In *Legitimating International Organizations*, edited by Dominik Zaum, pp. 111–31. Oxford: Oxford University Press.

Loveless, Matthew, and Robert Rohrschneider. 2011. Public Perceptions of the EU as a System of Governance. *Living Reviews in European Governance* 6(2): 1–37.

Lukes, Steven. 2005. *Power: A Radical View*. 2nd ed. Basingstoke: Palgrave Macmillan.

Lundgren, Magnus, Theresa Squatrito, and Jonas Tallberg. 2017. Stability and Change in International Policy-Making: A Punctuated Equilibrium Approach. *Review of International Organizations*. DOI: 10.1007/s11558-017-9288-x.

Luskin, Robert C. 1990. Explaining Political Sophistication. *Political Behavior* 12(4): 331–61.

Macdonald, Terry. 2008. *Global Stakeholder Democracy: Power and Representation beyond Liberal States*. Oxford: Oxford University Press.

Macdonald, Terry. 2012. Citizens or Stakeholders? Exclusion, Equality and Legitimacy in Global Stakeholder Democracy. In *Global Democracy. Normative and Empirical Perspectives*, edited by Daniele Archibugi, Mathias Koenig-Archibugi, and Raffaele Marchetti, pp. 47–68. Cambridge: Cambridge University Press.

Macdonald, Terry. 2015. Political Legitimacy in International Border Governance Institutions. *European Journal of Political Theory* 14(4): 409–28.

Maier, Michaela, Silke Adam, and Jürgen Maier. 2012. The Impact of Identity and Economic Cues on Citizens' EU Support: An Experimental Study on the Effects of Party Comminication in the Run-Up to the 2009 European Parliament Elections. *European Union Politics* 13(4): 580–603.

Majone, Giandomenico. 1998. Europe's "Democratic Deficit": The Question of Standards. *European Law Journal* 4(1): 5–28.

Mandel, Ernest. 1989. How to Make No Sense of Marx. *Canadian Journal of Philosophy* Supplementary Volume 15: 105–32.

Mann, Michael. 1986. *The Sources of Social Power, Volume I: A History of Power from the Beginning to AD 1760.* Cambridge: Cambridge University Press.

Mann, Michael. 1993. *The Sources of Social Power, Volume II: The Rise of Classes and Nation-States, 1760–1914.* Cambridge: Cambridge University Press.

Mansfield, Edward D., and Eric Reinhardt. 2008. International Institutions and the Volatility of International Trade. *International Organization* 62(4): 621–52.

Maslow, Abraham H. 1943. A Theory of Human Motivation. *Psychological Review* 50(4): 370–96.

Mastenbroek, Ellen. 2005. EU Compliance: Still a "Black Hole"? *Journal of European Public Policy* 12(6): 1103–20.

Mau, Steffen. 2005. Europe from the Bottom: Assessing Personal Gains and Losses and Its Effects on EU Support. *Journal of Public Policy* 25(3): 289–311.

Mayntz, Renate. 2010. Legitimacy and Compliance in Transnational Governance. Working paper. Köln: Max-Planck-Institut für Gesellschaftsforschung.

McCourt, David M. 2016. Practice Theory and Relationalism as the New Constructivism. *International Studies Quarterly* 60(3): 475–85.

McEwen, Craig A., and Richard J. Maiman. 1983. In Search of Legitimacy: Toward an Empirical Analysis. *Law and Policy* 8(3): 257–73.

McGee, Jeffrey, and Ros Taplin. 2009. The Role of the Asia Pacific Partnership in Discursive Contestation of the International Climate Regime. *International Environmental Agreements* 9(3): 213–38.

McInnes, Colin. 2015. WHO's Next? Changing Authority in Global Health Governance after Ebola. *International Affairs* 91(6): 1299–316.

McLaren, Lauren M. 2002. Public Support for the European Union: Cost/Benefit Analysis or Perceived Cultural Threat? *Journal of Politics* 64(2): 551–66.

McLaren, Lauren M. 2004. Opposition to European Integration and Fear of Loss of National Identity: Debunking a Basic Assumption Regarding Hostility to the Integration Project. *European Journal of Political Research* 43(6): 895–912.

Mearsheimer, John J. 1994/1995. The False Promise of International Institutions. *International Security* 19(3): 5–49.

Meine, Anna. 2016. Debating Legitimacy Transnationally. *Global Discourse* 3(6): 330–46.

Merritt, Richard L., and Donald J. Puchala. 1968. *Western European Perspectives on International Affairs: Public Opinion Studies and Evaluations.* New York: Frederick A. Praeger.

Mersiades, Michael. 2005. Peacekeeping and Legitimacy: Lessons from Cambodia and Somalia. *International Peacekeeping* 12(2): 205–21.

Merton, Robert K. 1949/1968. *Social Theory and Social Structure*. New York: Free Press.

Meyer, Jan-Henrik. 2014. "Where Do We Go from Wyhl?" Transnational Anti-Nuclear Protest Targeting European and International Organizations in the 1970s. *Historical Social Research* 39(1): 212–35.

Meyer, John W., and Brian Rowan. 1977. Institutionalized Organizations: Formal Structure as Myth and Ceremony. *American Journal of Sociology* 83(2): 340–63.

Michailidou, Asimina, and Hans-Jörg Trenz. 2013. Mediatized Representative Politics in the European Union: Towards Audience Democracy? *Journal of European Public Policy* 20(2): 260–77.

Mies, Maria. 2014. *Patriarchy and Accumulation on a World Scale: Women in the International Division of Labour*. London: Zed.

Migdal, Joel S. 2001. *State in Society: Studying How States and Societies Transform and Constitute One Another*. Cambridge: Cambridge University Press.

Milanovic, Branko. 2016. *Global Inequality: A New Approach for the Age of Globalization*. Cambridge, MA: Harvard University Press.

Miles, Edward L., Steinar Andresen, Elaine M. Carlin, Jon Birger Skjærseth, Arild Underdal, and Jørgen Wettestad. 2002. *Environmental Regime Effectiveness: Confronting Theory with Evidence*. Cambridge, MA: MIT Press.

Miller, David. 1999. *Principles of Social Justice*. Cambridge, MA: Harvard University Press.

Miller, David. 2010. Against Global Democracy. In *After the Nation? Critical Reflections on Nationalism and Postnationalism*, edited by Keith Breen and Shane O'Neill, pp. 141–60. Basingstoke: Palgrave Macmillan.

Mitchell, Ronald B. 2008. Evaluating the Performance of Environmental Institutions: What to Evaluate and How to Evaluate It. In *Institutions and Environmental Change: Principal Findings, Applications, and Research Frontiers*, edited by Oran R. Young, Leslie A. King, and Heike Schroeder, pp. 79–114. Cambridge, MA: MIT Press.

Mittelman, James H. 2004. *Whither Globalization? The Vortex of Knowledge and Ideology*. London: Routledge.

Mittelman, James H. 2011. *Contesting Global Order: Development, Global Governance, and Globalization*. Abingdon: Routledge.

Modelski, George. 1987. *Long Cycles in World Politics*. Basingstoke: Palgrave Macmillan.

Mondak, Jeffery J. 1999. Reconsidering the Measurement of Political Knowledge. *Political Analysis* 8(1): 57–82.

Morgenthau, Hans Joachim. 1948. *Politics among Nations: The Struggle for Power and Peace*. New York, NY: Alfred A. Knopf.

Morse, Julia C., and Robert O. Keohane. 2014. Contested Multilateralism. *Review of International Organizations* 9(1): 385–412.

Mouffe, Chantal. 1999. Deliberative Democracy or Agonistic Pluralism? *Social Research* 66(3): 745–58.

Muñoz, Jordi. 2017. Political Trust and Multilevel Government. In *Handbook on Political Trust*, edited by Sonja Zmerli and Tom W.G. van der Meer, pp. 69–88. Cheltenham: Edward Elgar.

Muñoz, Jordi, Mariano Torcal, and Eduard Bonet. 2011. Institutional Trust and Multilevel Government in the European Union: Congruence or Compensation? *European Union Politics* 12(4): 551–74.

Murphy, Craig. 2016. The Westfailure System, Fifteen Years On: Global Problems, What Makes Them Difficult to Solve and the Role of IPE. In *Susan Strange and the Future of Global Political Economy: Power, Control, and Transformation*, edited by Randall Germain, pp. 33–52. London: Routledge.

Mutz, Diana C. 2011. *Population-Based Survey Experiments*. Princeton, NJ: Princeton University Press.

Nanz, Patrizia, and Jens Steffek. 2004. Global Governance, Participation and the Public Sphere. *Government and Opposition* 39(2): 314–35.

Näsström, Sofia. 2015. Democratic Representation beyond Election. *Constellations* 22(1): 1–12.

Naurin, Daniel, and Helen Wallace. 2008. *Unveiling the Council of the European Union: Games Governments Play in Brussels*. London: Palgrave Macmillan.

Nicholson, Stephen P. 2011. Polarizing Cues. *American Journal of Political Science* 56(1): 52–66.

Niedermeyer, Oskar, and Richard Sinnott. 1995. Introduction. In *Public Opinion and Internationalized Governance*, edited by Oskar Niedermeyer and Richard Sinnott, pp. 1–9. New York, NY: Oxford University Press.

Niezen, Ronald and Maria Sapignoli, eds. 2017. *Palaces of Hope: The Anthropology of Global Organizations*. Cambridge: Cambridge University Press.

Norris, Pippa. 2000. Global Governance and Cosmopolitan Citizens. In *Governance in a Globalizing World*, edited by Joseph S. Nye and John D. Donahue, pp. 155–77. Washington, DC: Brookings Institution Press.

Norris, Pippa. 2009. Confidence in the United Nations: Cosmopolitan and Nationalistic Attitudes. In *The International System, Democracy, and Values*, edited by Yilmaz Esmer and Thorleif Pettersson, pp. 17–48. Uppsala: Acta Universitatis Upsaliensis.

Norris, Pippa. 2011. *Democratic Deficit: Critical Citizens Revisited*. Cambridge: Cambridge University Press.

Norris, Pippa, and Ronald Inglehart. 2009. *Cosmopolitan Communications*. Cambridge: Cambridge University Press.

Nullmeier, Frank, Dominika Biegon, Martin Nonhoff, Henning Schmidtke, and Steffen Schneider. 2010. *Prekäre Legitimitäten: Rechtfertigung von Herrschaft in der postnationalen Konstellation*. Frankfurt am Main: Campus.

O'Brien, Robert, Anne Marie Goetz, Jan Aart Scholte, and Marc Williams. 2000. *Contesting Global Governance: Multilateral Economic Institutions and Global Social Movements*. Cambridge: Cambridge University Press.

O'Neill, Kate. 2004. Transnational Protest: State, Circuses and Conflict at the Frontline of Global Politics. *International Studies Review* 6(2): 233–51.

Oates, John G. 2017. The Fourth Face of Legitimacy: Constituent Power and the Constitutional Legitimacy of International Institutions. *Review of International Studies* 43(2): 199–220.

Oberthür, Sebastian, and Thomas Gehring. 2006. Institutional Interaction in Global Environmental Governance: The Case of the Cartagena Protocol and the World Trade Organization. *Global Environmental Politics* 6(2): 1–31.

Oberthür, Sebastian, and Justyna Pozarowska. 2013. Managing Institutional Complexity and Fragmentation: The Nagoya Protocol and the Global Governance of Genetic Resources. *Global Environmental Politics* 13(3): 100–15.

Orr, Shannon. 2016. Institutional Control and Climate Change Activism at COP21 in Paris. *Global Environmental Politics* 16(3): 23–30.

Orsini, Amandine. 2013. Institutional Fragmentation and the Influence of "Multi-Forum" Non-State Actors: Navigating the Regime Complexes for Forestry and Genetic Resources. *Global Environmental Politics* 13(3): 34–55.

Orsini, Amandine, Jean-Frédéric Morin, and Oran Young. 2013. Regime Complexes: A Buzz, a Boom, or a Boost for Global Governance? *Global Governance* 19(1): 27–39.

Ostrom, Elinor. 2010. Polycentric Systems for Coping with Collective Action and Global Environmental Change. *Global Environmental Change* 20(4): 550–7.

Park-Fuller, Linda. 2003. Audiencing the Audience: Playback Theatre, Performative Writing, and Social Activism. *Text and Performance Quarterly* 23(3): 288–310.

Parsons, Talcott. 1937. *The Structure of Social Action*. New York, NY: Free Press.

Parsons, Talcott. 1960. *Structure and Process in Modern Societies*. Glencoe, IL: Free Press.

Paterson, Matthew. 2010. Legitimation and Accumulation in Climate Change Governance. *New Political Economy* 15(3): 345–68.

Pauwelyn, Joost, Ramses A. Wessel, and Jan Wouters. 2014. When Structures Become Shackles: Stagnation and Dynamics in International Lawmaking. *European Journal of International Law* 25(3): 733–63.

Payne, Rodger A., and Nayef H. Samhat. 2004. *Democratizing Global Politics*. Albany, NY: SUNY Press.

Peters, Dirk. 2013. *Rethinking the Legitimacy of Global Governance: On the Need for Sociological and Philosophical Foundations*. Global Cooperation Research Papers 2. Duisburg: Käte Hamburger Kolleg/Centre for Global Cooperation Research (KHK/GCR21).

Pevehouse, Jon C. 2005. *Democracy from Above: Regional Organizations and Democratization*. Cambridge: Cambridge University Press.

Piccolino, Giulia. 2016. *International Diffusion and the Puzzle of African Regionalism: Insights from West Africa*. Bruges: UNU Institute on Comparative Regional Integration Studies.

Picq, Manuela Lavinas, and Markus Thiel, eds. 2015. *Sexualities in World Politics: How LGBTQ Claims Shape International Relations*. Abingdon: Routledge.

Pitkin, Hanna Fenichel. 1967. *The Concept of Representation*. Berkeley, CA: University of California Press.

Pogge, Thomas. 2002. *World Poverty and Human Rights: Cosmopolitan Responsibilities and Reforms*. Cambridge: Polity Press.

Poovey, Mary. 1998. *A History of the Modern Fact: Problems of Knowledge in the Sciences of Wealth and Society*. Chicago, IL: University of Chicago Press.

Postel-Vinay, Karoline. 2011. *Le G20, laboratoire d'un monde émergent*. Paris: Presses de Sciences Po.

Poulantzas, Nicos. 1973. *Classes in Contemporary Capitalism*. London: Verso.

Putnam, Robert D. 1993. *Making Democracy Work: Civic Traditions in Modern Italy*. Princeton, NJ: Princeton University Press.

Quack, Sigrid. 2010. Law, Expertise and Legitimacy in Transnational Economic Governance: An Introduction. *Socio-Economic Review* 8(1): 3–16.

Rapaport Press Release. 2010. Martin Rapaport Begins Three-Day Protest Fast Outside Kimberley Process. June 20. http://www.diamonds.net/News/NewsItem.aspx? ArticleID=31414&ArticleTitle=Martin+Rapaport+Begins+Three-Day+Protest+Fast +Outside+ Kimberley+Process+Meeting+. Accessed January 30, 2017.

Raustiala, Kal, and David G. Victor. 2004. The Regime Complex for Plant Genetic Resources. *International Organization* 58(2): 277–309.

Raymond, Mark, and Laura DeNardis. 2015. Multistakeholderism: Anatomy of an Inchoate Global Institution. *International Theory* 7(3): 572–616.

Raz, Joseph. 2009. *The Authority of Law: Essays on Law and Morality*. Oxford: Oxford University Press.

Reus-Smit, Christian. 2007. International Crises of Legitimacy. *International Politics* 44(2): 157–74.

Reyes, Antonio. 2011. Strategies of Legitimization in Political Discourse: From Words to Action. *Discourse and Society* 22(6): 781–807.

Riggirozzi, Pia. 2014a. The Social Turn and Contentious Politics in Latin American Post-Neoliberal Regionalism. In *The Legitimacy of Regional Integration in Europe and the Americas*, edited by Achim Hurrelmann and Steffen Schneider, pp. 229–49. Basingstoke: Palgrave.

Riggirozzi, Pia. 2014b. Rescaling Responsibilities and Rights: The Case of UNASUR Health. In *Exploring the New South American Regionalism (NSAR)*, edited by Ernesto Vivares, pp. 129–46. Farnham: Ashgate.

Rigney, Daniel. 2001. *The Metaphorical Society: An Invitation to Social Theory*. Lanham, MD: Rowman and Littlefield.

Risse, Thomas. 2002. Nationalism and Collective Identities: Europe versus the Nation-State? In *Developments in West European Politics*, edited by Paul Heywood, Erik Jones, and Martin Rhodes, pp. 77–93. London: Palgrave Macmillan.

Risse, Thomas. 2016. The Diffusion of Regionalism, Regional Institutions, Regional Governance. In *Oxford Handbook of Comparative Regionalism*, edited by Tanja Börzel and Thomas Risse, pp. 87–107. Oxford: Oxford University Press.

Rittberger, Berthold, and Philipp Schroeder. 2016. The Legitimacy of Regional Institutions. In *Oxford Handbook of Comparative Regionalism*, edited by Tanja Börzel and Thomas Risse, pp. 579–99. Oxford: Oxford University Press.

Rittberger, Volker, Bernhard Zangl, and Andreas Kruck. 2012. *International Organization*. 2nd ed. Basingstoke: Palgrave.

Robertson, Roland. 1992. *Globalization: Social Theory and Global Culture*. London: Sage.

Robinson, William I. 2011. Giovanni Arrighi: Systemic Cycles of Accumulation, Hegemonic Transitions, and the Rise of China. *New Political Economy* 16(2): 267–80.

Rocabert, Jofre, Frank Schimmelfennig, Thomas Winzen, and Loriana Crasnic. 2016. The Rise of International Parliamentary Institutions: Authority and Legitimation. Unpublished.

Rodrik, Dani. 2002. Feasible Globalizations. NBER Working Paper No. 9129. www.nber. org/papers/w9129 Accessed September 30, 2017.

Rohrschneider, Robert. 2002. The Democracy Deficit and Mass Support for an EU-Wide Government. *American Journal of Political Science* 46(2): 462–75.

Rohrschneider, Robert, and Matthew Loveless. 2010. Macro Salience: How Economic and Political Contexts Mediate Popular Evaluations of the Democracy Deficit in the European Union. *Journal of Politics* 72(4): 1029–45.

Rokeach, Milton. 1968. *Beliefs, Attitudes, and Values*. San Francisco, CA: Jossey-Bass.

Rosenau, James N. 1999. Toward an Ontology for Global Governance. In *Approaches to Global Governance Theory*, edited by Martin Hewson and Timothy J. Sinclair, pp. 287–301. Albany, NY: SUNY Press.

Rosenau, James N., and Ernst-Otto Czempiel, eds. 1992. *Governance without Government: Order and Change in World Politics*. Cambridge: Cambridge University Press.

Rosendal, Kristin. 2006. The Convention on Biological Diversity: Tensions with the WTO TRIPS Agreement over Access to Genetic Resources and the Sharing of Benefits. In *Institutional Interaction in Global Environmental Governance: Synergy and Conflict among International and EU Policies*, edited by Sebastian Oberthür and Thomas Gehring, pp. 79–102. Cambridge, MA: MIT Press.

Rostow, Walt Whitman. 1960. *The Stages of Economic Growth: A Non-Communist Manifesto*. Cambridge: Cambridge University Press.

Rothstein, Bo. 2003. Political Legitimacy for Public Administration. In *Handbook of Public Administration*, edited by Guy Peters and Jon Pierre, pp. 407–17. London: Sage.

Ruggie, John G. 1982. International Regimes, Transactions, and Change: Embedded Liberalism in the Postwar Economic Order. *International Organization* 36(2): 379–415.

Ruggie, John G. 2004. Reconstituting the Global Public Domain: Issues, Actors and Practices. *European Journal of International Relations and Development* 10(4): 499–531.

Runyan, Anne Sisson, and V. Spike Peterson. 2014. *Global Gender Issues in the New Millennium*. Boulder, CO: Westview.

Rupert, Mark. 1995. *Producing Hegemony: The Politics of Mass Production and American Global Power*. Cambridge: Cambridge University Press.

Rupert, Mark. 2005. *Ideologies of Globalization: Contending Visions of a New World Order*. London: Routledge.

Said, Edward W. 1978. *Orientalism*. London: Routledge and Kegan Paul.

Salancik, Gerald R., and Jeffrey Pfeffer. 1978. A Social Information Processing Approach to Job Attitudes and Task Design. *Administrative Science Quarterly* 23(2): 224–53.

Sánchez-Cuenca, Ignacio. 2000. The Political Basis of Support for European Integration. *European Union Politics* 1(2): 147–71.

SAPSN. 2000. Making Southern African Development Cooperation and Integration a People-Centered and People-Driven Regional Challenge to Globalisation. Declaration to the Governmental Summit of the Southern African Development Community, Windhoek, Namibia, August 1–7.

Sattler, Thomas, and Johannes Urpelainen. 2012. Explaining Public Support for International Integration: How Do National Conditions and Treaty Characteristics Interact with Individual Beliefs? *Journal of Politics* 74(4): 1108–24.

Saward, Michael. 2000. A Critique of Held. In *Global Democracy: Key Debates*, edited by Barry Holden, pp. 32–46. London: Routledge.

Saward, Michael. 2010. *The Representative Claim*. Oxford: Oxford University Press.

Scharpf, Fritz W. 1997. *Games Real Actors Play: Actor-Centered Institutionalism in Policy Research*. Boulder, CO: Westview Press.

Scharpf, Fritz W. 1999. *Governing in Europe: Effective and Democratic?* Oxford: Oxford University Press.

Schill, Stephan W. 2017. Authority, Legitimacy, and Fragmentation in the (Envisaged) Dispute Settlement Disciplines in Mega-Regionals. In *Mega-Regional Trade Agreements: CETA, TTIP, and TiSA*, edited by Stefan Griller, Walter Obwexer, and Erich Vranes, pp. 111–50. Oxford: Oxford University Press.

Schlipphak, Bernd. 2015. Measuring Attitudes toward Regional Organizations outside Europe. *Review of International Organizations* 10(3): 351–75.

Schlyter, Peter, Ingrid Stjernquist, and Karin Bäckstrand. 2009. Not Seeing the Forest for the Trees? The Environmental Effectiveness of Forest Certification in Sweden. *Forest Policy and Economics* 11(5): 375–82.

Schmidt, Vivien. 2010. Democracy and Legitimacy in the European Union Revisited: Output, Input *and* "Throughput." *Political Studies* 61: 2–22.

Schneider, Steffen, Frank Nullmeier, and Achim Hurrelmann. 2007. Exploring the Communicative Dimension of Legitimacy: Text Analytical Approaches. In *Legitimacy in an Age of Globalization*, edited by Achim Hurrelmann, Steffen Schneider, and Jens Steffek, pp. 126–54. Basingstoke: Palgrave Macmillan.

Scholte, Jan Aart. 1993. *International Relations of Social Change*. Buckingham: Open University Press.

Scholte, Jan Aart. 2002. Civil Society and the Governance of Global Finance. In *Civil Society and Global Finance*, edited by Jan Aart Scholte and Albrecht Schnabel, pp. 11–32. London: Routledge.

Scholte, Jan Aart. 2004a. Civil Society and Democratically Accountable Global Governance. *Government and Opposition* 39(2): 211–33.

Scholte, Jan Aart. 2004b. *Democratizing the Global Economy: The Role of Civil Society*. Coventry: Centre for the Study of Globalisation and Regionalisation.

Scholte, Jan Aart. 2005. *Globalization: A Critical Introduction*. Basingstoke: Palgrave Macmillan.

Scholte, Jan Aart. 2007. Civil Society and the Legitimation of Global Governance. *Journal of Civil Society* 3(3): 305–26.

Scholte, Jan Aart, ed. 2011a. *Building Global Democracy? Civil Society and Accountable Global Governance*. Cambridge: Cambridge University Press.

Scholte, Jan Aart. 2011b. Towards Greater Legitimacy in Global Governance. *Review of International Political Economy* 18(1): 110–20.

Scholte, Jan Aart. 2016. Whither Global Theory? *ProtoSociology* 33: 213–24.

Scholte, Jan Aart, Lorenzo Fioramonti, and Alfred G. Nhema, eds. 2016. *New Rules for Global Justice: Structural Redistribution in the Global Economy*. London: Rowman and Littlefield International.

Schubert, Gunter. 2008. One-Party Rule and the Question of Legitimacy in Contemporary China: Preliminary Thoughts on Setting Up a New Research Agenda. *Journal of Contemporary China* 17(54): 191–204.

Schuck, Andreas R.T., and Claes H. de Vreese. 2006. Between Risk and Opportunity: News Framing and Its Effects on Public Support for EU Enlargement. *European Journal of Communication* 21(1): 5–32.

Schulz, Heiner, and Thomas König. 2000. Institutional Reform and Decision-Making Efficiency in the European Union. *American Journal of Political Science* 44(4): 653–66.

Scott, James C. 1985. *Weapons of the Weak. Everyday Forms of Peasant Resistance.* New Haven, CT: Yale University Press.

Scott, Richard. 1991. Unpacking Institutional Arguments. In *The New Institutionalism in Organizational Analysis*, edited by Walter W. Powell and Paul DiMaggio, pp. 164–82. Chicago, IL: Chicago University Press.

Seabrooke, Leonard. 2007. Legitimacy Gaps in the World Economy: Explaining the Sources of IMF's Legitimacy Crisis. *International Politics* 44(2): 250–68.

Sears, David O., and Carolyn L. Funk. 1999. Evidence of the Long-Term Persistence of Adults' Political Predispositions. *Journal of Politics* 61(1): 1–28.

Sell, Susan. 2016. Ahead of Her Times? Susan Strange and Global Governance. In *Susan Strange and the Future of Global Political Economy: Power, Control and Transformation*, edited by Randall Germain, pp. 21–32. London: Routledge.

Sénit, Carole-Anne, Agni Kalfagianni, and Frank Biermann. 2016. Cyberdemocracy? Information and Communication Technologies in Civil Society Consultations for Sustainable Development. *Global Governance* 22(4): 533–54.

Sénit, Carole-Anne, Frank Biermann, and Agni Kalfagianni. 2017. The Representativeness of Global Deliberation: A Critical Assessment of Civil Society Consultations for Sustainable Development. *Global Policy* 8(1): 62–72.

Seth, Sanjay, ed. 2013. *Postcolonial Theory and International Relations: A Critical Introduction.* Abingdon: Routledge.

Sethi, S. Prakash, and Donald H. Schepers. 2014. United Nations Global Compact: The Promise-Performance Gap. *Journal of Business Ethics* 122(2): 193–208.

Simmons, A. John. 1999. Justification and Legitimacy. *Ethics* 109(4): 739–71.

Simmons, Beth A. 1998. Compliance with International Agreements. *Annual Review of Political Science* 1(1): 75–93.

Simmons, Beth A. 2009. *Mobilizing for Human Rights: International Law in Domestic Politics.* Cambridge: Cambridge University Press.

Singh, Jitendra V., David J. Tucker, and Robert J. House. 1986. Organizational Legitimacy and the Liability of Newness. *Administrative Science Quarterly* 31(2): 171–93.

Sivaraksa, Sulak. 1999. *Global Healing.* Bangkok: Thai Inter-Religious Commission for Development and Sathirakoses-Nagapradipa Foundation.

Sklair, Leslie. 2001. *The Transnational Capitalist Class.* Oxford: Blackwell.

Sklair, Leslie. 2002. *Globalization: Capitalism and Its Alternatives.* Oxford: Oxford University Press.

Skodvin, Tora, and Steinar Andresen. 2009. An Agenda for Change in US Climate Policies? Presidential Ambitions and Congressional Powers. *International Environmental Agreements* 9(3): 263–80.

Slater, Jerome. 1969. The Limits of Legitimization in International Organizations: The Organization of American States and the Dominican Crisis. *International Organization* 23(1): 48–72.

Slaughter, Anne-Marie. 2004. *A New World Order*. Princeton, NJ: Princeton University Press.

Slaughter, Anne-Marie, and Thomas N. Hale. 2011. Transgovernmental Networks. In *The Sage Handbook of Governance*, edited by Mark Bevir, pp. 342–51. London: Sage.

Slaughter, Steven. 2015. The G20's Role in Legitimating Global Capitalism: Beyond Crisis Diplomacy? *Contemporary Politics* 21(4): 384–98.

Sleat, Matt. 2014. Legitimacy in Realist Thought: Between Moralism and Realpolitik. *Political Theory* 42(3): 314–37.

Smith, Tom W. 1984. Recalling Attitudes: An Analysis of Retrospective Questions on the 1982 GSS. *Public Opinion Quarterly* 48(3): 639–49.

Söderbaum, Fredrik. 2016. *Rethinking Regionalism*. Basingstoke: Palgrave Macmillan.

Sommerer, Thomas, Jonas Tallberg, Magnus Lundgren, and Theresa Squatrito. 2016. The Decision-Making Capacity of International Organizations. Unpublished.

Steffek, Jens. 2003. The Legitimation of International Governance: A Discourse Approach. *European Journal of International Relations* 9(2): 249–75.

Steffek, Jens. 2004. Why IR Needs Legitimacy: A Rejoinder. *European Journal of International Relations* 10(3): 485–90.

Steffek, Jens. 2007. Legitimacy in International Relations: From State Compliance to Citizen Consensus. In *Legitimacy in an Age of Global Politics*, edited by Achim Hurrelmann, Steffen Schneider, and Jens Steffek, pp. 175–92. London: Palgrave Macmillan.

Steffek, Jens. 2009. Discursive Legitimation in Environmental Governance. *Forest Policy and Economics* 11(5–6): 313–18.

Steffek, Jens, and Patrizia Nanz. 2008. *Emergent Patterns of Civil Society Participation in Global and European Governance*. London: Palgrave Macmillan.

Stephen, Matthew. 2016. Legitimacy in Time: Design, Drift, and Decoupling at the UN Security Council. Paper presented at the ECPR General Conference, Prague, September 10.

Stevenson, Hayley. 2016. The Wisdom of the Many in Global Governance: An Epistemic-Democratic Defence of Diversity and Inclusion. *International Studies Quarterly* 60(3): 400–12.

Stiles, Kendall W., and Adam Thayne. 2006. Compliance with International Law: International Law on Terrorism at the United Nations. *Cooperation and Conflict* 41(2): 153–76.

Stokke, Olav Schram, and Sebastian Oberthür. 2011. Introduction: Institutional Interaction in Global Environmental Change. In *Managing Institutional Complexity: Regime Interplay and Global Environmental Change*, edited by Olav Schram Stokke and Sebastian Oberthür, pp. 1–23. Cambridge, MA: MIT Press.

Streeck, Wolfgang. 2011. The Crises of Democratic Capitalism. *New Left Review* 71: 5–29.

Streeck, Wolfgang. 2014. How Will Capitalism End? *New Left Review* 87: 35–64.

Suchman, Marc C. 1995. Managing Legitimacy: Strategic and Institutional Approaches. *Academy of Management Review* 20(3): 571–610.

Suliman, Samid. 2014. Protest. *Global Discourse* 4(2–3): 109–19.

Sum, Ngai-Ling, and Bob Jessop. 2013. *Towards a Cultural Political Economy: Putting Culture in Its Place in Political Economy*. Cheltenham: Elgar.

Sunshine, Jason, and Tom R. Tyler. 2003. The Role of Procedural Justice and Legitimacy in Shaping Public Support for Policing. *Law and Society Review* 37(3): 513–48.

Sunstein, Cass R. 1996. Social Norms and Social Roles. *Columbia Law Review* 96(4): 903–68.

Symons, Jonathan. 2011. The Legitimation of International Organisations: Examining the Identity of the Communities that Grant Legitimacy. *Review of International Studies* 37(5): 2557–83.

Tallberg, Jonas, and Michael Zürn. 2017. The Legitimacy and Legitimation of International Organizations. Unpublished.

Tallberg, Jonas, Thomas Sommerer, Theresa Squatrito, and Christer Jönsson. 2013. *The Opening Up of International Organizations: Transnational Access in Global Governance*. Cambridge: Cambridge University Press.

Tallberg, Jonas, Thomas Sommerer, Theresa Squatrito, and Christer Jönsson. 2014. Explaining the Transnational Design of International Organizations. *International Organization* 68(4): 741–74.

Tallberg, Jonas, Thomas Sommerer, and Theresa Squatrito. 2016a. Democratic Memberships in International Organizations: Sources of Institutional Design. *Review of International Organizations* 11(1): 59–87.

Tallberg, Jonas, Thomas Sommerer, Theresa Squarito, and Magnus Lundgren. 2016b. The Performance of International Organizations: An Output-Based Approach. *Journal of European Public Policy* 23(7): 1077–96.

Tanenhaus, Joseph, and Walter F. Murphy. 1981. Patterns of Public Support for the Supreme Court: A Panel Study. *Journal of Politics* 43(1): 24–39.

Tarrow, Sydney. 2005. *The New Transnational Activism*. Cambridge: Cambridge University Press.

Taylor, Charles. 1985. Alternative Futures: Legitimacy, Identity, and Alienation in Late Twentieth-Century Canada. In *Constitutionalism, Citizenship, and Society in Canada*, edited by Cynthia Williams and Alan C. Cairns, pp. 183–229. Toronto: University of Toronto Press.

Taylor, Peter J. et al. 1996. On the Nation-State, the Global, and the Social Sciences. *Environment and Planning A* 28(11): 1917–95.

Thérien, Jean-Philippe. 2015. The United Nations Ideology: From Ideas to Global Policies. *Journal of Political Ideologies* 20(3): 221–43.

Tilly, Charles. 2005. *Trust and Rule*. Cambridge: Cambridge University Press.

Torgler, Benno. 2008. Trust in International Organizations: An Empirical Investigation Focusing on the United Nations. *Review of International Organizations* 3(1): 65–93.

Tormey, Simon. 2012. Occupy Wall Street: From Representation to Post-Representation. *Journal of Critical Globalisation Studies* 5: 132–6.

Tyler, Tom R. 1990. *Why People Obey the Law: Procedural Justice, Legitimacy, and Compliance*. New Haven, CT: Yale University Press.

Tyler, Tom R. 2006. Psychological Perspectives on Legitimacy and Legitimation. *Annual Review of Psychology* 57: 375–400.

Uhlin, Anders. 2016. *Civil Society and Regional Governance: The Asian Development Bank and the Association of Southeast Asian Nations*. Lanham, MD: Lexington Books.

UIA. 2015. *Yearbook of International Organizations*. New York, NY: K.G. Saur.

Underdal, Arild. 2004. Methodological Challenges in the Study of Regime Effectiveness. In *Regime Consequences: Methodological Challenges and Research Strategies*, edited by Arild Underdal and Oran R. Young, pp. 27–48. Dordrecht: Kluwer.

UNDP. 2016. *Human Development Reports*. http://www.hdr.undp.org/en/composite/trends. Accessed September 6, 2016.

Uslaner, Eric M. 2002. *The Moral Foundations of Trust*. Cambridge: Cambridge University Press.

Vaara, Eero. 2014. Struggles over Legitimacy in the Eurozone Crisis: Discursive Legitimation Strategies and their Ideological Underpinnings. *Discourse Society* 25(4): 500–18.

Valentini, Laura. 2014. No Global Demos, No Global Democracy? A Systematization and Critique. *Perspectives on Politics* 12(4): 789–807.

Van Asselt, Harro. 2007. From UN-ity to Diversity? The UNFCCC, the Asia-Pacific Partnership, and the Future of International Law on Climate Change. *Carbon and Climate Law Review* 1(1): 17–28.

Van Asselt, Harro. 2014. *The Fragmentation of Global Climate Governance: Consequences and Management of Regime Interactions*. Cheltenham: Edward Elgar.

Van Asselt, Harro, and Stefan Bößner. 2016. The Shape of Things to Come: Global Climate Governance after Paris. *Carbon and Climate Law Review* 10(1): 46–61.

Van de Graaf, Thijs. 2013. Fragmentation in Global Energy Governance: Explaining the Creation of IRENA. *Global Environmental Politics* 13(3): 14–33.

Van der Lugt, Cornis, and Klaus Dingwerth. 2015. Governing Where Focality Is Low: UNEP and the Principles for Responsible Investments. In *International Organizations as Orchestrators*, edited by Kenneth Abbott, Philipp Genschel, Duncan Snidal, and Bernhard Zangl, pp. 237–61. Cambridge: Cambridge University Press.

Van der Pijl, Kees. 1998. *Transnational Classes and International Relations*. Abingdon: Routledge.

Van Dijck, José. 2013. *The Culture of Connectivity: A Critical History of Social Media*. Oxford: Oxford University Press.

Van Evera, Stephen. 1997. *Guide to Methods for Students of Political Science*. Ithaca, NY: Cornell University Press.

Van Leeuwen, Theo. 2007. Legitimation in Discourse and Communication. *Discourse and Communication* 1(1): 91–112.

Van Leeuwen, Theo. 2008. *Discourse and Practice: New Tools for Critical Discourse Analysis*. Oxford: Oxford University Press.

Van Rooy, Alison. 2004. *The Global Legitimacy Game: Civil Society, Globalization and Protest*. Basingstoke: Palgrave Macmillan.

Verba, Sidney, Kay Schlozman, and Henry Brady. 1995. *Voice and Equality: Civic Volunteerism in American Politics*. Cambridge, MA: Harvard University Press.

Victor, David G. 2016. What the Framework Convention on Climate Change Teaches Us about Cooperation on Climate Change. *Politics and Governance* 4(3): 133–41.

Viola, Lora. 2015. Orchestration by Design: The G20 in International Financial Regulation. In *International Organizations as Orchestrators*, edited by Kenneth Abbott, Philipp Genschel, Duncan Snidal, and Bernhard Zangl, pp. 88–113. Cambridge: Cambridge University Press.

Voeten, Erik. 2013. Public Opinion and the Legitimacy of International Courts. *Theoretical Inquiries in Law* 14(2): 411–36.

Vreeland, James, and Axel Dreher. 2014. *The Political Economy of the United Nations Security Council: Money and Influence*. Cambridge: Cambridge University Press.

Walker, R.B.J. 1993. *Inside/Outside: International Relations as Political Theory*. Cambridge: Cambridge University Press.

Wallerstein, Immanuel. 1974. *The Modern World-System*. Berkeley, CA: University of California Press.

Wallerstein, Immanuel. 1983. The Three Instances of Hegemony in the History of the Capitalist World-Economy. In *The Politics of the World-Economy: The States, the Movements, and the Civilizations*, pp. 37–46. Cambridge: Cambridge University Press.

Wallerstein, Immanuel. 2004. *World-Systems Analysis: An Introduction*. Durham, NC: Duke University Press.

Walton, John, and Charles Ragin. 1990. Global and National Sources of Political Protest: Third World Responses to the Debt Crisis. *American Sociological Review* 55: 876–90.

Waltz, Kenneth N. 1979. *Theory of International Politics*. New York, NY: McGraw-Hill.

Weber, Max. 1922/1978. *Economy and Society*. Berkeley, CA: University of California Press.

Weiss, Thomas G., and Rorden Wilkinson, eds. 2014. *International Organization and Global Governance*. Abingdon: Routledge.

Welsh, Jennifer, and Dominik Zaum. 2013. Legitimation and the Security Council. In *Legitimating International Organizations*, edited by Dominik Zaum, pp. 65–87. Oxford: Oxford University Press.

Wendt, Alexander. 2001. Driving with the Rearview Mirror: On the Rational Science of Institutional Design. *International Organization* 55(4): 1019–49.

Westergren, Martin. 2016. The Political Legitimacy of Global Governance Institutions: A Justice-Based Account. PhD dissertation, Department of Political Science, Stockholm University.

Westle, Bettina. 2007. Political Beliefs and Attitudes: Legitimacy in Public Opinion Research. In *Legitimacy in an Age of Global Politics*, edited by Achim Hurrelmann, Steffen Schneider, and Jens Steffek, pp. 93–125. Basingstoke: Palgrave.

White House. 2001. President Bush Discusses Global Climate Change. http://georgewbush-whitehouse.archives.gov/news/releases/2001/06/20010611-2.html. Accessed January 20, 2017.

WHO. 2017. Programmatic and Financial Report. http://www.who.int/about/finances-accountability/reports/en/. Accessed April 28, 2017.

Wigen, Einar. 2015. Two-Level Language Games: International Relations as Inter-Lingual Relations. *European Journal of International Relations* 27(2): 427–50.

Williams, Michael C. 2003. Words, Images, Enemies, Securitization and International Politics. *International Studies Quarterly* 47(4): 511–31.

Williams, Paul. 2013. Regional and Global Legitimacy Dynamics: The United Nations and Regional Arrangements. In *Legitimating International Organizations*, edited by Dominik Zaum, pp. 41–64. Oxford: Oxford University Press.

Wolf, Klaus Dieter. 1991. *Internationale Regime zur Verteilung globaler Ressourcen*. Baden-Baden: Nomos.

Worth, Owen. 2015. *Rethinking Hegemony*. Basingstoke: Palgrave Macmillan.

Wright, Clive. 2004. Tackling Conflict Diamonds: The Kimberley Process Certification Scheme. *International Peacekeeping* 11(4): 697–708.

WTO. 2017a. WTO Documents and Resources. https://www.wto.org/english/res_e/res_e.htm. Accessed April 28, 2017.

WTO. 2017b. WTO Annual Report. https://www.wto.org/english/res_e/ publications_e/anrep16_e.htm. Accessed April 28, 2017.

WTO. 2017c. Regional Trade Agreements Information System. http://rtais.wto.org/UI/PublicMaintainRTAHome.aspx. Accessed April 28, 2017.

WTO and UNEP. 2016. *Trade and Green Economy: A Handbook*. 3rd ed. Geneva: World Trade Organization.

WVS. 2016. Findings and Insights. http://www.worldvaluessurvey.org/WVSContents.jsp?CMSID=Findings. Accessed September 6, 2016.

Young, Oran. 1999. *The Effectiveness of International Environmental Regimes: Causal Connections and Behavioral Mechanisms*. Cambridge, MA: MIT Press.

Young, Oran. 2002. *The Institutional Dimensions of Environmental Change: Fit, Interplay, and Scale*. Cambridge, MA: MIT Press.

Young, Oran. 2011. Effectiveness of International Environmental Regimes: Existing Knowledge, Cutting-Edge Themes, and Research Strategies. *Proceedings of the National Academy of Sciences* 108(50): 19853–60.

Zaller, John R. 1992. *Nature and Origins of Mass Opinion*. New York, NY: Cambridge University Press.

Zangl, Bernhard, Frederick Haussner, Andreas Kruck, and Xenia Lanzendörfer. 2016. Imperfect Adaptation: How the WTO and IMF Adjust to Shifting Power Distributions among Their Members. *Review of International Organizations* 11(2): 171–96.

Zaum, Dominik, ed. 2013a. *Legitimating International Organizations*. Oxford: Oxford University Press.

Zaum, Dominik. 2013b. International Organizations, Legitimacy, and Legitimation. In *Legitimating International Organizations*, edited by Dominik Zaum, pp. 3–25. Oxford: Oxford University Press.

Zaum, Dominik. 2013c. Conclusion. In *Legitimating International Organizations*, edited by Dominik Zaum, pp. 221–30. Oxford: Oxford University Press.

Zaum, Dominik. 2016. Legitimacy. In *Oxford Handbook of International Organizations*, edited by Jacob Katz Cogan, Ian Hurd, and Ian Johnstone, pp. 1107–26. Oxford: Oxford University Press.

Zelli, Fariborz. 2011. The Fragmentation of the Climate Governance Architecture. *Wiley Interdisciplinary Reviews: Climate Change* 2(2): 255–70.

Zelli, Fariborz. 2015. Institutional Fragmentation. In *Encyclopedia of Global Environmental Governance and Politics*, edited by Philipp Pattberg and Fariborz Zelli, pp. 469–77. Cheltenham: Edward Elgar.

Zelli, Fariborz, and Harro van Asselt. 2013a. Introduction: The Institutional Fragmentation of Global Environmental Governance—Causes, Consequences and Responses. *Global Environmental Politics* 13(3): 1–13.

Zelli, Fariborz, and Harro van Asselt, eds. 2013b. The Institutional Fragmentation of Global Environmental Governance. Special Issue, *Global Environmental Politics* 13(1).

Zelli, Fariborz, and Harro van Asselt. 2015. Fragmentation. In *Research Handbook on Climate Governance*, edited by Karin Bäckstrand and Eva Lövbrand, pp. 121–31. Cheltenham: Edward Elgar.

Zelli, Fariborz, Ina Möller, and Harro van Asselt. 2017. Institutional Complexity and Private Authority in Global Climate Governance: The Cases of Climate Engineering, REDD+, and Short-Lived Climate Pollutants. *Environmental Politics* 26(4): 669–93.

Zmerli, Sonja. 2010. EU Legitimacy and Social Capital: Empirical Insights into a Complex Relationship. In *Civil Society and Activism in Europe: Contextualizing Engagement and Political Orientations*, edited by William A. Maloney and Jan W. Van Deth, pp. 156–79. London: Routledge.

Zürn, Michael. 1993. Problematic Social Situations and International Institutions: On the Use of Game Theory in International Politics. In *International Relations and Pan-Europe: Theoretical Approaches and Empirical Findings*, edited by Frank R. Pfetsch, pp. 63–84. Münster: Lit.

Zürn, Michael. 2000. Democratic Governance beyond the Nation-State: The EU and Other International Institutions. *European Journal of International Relations* 6(2): 183–221.

Zürn, Michael. 2004. Global Governance and Legitimacy Problems. *Government and Opposition* 39(2): 261–87.

Zürn, Michael. 2014. The Politicization of World Politics and Its Effects: Eight Propositions. *European Political Science Review* 6(1): 47–71.

Zürn, Michael, and Matthew Stephen. 2010. The View of Old and New Powers on the Legitimacy of International Institutions. *Politics* 30(S1): 91–101.

Zürn, Michael, Martin Binder, and Matthias Ecker-Ehrhardt. 2012. International Authority and Its Politicization. *International Theory* 4(1): 69–106.

Zürn, Michael, Martin Binder, Alexandros Tokhi, Xaver Keller, and Autumn Lockwood Payton. 2015. The International Authority Data Project. Paper presented at the International Authority Workshop, Berlin, December 10–11.

Index

Index

Printed and bound by CPI Group (UK) Ltd, Croydon, CR0 4YY